Daniel Romano

BLACKPOOL

Town and City Histories

Titles in print or forthcoming include:

Town and City Histories
Series editor: Stephen Constantine

Blackpool

John K. Walton

Edinburgh University Press/
Carnegie Publishing

Dedication

In memoriam
Tony Rybaczek
(1957–1997)
Footballer, historian and the most loyal of friends

© John K. Walton, 1998

Published by Edinburgh University Press
22 George Square, Edinburgh
http://www.eup.ed.ac.uk
and Carnegie Publishing Ltd
Chatsworth Road, Lancaster

Typeset in Minion by
Carnegie Publishing
Printed and bound in Great Britain by
Cambridge University Press

British Library Cataloguing-in-Publication data
A catalogue record for this book is available from the British Library

ISBN 1 85331 215 0

Contents

Series Editor's Foreword

THE BOOKS in this series are designed and written with a broad readership in mind: local people interested to know how the character of their town has been shaped by major historical forces and the energies of their predecessors; newcomers and visitors curious to acquire a historical introduction to their new surroundings; general readers wishing to see how the sweeps of national and international history have manifested themselves in particular urban communities; and the scholar seeking to understand urbanisation by comparing and contrasting local experiences.

We live, most of us, in intensely urban environments. These are the products largely of the last two centuries of historical development, although the roots of many towns, of course, go back deep into the past. In recent years there has been considerable historical research of a high standard into this urban history. Narrative and descriptive accounts of the history of towns and cities can now be replaced by studies such as the TOWN AND CITY HISTORIES which investigate, analyse and, above all, explain the economic, political, social and cultural processes and consequences of urbanisation.

Writers for this series consider the changing economic foundations of their town or city and the way change has affected its physical shape, built environment and interests of those who wielded power locally and the structure and functions of local government in different periods are also examined, since locally exercised authority could determine much about the fortunes and quality of urban life. Particular emphasis is placed on the changing life experiences of ordinary men, women and children – their homes, education, occupations, social relations, living standards and leisure activities. Towns and cities control and respond to the values, aspirations and actions of their residents. The books in this series therefore explore social behaviour as well as the economic and political history of those who live in and helped make the towns and cities of today.

Stephen Constantine
University of Lancaster

Acknowledgements

I HAVE LIVED with the social history of Blackpool since 1971, when I began a doctoral thesis on its origins and growth between the late eighteenth century and the First World War, under the supervision of John Marshall and Harold Perkin at the University of Lancaster. Early debts were acknowledged in my first book, *The Blackpool Landlady: A Social History* (Manchester University Press, 1978), which now seems a very long time ago. Since then my work has diversified into a variety of fields, but Blackpool has never quite released its grip. This urban biography – which looks at the earlier period from a different angle and in the light of the changing preoccupations of historians over the last two decades, and brings the story up to date as far as the General Election of 1997 – is not an attempt at exorcism: I have further work to do on the comparative history of seaside resorts, and it will be impossible to keep Blackpool out. But it is an attempt to explain and interpret Blackpool's history, and to suggest ways in which it has been significant. It is not definitive: no history can be, and many other histories of Blackpool could be presented. It is a product of place, time and personality. As such, some of the influences on the author need to be acknowledged.

I should begin by reiterating that my interest in Blackpool arose originally from members of my family retiring and setting up in business there during the 1960s, and from riding up and down the sea-front as a temporary tram conductor during the summer of 1968 (when everyone else seems to have been busy in other ways), gradually realising the importance of what I was seeing and the need to try to explain it. Historical practice has moved on since then, but I remain wedded to the duty to try to explain. In their contrasting ways, John Marshall and Harold Perkin helped me to initiate that process, which was made possible by a Ph.D. grant from the then Social Science Research Council (how encouraging it would be if a new government were to reinstate the old name). In 1974, I joined them as a colleague at the University of Lancaster, and continued to teach there with unabated enjoyment until 1998, in spite of the efforts of successive governments to make it impossible to do the job properly. My colleagues deserve a collective acknowledgement, if only for putting up with occasional blunt speaking and a blustery temper. The book was completed in the aftermath of two terms of study leave, which enabled me to clear the decks for a final push over the summer of 1997, and which I acknowledge with gratitude in these difficult times.

The book is dedicated to a former student. His untimely death – as the volume approached completion – formed a salutary reminder of the context in which we now work. Tony Rybaczek came to study history at Lancaster from driving buses in Greater Manchester. He wrestled with academic history and came out triumphant: although he just missed an Upper Second, he paid his way through the MA in Modern Social History (by driving buses) and just missed a Distinction for a dissertation which looked at the history of council housing in his home town. He subsequently published this work, *Homes for Heroes in Inter-War Ashton: Did They Stop a Revolution?* (Ashton-under-Lyne, 1995), and it makes a very useful contribution to the literature. He submitted his dissertation on time in spite of suffering a heart attack, and coming very close to death, while working on it. Subsequently he was unable to find work to match his abilities and qualifications, and two years later a second heart attack killed him. He could not have entered university under present conditions; and if he had been prepared to undertake the burden of debt envisaged by a so-called 'New Labour' administration, the escalating fees would have debarred him from postgraduate work. When it came to seeking employment, his face, literally, did not fit. But his enthusiasm remained contagious, and affected all around him. We must not exclude the Tony Rybaczeks from higher education (in the fullest sense: personal development and fulfilment, not just training for business); we must encourage them, recognise their talents, and use (and reward) them to the full. I have little hope that this will come to pass in my lifetime. When I began my career it seemed a plausible goal, and it is particularly sad that a 'Labour' government should have dealt it such a damaging blow.

It is a pleasure to acknowledge people who have provided practical help in the making of this book. My research students Julian Demetriadi and Nora Essafi have contributed generously to Chapter 6, as has Liz Samuels, who was my research assistant during the summer of 1997 and will be able to identify her contribution to the same chapter. Three years earlier Karen Guerin did invaluable work for me on the inter-war years, and I have also drawn on Sharon Messenger's unpublished MA dissertation. I have vivid memories of the tour of Blackpool's most disreputable places which Richard Emmess organised for a group of us in the early 1990s, and it is a pleasure to thank him here. Gerry Mars's reminiscences and ideas contributed important insights to Chapter 6. Gary Cross's work on Mass-Observation has been of central importance, and Robert Poole has helped in various ways. Steve Constantine has been patient and constructive as series editor. I must have forgotten to acknowledge many other people, to whom I apologise; but the staff of Blackpool Central Library must not be omitted from this litany of gratitude. Above all, I thank Sue, who has kept pushing me towards open-mindedness and innovation, combined with accessibility. This text will not satisfy her, but nor should it. I hope the next book will do better.

John K. Walton

CHAPTER ONE

The fascination of Blackpool

BLACKPOOL scarcely needs an introduction to the British reader. Its fame as Britain's largest, brashest, busiest and best-publicised popular resort is long-established, unchallenged and has practically passed into folklore. It became, in a tempting and not entirely misleading phrase, the Mecca of the English working class on pleasure bent during the half-century or so after 1870, starting as a magnet for cotton workers and extending its spell nationwide (including industrial Scotland and Wales) by the inter-war years. Everyone has heard of Blackpool, and it projects, enduringly, a permissive but unthreatening image of proletarians at play. That the image is unduly simple goes without saying, and there are many intersecting Blackpools, including residential, respectable and poverty-stricken ones, behind and to either side of the pullulating, pulsating sea-front of the Golden Mile and Pleasure Beach, living out a more prosaic existence alongside the glitter and gowns of the night-clubs and cabarets which represent a more recent dominant image of Blackpool's pleasure identity.[1] As this intimation of novelty suggests, Blackpool, like all resorts which have sustained popularity over a long period, has had to remake itself and reinvent its image at regular intervals, without losing the 'trad-itional' characteristics – themselves historical creations – which form part of its appeal for the many visitors who return regularly year after year, whether once, twice or several times. Meanwhile, Blackpool's nature as a town, and the social composition of its inhabitants and visitors, have changed in interesting and significant ways in the long run. We need to look behind the instant perceptions and assumptions, and to take account of changing economic arrangements and patterns of conflict in Blackpool's hinterland as well as in the town itself, if we are to understand where the Blackpool of today has come from, what it is and where it might be going.

Blackpool is, and has been, essentially a British institution, for all its attempts to claim an American vigour and vitality, to attract visitors from other countries and to borrow appealing kinds of popular festivity from other cultures (as in the case of the controversial Carnivals of 1923–4, to say nothing of the local version of the Eiffel Tower). Its raw vitality and obvious importance as an artefact of social history are capable of impressing the most cosmopolitan of observers. Sir Nikolaus Pevsner, the architectural writer, spoke of the 'lack of aesthetic discrimination which we shall find everywhere at Blackpool', but pointed out that the then absence of an official

Blackpool Tower, which dominates the town's skyline at every turn.

list of buildings of architectural and historic interest in the town did not mean that no such interest could be found, concluding roundly that, 'English social history of the second half of the nineteenth century and the first half of the twentieth century could not be written without Blackpool.'[2] Social historians themselves have not always been so perceptive, however, and Blackpool's appeal has not generally been an exportable commodity. It is persistently perceived in southern England as essentially a regional phenomenon, an assessment in which northern commentators sometimes proudly collude, and it has had some difficulty in escaping from a provincial cloth-cap-and-whippet, Coronation Street image culled from earlier generations, which has just enough truth to ensnare sociologists in pursuit of symbols of northern popular culture.[3]

The rise of Blackpool

What is undeniable is Blackpool's popularity. Compared with south coast resorts like Brighton and Margate which pioneered the sea-bathing fashion and the seaside holiday industry, or with Scarborough which was their northern counterpart, Blackpool was a late developer; but it caught up very rapidly indeed in the later nineteenth century, capitalising mainly (though never entirely) on the growing working-class spending power which was released through falling prices in the extended period of deflation after 1873. Its earlier growth was less remarkable. In the late eighteenth century Blackpool's line of scattered houses facing the Irish sea was well filled with a few hundred August visitors, drawn from the mercantile and professional classes of Lancashire and the West Riding of Yorkshire, with a leavening of gentry, farmers and textile manufacturers. At the start of the railway age, when Brighton already had an off-season resident population of 40,000, Blackpool had little more than 1,000 regular inhabitants in 1841 and was full in mid-August with just over 3,000 visitors. Over the next generation Blackpool continued to grow as a second-rank provincial resort, with a visiting public drawn mainly from the expanding and prospering Lancashire middle classes, augmented at weekends in high summer by working-class trippers from the cotton towns. Between 1861 and 1865, despite the intervening Cotton Famine, rail passenger arrivals more than doubled to over 285,000 per year, and by the mid-1860s up to 25,000 staying visitors might be in the town at peak periods, perhaps five times the resident population. This was, comparatively, an unusually high ratio, and by this time Blackpool was beginning to stand out as a distinctive and (as we shall see) an enterprising seaside resort. But what took it from distinctiveness to uniqueness, in the scale and nature of its holiday industry, was what happened between 1870 and the First World War.[4]

From the 1870s Blackpool opened its doors, with early trepidation but growing conviction, to the working-class holidaymaker *en masse*, first from

the Lancashire cotton towns, then from further afield. We shall explore
the reasons for expanding working-class spending power, and for the
channelling of leisure time and leisure money into seaside resorts and
(overwhelmingly) into Blackpool, later in the book. What matters here is
the fact of it. All the Victorian and Edwardian figures for visitor numbers
are guesstimates (and even the most recent and sophisticated-looking have
very high margins of error), but it seems that annual totals (including
day-trippers) roughly trebled to about 850,000 between 1865 and 1873, more
than doubled again to nearly 2 million over the next twenty years, and
continued this process to reach nearly 4 million on the eve of the First
World War. By the 1880s daylight was showing between Blackpool and its
nearest rivals in the popularity stakes, and by the early twentieth century
it was in a league of its own, which is where it has remained.[5] Meanwhile,
the census population (taken in April in the absence of visitors and of a
large number of seasonal residents) trebled from just over 7,000 to nearly
22,000 between 1871 and 1891, and then more than doubled to top 47,000
in the explosive decade between 1891 and 1901 which saw the opening of
the Tower and the Gigantic Wheel. A consolidatory period of slower
population growth followed, and in 1911 Blackpool's April population of
58,371 left it ranking sixth among British seaside resorts.[6]

This was not achieved solely on the basis of the working-class market,
important though that was. Blackpool retained and indeed developed
middle-class holidaymaking and residential areas at either end of its long
promenade, while the industrial workers and those who catered for them
took over the town centre, between the railway stations and between the
first two piers, although from the turn of the century the Pleasure Beach
amusement park began to pull its surroundings around the southern tram
terminal a little way down-market. The growth of the middle-class market
nationally was dynamic enough to enable Bournemouth to outpace Blackpool in population terms during this period, although the southern resort
was developing a subsidiary working-class market of its own at this time.
No resort could grow on the grand scale by concentrating on one visiting
public to the exclusion of all others.[7] The truth of this observation is
underlined by Blackpool's visible and successful cultivation of a comfortably-off residential sector of commuters and retired people, as well as
mobile white-collar workers such as commercial travellers, during these
years. Even so, the dramatic and obvious changes in Blackpool's image
and demeanour, and the ones associated most directly with the town's very
rapid growth, arose from the transformative power of working-class leisure
spending in the town centre and its immediate surroundings. These
developments, and the conflicts and controversies surrounding them, form
a central theme of the book: they are crucial to understanding Blackpool
in a longer perspective, in visual as well as social and economic terms.
Despite subsequent developments, Blackpool remains, beneath the surface

gloss and enjoyable tackiness, overwhelmingly a late Victorian and Edwardian town.

Twentieth-century Blackpool

This is not to suggest that what has happened since is unimportant. The First World War was a surprisingly prosperous period for Blackpool, as it benefited from the billeting of troops and refugees and the redistribution of resources which produced enhanced spending power for industrial workers while rationing restricted access to consumer goods. Meanwhile transport restrictions gave Blackpool a captive market from the nearby industrial centres. The later years of the war and its aftermath brought unprecedented industrial conflict which extended to seasonal workers, who were usually notoriously difficult to organise; and Labour politics seemed to pose a brief and flickering threat to the town's Tory rulers, who were drawn overwhelmingly from the entertainment and building interests.[8]

This storm was weathered with relative ease, however, and Blackpool continued to grow impressively during the inter-war years, still relying to a unique extent on the working-class market but sustaining a broad appeal to more affluent groups and making a determined pitch for more comfortably-off residents. Population trends and visitor numbers are harder to chart for these years: the 1921 census was taken in June, and there was a fierce dispute between informed but self-interested municipal opinion and the census-takers over how many 'visitors' should be deducted to arrive at a 'normal' residential population, which was a particularly problematic concept in a highly seasonal resort.[9] Meanwhile, attempts to calculate visitor numbers from railway traffic flows, which were reasonably plausible before the war, were invalidated by the rapidly growing importance of motor traffic on the roads. The June population in 1921 had been on the verge of 100,000, until its controversial deflation to 73,800, which was still an impressive advance during a decade disrupted by war; and the April population in 1931 did reach six figures, while continuing expansion during the 1930s must have moved the total a long way towards the 147,184 of 1951, the 1941 census having been lost to the Second World War. Most observers agreed on a working estimate of 7 million visitors per year during the 1930s, nearly double the pre-war figure; and by this time Blackpool's place in the public eye had become truly national. Since 1879 the Corporation had had the unique privilege of being able to allocate property-based local taxation to municipal advertising, using the product of a rate of twopence in the pound; and by the turn of the century Blackpool's poster campaigns were invading the Midlands and South after a saturation bombardment of the best hoardings in Lancashire and Yorkshire, supported by publicity stunts and press coverage of special events. The fruits of this were already being gathered before the war, and by the 1920s Glasgow's love affair with Blackpool (a sometimes violent relationship) was well under way, while visitors were coming from London, the Bristol area, the south coast and industrial South Wales. The revival of the autumn Illuminations, which had been a huge success just before the war, extended the catchment area as well as the season after 1925, and in 1926 a local newspaper triumphantly reported large party bookings from both Plymouth and St Andrews.[10] From the mid-1920s Blackpool's unique position was even more clearly defined than hitherto: it had by far the longest season, the widest visitor catchment area and (above all) the largest visitor numbers of any British resort. There was nothing like it in Europe, and worthwhile comparisons would have to be sought in the United States.[11]

Comment on Blackpool at national level, whether from gossip columnists like Charles Graves, popular journalists like William Holt, the eye of the camera through *Picture Post*, the populist anthropology of Mass-Observation, the cinema (as in the Gracie Fields vehicle *Sing as we Go*) or the music-hall, tended to focus on its central role as boisterous, cheerful, beery, bonhomous popular resort. It presented the holiday crowds, their amusements and those who catered for them.[12] But, increasingly in the inter-war years, there was more to Blackpool than this. The new holiday accommodation on the extended promenades to north and south was relatively up-market, and the number of self-described 'private hotels' grew rapidly, while even in the early 1920s car parking became a headache for the local police and the first traffic jams were experienced. The local press pushed the idea of residential Blackpool, emphasising its attractions not only as a place of retirement but also as a healthy and well-equipped place to bring up children, with good schools as well as other amenities. The suburbs did indeed proliferate, as Blackpool enjoyed a building boom in private three-bedroomed semi-detached houses: it was one of the seaside resorts whose inter-war growth kept pace with London's and Manchester's outer suburbia, holding a lot of characteristics in common.[13] Inter-war Blackpool was increasingly a residential town with a popular resort image. At the same time, its boosters extolled the glorious role of private enterprise in its development, while the great initiatives of the inter-war years came from the Corporation in the form of parks, swimming pools, promenade extensions, parking, public transport and planning schemes. Blackpool was being celebrated for claims and attributes which, while they remained important, were becoming less representative of the social characteristics of the town as a whole, although we shall see that the values and preoccupations of the popular holiday industry were by no means confined to the areas where it was most obviously in evidence.

After a prosperous Second World War, with the local economy boosted by military training, convalescents, transferred civil servants and large-scale aircraft production, the continuing prosperity of Blackpool's holiday season masked the continuing growth of its commuter, retired and service sector population during the 1950s and 1960s. The population stabilised at around 150,000, although some residential growth took place in a 'greater Blackpool' beyond the borough boundary. Meanwhile, visitor numbers remained buoyant, despite the warning lights which were detected by the first professionally compiled and relatively sophisticated visitor survey in 1972, which suggested that Blackpool's visitors were too elderly and down-market to augur well for the future. A marked improvement on both counts was detected by further surveys at the end of the 1980s, however, and it appeared that Blackpool was continuing its successful career of introducing appropriate and timely innovations while retaining the loyalty of its established clientele. The 1972 survey calculated, on very dubious assumptions, that about 16 million tourist visits were made to Blackpool by nearly 6 million visitors, but that 80 per cent of the visits were for single days or evenings only. Fifteen years later a second survey calculated 3.46 million staying visits out of a total of 12.4 million which included those who merely drove along the promenade to see the Illuminations.[14] The balance of the season was shifting away from the traditional July and August holidays of the industrial towns, towards shorter stays during the autumn Illuminations, while the switch of transport from rail to road continued to pose increasing problems. During a period of intensifying competition for holiday business from overseas destinations, which saw a decline in the taking of domestic holidays by Britons from the mid-1970s, while within Britain new kinds of holidaymaking diverted the remaining demand away from what was now the traditional resort-based seaside holiday, Blackpool sustained its popularity remarkably well while others struggled.[15] It was not plain sailing, as crises over environmental pollution and Corporation entertainment policy reminded followers of Blackpool's fortunes in the late 1980s and early 1990s; but an unexpected willingness to embrace the 'pink pound' and a new identity as a centre for gay night-life helped the town to sustain its status as Britain's most popular seaside resort, and as a leading player on the world stage, despite the problems of adapting an ageing infrastructure to rising expectations.

It would be easy to write a celebratory history of Blackpool which made much of its business acumen, adaptability, cultural uniqueness, sheer vigour and appetite for sustained growth on the grand scale. It would be utterly misleading to deny these attributes; but it would be equally distorting to ignore the social and environmental problems which have marched in step with the profits of entertainment companies and building firms and the high profile adopted by local government in servicing and encouraging the holiday industry. All seaside resorts have generic problems of seasonality and insecurity in their labour markets and in the rhythms of their businesses, but in Blackpool this was particularly marked: the phrase 'three months' hard labour and nine months' solitary confinement' was passing into the status of a proverb by the turn of the century, and the problem it defined has been enduring. A widespread reluctance to encourage the growth of manufacturing industry at the seaside was shared in Blackpool, where a local reserve of cheap, flexible labour was a valued commodity for local employers. Regular, year-round work was likely to diminish it. Many local family economies had to be augmented by work at a distance, especially out of season, a phenomenon which was already in evidence in Edwardian times. Meanwhile, the sheer pressure of seasonal demand for labour was visible at a distance, and large numbers of migrant workers in catering, entertainment and other trades have descended on the town every summer, worsening accommodation problems and generating regular panics about threats to the morality of servants and waitresses. Beggars and prostitutes were part of this picture, and the police worked hard to push them to the margins. High rents and housing shortages for the working class were also common problems in resorts, and Blackpool experienced them in its own distinctive way, while the eagerness of the holiday trades to employ school-age children has been an enduring source of worry for social reformers. Seaside resort economies generally put pressure on families – through migration, insecurity, intermittent bouts of hard work and overcrowding, and lack of alternative resources to take the strain – while in Blackpool especially, competition for work and customers (especially in the boarding-house sector) made it more difficult to build up the broader community ties and organisations so characteristic of the industrial towns. Trade unions were weak, for example, and only the Co-operative movement (belatedly, but impressively) did well. Recent research shows that even in the apparently-prosperous 1950s and 1960s there was no shortage of poverty in Blackpool's back streets. These themes will keep recurring in the chapters which follow.[16]

Blackpool's environmental problems should not be set aside, ironical as their existence may seem in a resort whose origins lay in celebrating the salubrity of the seaside, and whose propaganda continued to emphasise fresh air and clean beaches well beyond the Second World War. There is a sense in which Blackpool was named after its main sewer outlet, the black or peaty 'pull' or 'pool' in the Spen Dyke whose concrete entombment beneath the promenade is now marked by a black and white lighthouse-shaped building which provides a picturesque disguise for the sewer ventilator.[17] The problems arising from the disposal of Blackpool's untreated sewage in the sea could be all too apparent more than a century ago. Complaints about stenches from the sea were already being made in the 1840s, and the General Board of Health's inspector recommended treatment of the town's sewage in 1850. Drainage was laid out but no sewage farm was provided, and a renewed agitation led by W. H. Cocker, Blackpool's leading citizen of the time, in the early 1880s likewise achieved little, although the outfall pipe was extended. Similar palliative responses were made to subsequent complaints, which tended to follow the appearance of obvious gross pollution on the beach, and screening was introduced in 1909; but systematic pollution of the bathing water by the visitors' (and locals') own excrement has been an enduring theme in Blackpool's history. It will necessarily be addressed here.[18]

It may seem a paradox that a local authority whose concern to nurture the holiday industry led it into heavy expenditure on promenades, sea defences, advertising, and later parks and other amenities, should have been so neglectful in this seemingly vital respect; and the neglect is even more striking when we consider the early activity of Blackpool's municipality in such matters as the testing of household drains and the compulsory notification of infectious diseases. We shall see that there were other interesting gaps in the Corporation's record, reflecting greater concern for the economic health of the holiday industry than for the amenities of local inhabitants; but the abuse of the sea has special power to shock. In fairness, the problem was not unique to Blackpool: such neglect has been common in Britain, and it can be found on the grand scale in recent beach resort developments elsewhere.[19] In Blackpool's own case a combination of widely shared faith in the sea's power to absorb and neutralise pollutants, and an awareness of the growing importance of artificial rather than natural attractions to the resort's prosperity, helps to explain matters. So do the perceived expense of treatment works and the expected impact of a sewage farm on surrounding housing and land values.[20] All this draws attention to the vitally important role of local government in Blackpool's development, and what it did achieve was even more important than what it omitted. The identity, priorities and policies of Blackpool's rulers helped to chart the course of the resort's development to such an extent that local government (in a particularly interesting guise) will form a strong and recurrent theme in the chapters that follow.

Local government was all the more important in Blackpool because of the absence of a large landed estate to oversee development and impose a preferred image and identity in the formative years. The obviously central role of landed families and their agents in imposing formal layouts and minimum standards, zoning development, proscribing undesirable land uses and even providing entertainments and other amenities has attracted the attention of several historians.[21] Harold Perkin has even argued that the eventual 'social tone' of a resort was dominated by the initial pattern of landownership, so that Blackpool's small estates were wide open to speculative lowest-common-denominator development and easily colonised by working-class visitors and those who catered for them, while neighbouring resorts like Southport, Lytham and St Anne's could develop in more planned and spacious ways for a decorous middle-class market under the auspices of landed estates and land companies.[22] This interpretation provides a theme for discussion rather than a set of easy answers, and the role of landowners, developers and builders in Blackpool's growth will be another theme running through the book.

Local government and landownership are already well-established themes in historical debate about the English seaside. Less in evidence have been concerns about age, gender, race, ethnicity and sexual orientation which have been attracting increasing attention among social historians in recent years. The distinctive population structure of seaside resorts, coupled with issues raised by sexual division of both labour and leisure and the pressures towards and opportunities for the employment of children, push the former themes to the fore in resort settings, however, and Blackpool is no exception. Women in their teens and early twenties and in their forties and fifties have been particularly over-represented in Blackpool's population, reflect-ing demand for domestic service and catering work in the younger age-groups and the economic opportunities offered by the accommodation industry for the middle-aged. More than any other resort, late Victorian Blackpool became a town of 'landladies', women who ran their businesses and (popular folklore had it) dominated their husbands: a perception which was propagated through comic postcards, dialect literature, music-hall sketches and the cinema. No doubt this mockery played on fear of the female power and independence which running a boarding-house seemed to provide: it was certainly very much a woman's business.[23] Children were less in evidence in the censuses: there was a much smaller private school population than in (for example) some of the up-market south coast resorts. But children of landladies and the local working class were much in demand in the summer, often to the detriment of school attendance, and we shall see that this was an enduring problem, as was the poverty associated with old age and fixed incomes.

Race and ethnicity are less obviously to the fore as issues in Blackpool, although the presentation of minority groups and distant cultures through the entertainment industry both responded to and reinforced stereotypes which were engendered by other means, and this applied especially where imperial motifs were presented. The resident population remained over-whelmingly British by birth and identification, in contrast with many of the inland towns from which visitors were drawn. Gypsies were often controversial, especially when they offered to tell fortunes in public places, while by the turn of the century Italians had put down firm roots among the ice-cream vendors. Some stigma attached to both groups at times. Blackpool's Jewish population seems to have been well-off and less con-troversial, and the resort did not share in the Irish migrations which made an important impact on society and politics in many mid-Victorian towns in Lancashire and beyond. Nor were migrants from the New Common-wealth much in evidence as residents after the Second World War. The 1991 Census found only 975 people in Blackpool with a New Commonwealth birthplace, including 45 from the Caribbean and only 332 from South Asia. Indeed, migrants from the Indian subcontinent were outnumbered by the 407 German-born.[24] A growing New Commonwealth presence has been visible among the visitors over the last twenty years, reflecting developments in Blackpool's hinterland, but there seems to have been amiable co-existence among the various visitor groupings. Gurinder Chadha's recent film *Bhaji on the Beach*, which portrays an outing for Hindu women from Birmingham to Blackpool, makes a lot of well-taken points about race and gender relations without damaging Blackpool's own reputation for relatively harmonious and comfortable mixing, despite the presence of crowds of people from inland cities with tensions of their own.

Bhaji on the Beach is one of a spate of recent feature films and television dramas filmed in Blackpool. The reasons given by some of the film-makers are revealing. Chadha commented: 'It had to be Blackpool because of its place in British social history. Of all the seaside resorts it has the strongest identity in belonging to a specific time and place ...'; and Colin Nutley, returning from several years working in Sweden, said that, 'Blackpool still smells of England in the Fifties. I find that thrilling. It has history and beaches and piers and pubs. It has life.'[25] The town is perceived to have kept a particular kind of vulgar but vivid Englishness which it has protected against American cultural imperialism (despite J. B. Priestley's fears in the 1930s); and its distinctive history is now being regarded as something to celebrate in its own right, by film-makers if not by most British historians. The place has kept a fascination of its own, and a sense of its own past, even as it keeps on reconstructing itself and its image for each new generation, combining novelty and tradition, excitement and reassurance, keeping its old visitors and drawing in new ones. Among these are the gays, who have built on Blackpool's older reputation for providing secure meeting-places and a pool of contacts and now flaunt a new exoticism on the night-club and cabaret scene of the 1990s, in a setting where all seem to be welcome and gay excess is a matter for shared enjoyment rather than apprehension or disapproval. Thus has Blackpool overcome almost the last frontier in its quest to open out the broadest spectrum of entertainment to the widest possible constituency.

Blackpool and the 'resort cycle'

Successive remakings have been essential to Blackpool's continuing dynamism and success as a popular resort. They can be identified in Blackpool's past as it proceeded through the stages of resort development identified by R. W. Butler and elaborated by B. Goodall. These begin with exploration in the later eighteenth century, as Blackpool began to be 'discovered' by comfortably-off sea-bathers. They continue through local development initiatives in the first half of the nineteenth century, and the involvement of outside capital by the 1860s and 1870s, to a fourth level of consolidation which had been reached by the turn of the century, involving the growth of mass tourism and the predominance of the built environment and artificial attractions over the natural attributes which had stimulated the original activity.[26] Blackpool was, of course, unusual in passing through so many stages of the cycle, and beyond the fourth stage the Butler/Goodall model becomes too schematic to deal adequately with developments here. The model makes no provision for the twentieth-century sophistication of the mass market, with season extension, municipal provision of amenities and the attraction of middle-class visitors and residents. Not until the 1970s, perhaps, was the postulated fifth stage reached, that of stagnation, with peak visitor numbers and growing pressure on environment and amenities; and we shall see that active and (in some ways) successful measures were taken to counter the emergent problems. Even in the crisis-ridden (but dynamic) 1990s it is far from clear that the sixth stage, of decline expressed through loss of competitiveness, environmental degeneration and a shrinking catchment area for visitors, is yet more than a threat to be combated. Goodall himself is clear that, valid though the model may be for some British resorts (New Brighton is a classic example), there is nothing inevitable about it; and he cites Blackpool itself as a prime example of 'rejuvenation' as an alternative to the decline phase, with a round of new investment over the last few years.[27]

These ideas will be kept in mind through the rest of the book, as we explore the reasons for Blackpool's unique experience as the world's first working-class seaside resort, while paying due heed to the other Blackpools which coexist with this incarnation and trying to identify the nature of the resort's appeal and influence. The inner workings of the town will be examined, but so will its relations with the outside world. This is always essential for an urban biography, but in the case of this remarkable example of an important and neglected kind of town, it is an overriding need. This will be apparent already in the next chapter, when we look at the origins and early development of Blackpool and try to explain why the first visitors were drawn to this unpromising and unremarkable stretch of remote Lancashire coastline.

CHAPTER TWO

Blackpool before the railway

B LACKPOOL'S EMERGENCE as a distinctive kind of popular resort is rightly associated with the railway age. But, like almost all English resorts, it was not conjured into existence at a stroke by the magic wand of railway wizardry. Its sea-bathing season had been developing noticeably for sixty years and more before the railway arrived, and we shall see that it had a long tradition of popular sea-bathing in August, whose origins are impossible to locate. By the last quarter of the eighteenth century Blackpool was already attracting moneyed visitors from inland Lancashire, the West Riding of Yorkshire and sometimes more distant parts: indeed, its first historian, William Hutton, was a Birmingham bookseller.[1] Blackpool's growth in the railway age was strongly influenced by the links it had forged, the reputation it had obtained and the patterns of development which had already been established over a lifetime between the 1770s and the advent of the railway during the 1840s. To understand subsequent events and processes it is necessary to begin with the origins of the visiting season, and to see how far Blackpool had come by the middle of the nineteenth century.

Blackpool in perspective

In 1851 Blackpool ranked 43rd among English and Welsh seaside resorts, on the basis of a population count in the early spring. At the national census of that year it had 2,564 inhabitants: fewer than (for example) Sidmouth, Herne Bay, Tenby and even Lyme Regis, which were to have much less dynamic subsequent careers, and fewer than nearby Lytham. Southport, Blackpool's great rival across the Ribble Estuary, had more than three times as many inhabitants at this stage, while Scarborough, for many years the most fashionable northern sea-bathing centre, had nearly 13,000 people, although many of these were engaged in fishing and other maritime and trading activities. A further perspective is provided by Brighton, the world's first large specialised coastal health and pleasure resort, which already had 65,569 inhabitants and topped the resort league table comfortably.[2] Even as the railway began to work its magic (and its full influence for growth and transformation was not to be deployed until much later in the century), the Blackpool of 1851, which had been fully linked up with the national network five years previously, remained comparatively unimportant on the wider stage. But its regional influence was not negligible, and its journey to greatness had begun.

Origins

Blackpool's origins were tiny and obscure. It was a scattered hamlet of farms and fishermen's huts in the township of Layton with Warbreck, 20 miles west of the important provincial centre of Preston, which was already in the eighteenth century one of Lancashire's chief towns and a gathering-place for high society in the county. As there was no port and very little commerce in Blackpool, however, this relative proximity counted for little, especially as the roads were circuitous and destitute of milestones or signposts. There was a little hand-loom weaving, but the place was at the end of the road to nowhere, especially as most of the land was divided up among yeoman farmers and there were no local resident families of consequence in the wider world. Significantly, a persistent local legend had it that the only house of any size, Fox or Vaux Hall, had been fitted out as a hideout for Bonnie Prince Charlie in 1745 on the assumption that no-one would think of looking for him there. The shoreline was flat and treeless, rising slightly to a line of unimpressive cliffs at the northern end, and the only outstanding natural features were (importantly) a very extensive sandy beach with a westward aspect, and a lively sea which came right up to the shore at every tide. Only with the arrival of the first sea-bathers of means did more substantial buildings start to accumulate, and at first these were all inns which accommodated bathers during a season which ran from July to early October. Here lay the roots of Blackpool's metamorphosis into a thriving town and popular destination, but it took time for the process to gather momentum.

Early historians of Blackpool and its neighbourhood claim that sea-bathers began to arrive in the early eighteenth century, although evidence is at best anecdotal and might better be described as legendary. Thus when we are told that 'a mere sprinkling of visitors' was already coming in the summers of George I's reign, or that the first inhabitant to specialise in catering for visitors was the unexpectedly styled Ethart a Whiteside in 1735, we are encountering oral history at several removes from personal experience, if indeed the tales are not pure invention. Ethart's alleged successor, the eccentric 'Tom the Cobbler', who was said to have given out bread to the visitors 'with grimy fingers ... from the depths of his well-rosined apron', is an equally shadowy figure.[3] More plausible is Edwin Butterworth's claim, based on evidence gathered in 1835 for Edward Baines's history of Lancashire, that Blackpool's origins as a fashionable bathing-place occurred in the 1750s, when 'some gentlemen, casually visiting the coast, perceived how advantageously it was situated for bathing, and exerted themselves strenuously on its behalf ...'.[4] If this were so, however, as Butterworth himself remarked, early progress was slow, and it was not until the 1770s and 1780s that Blackpool began to make headway in earnest. We cannot rule out the possibility that Blackpool matched Scarborough and southern pioneers such as Brighton and Margate in starting a formal sea-bathing season in the 1730s; after all, this was happening a decade later at Allonby, on an even more remote site on the Solway Firth. But it is safer to regard Blackpool's first serious stirrings as a bathing resort for the comfortably-off as occurring nearly half a century after the origins of the fashion.[5]

It was certainly in the last quarter of the eighteenth century that Blackpool's growth as a resort really began. Inns and other providers of accommodation were beginning to multiply during the 1770s, when gentry, professionals, merchants and manufacturers from Preston and beyond were making the summer journey along the difficult roads. The Langton family, flax merchants of nearby Kirkham in the Fylde, found the basic trappings of a summer season at this time; but the pace of development began to quicken after 1780.[6] Stage-coach services began to run during the summer from inland Lancashire and the West Riding after 1781, giving Blackpool an impressive catchment area which extended to Manchester and Halifax. Two years later, bathing accommodation was being advertised in the Manchester press; and all this was happening at the very time when industrial and urban growth was beginning to accelerate in central and eastern Lancashire and the West Riding of Yorkshire as the Industrial Revolution got under way. The 1780s also saw the opening of the village's first shop and the first (unavailing) attempt to raise a subscription to build a church, and in 1788 William Hutton published the first history and description of the aspiring resort. He thought it contained about 400 visitors at the height of the season in August 1788, drawn mainly from Lancashire, with Manchester contributing the largest share.[7] His daughter Catherine amplifies, reckoning that in the same year there were four main 'houses for the reception of company', with a total capacity of 270, and that most of the visitors were Bolton manufacturers, 'Lancashire gentry, Liverpool merchants, and Manchester manufacturers', with a considerable admixture of lawyers who provided the most congenial company.[8]

Early expansion

This snapshot of Blackpool's early visitors came during a period whose dynamism is attested by the account-books of Bonny's-in-the-fields, which had been one of the two hostelries already plying their trade in 1769. By 1784 it was known as Bonny's Wine House. It took £111.30 from sea-bathing visitors during the 1785 season (exclusive of supplying them with wine), and two-fifths of this sum was taken during August. In the following year the establishment seems to have been rebuilt on a grander scale, offering twenty beds, and by the late 1780s receipts had more than doubled. In 1792

the detailed accounts suggest that £364.95 came in as payment for accommodation, with a further £94.54 from the wine account, which was clearly
big business in its own right: on 9 May 1791, the proprietor paid £41 for
655 bottles of port and £4.25 for 50 bottles of sherry. Detailed records for
1793 suggest that 140 visitors (with 12 servants) passed through Bonny's-
in-the-fields between 7 June and 30 October, with August again clearly the
busiest month. All this evidence confirms the growth of sea-bathing's
importance to the local economy, in ways which were stimulating investment, advertising and transport links.[9]

This spurt of development in the 1780s was followed by steady rather
than spectacular growth. Stage-coaches on the unimproved roads were still
irregular until a daily service began from Preston in the summer of
1816.[10] The resident population of the whole township of Layton with
Warbreck, including an extensive agricultural area as well as the village of
Blackpool itself, doubled from 473 in 1801 to 943 in 1831, accelerating to
reach 1,378 (excluding visitors) at the June census of 1841. Six years earlier
Butterworth had estimated the population of the village itself, again excluding visitors, at about 1,000.[11] Visitor numbers grew in step. Estimates at the
height of the season went up from 800–1,000 in 1830, through Butterworth's
'often 1800 people here in the height of the season – the average number
is 1600', and the propagandist vicar Thornber's more enthusiastic 2,000 in
the mid-1830s, to just over 3,000 recorded in the census of visitors in August
1840, when the railway was within easy reach for the first time. At this time
the corresponding estimate for Brighton was over 20,000, which would
have had a much higher purchasing power per head.[12]

The social pretensions of Blackpool's visitors certainly remained far
inferior to Brighton's, although there is some dispute in the sources over
the direction of change over time. Catherine Hutton (who was, after all,
only the daughter of a prosperous Birmingham bookseller and paper merchant who had speculated well in land) was scathing about the manners
of the Bolton contingent at the Lane Ends, where she stayed in 1788:

> These people are, in general, of a species called Boltoners, that is, rich,
> rough, honest manufacturers of the town of Bolton, whose coarseness
> of manners is proverbial even among their countrymen. The other houses
> are frequented by better company ... I find here that I have no equals
> but the lawyers; for those that are my equals in fortune are distinguished
> by their vulgarity, and those who are my equals in manners are above
> me in situation ... The Boltoners are sincere, good-humoured and noisy;
> the Manchestrians reserved and purse-proud; the Liverpoolians free and
> open as the ocean on which they get their riches. I know little of the
> gentry, but I believe them to be generous, hospitable and rather given
> to intemperance.[13]

Even the gentry, who seem to have segregated themselves from their social inferiors even in this intimate setting, were not the sophisticates of Brighton or even Scarborough, and aristocrats were rare birds of passage. This was still the case half a century later, when the social calibre of the visiting public seems not to have improved. Butterworth in 1835 did describe them as 'fashionable and respectable ... The mass of company comes from the manufacturing districts of both Lancashire and Yorkshire ...'.[14] Others were less easily impressed than the Oldham journalist, however, and his may be an unduly provincial voice for these purposes. In 1830 it was alleged that 'persons of distinction and fashion' had become fewer, tending to prefer Scotland, Ireland, the Lake District or European destinations, perhaps to avoid the proximity of their social inferiors.[15] The redoubtable Dr Granville had no doubts about Blackpool's relatively low status when he passed through in 1839 during his exhaustive tour of the spas and sea-bathing resorts of England. He stayed at Nixon's, the less select of the two leading hotels, and was amazed at the informality and greedy appetite of the 'motley of honest-looking people' who were drawn 'mob-fashion' into the dining-room by a 'loud scavenger-like bell' at dinner-time. 'Methinks the highest in rank here might have been an iron-founder, from near Bradford or Halifax, or a retired wine-merchant, from Liverpool ...' Dickson's was more select, but Granville concluded that although Blackpool's natural advantages in terms of beach and sea made it 'to the west coast of England, what Scarborough is to the east', its geographical and social appeal was more limited:

> I take it that the manufacturing inhabitants of Lancashire supply most of the company at Blackpool. It is rarely that the superior classes of Preston come hither. They prefer going to roast themselves on the less primitive shores of Brighthelmstone, or under St Leonard's cliff. None but such as cannot proceed farther south, or farther east, across Yorkshire, take up their abode here.

Nearer home, Lytham was a rival attraction for Preston lawyers and business-men, although it lacked the glories of the open sea, while Granville himself emphasized the hold Southport had acquired on the affections of Manchester, although he was dismissive about its attractions and social tone.[16]

Attractions and amenities

Blackpool's attractions in 1840 were still based entirely on its natural attributes, in striking contrast to the investment in entertainments and embellishments which was to mark its later rise to popularity as a caterer for the mass market. Its boosters celebrated the health of its maritime environment: a combination of lively sea, safe bathing, firm clean sands for exercise, and pure strong air. Granville endorsed all this, although he feared that many visitors would forfeit the benefits of their stay owing to their addiction to the pleasures of the table, which the sea air encouraged. He was appalled by the 'five solid repasts' and the requests for 'a *little* of the breast with some more of the green sauce' which he found to be so popular at Nixon's, and which was to form the groundwork of a Blackpool tradition of robust eating.[17] There was also an aesthetic dimension to Blackpool's appeal, although Catherine Hutton seems to have been impervious to it, telling a correspondent that the village was situated on 'a level, dreary, moorish coast: the cliffs are of earth, and not very high'.[18] Her father was much more expansive:

> As the land at Blackpool gradually rises from the shore, the eastern views are confined: the principal object is the sea, which is ever under the eye; its infinite diversity from the weather, its own flux and reflux, with the vessels upon its surface ... afford a continual source of amusement. To the north are seen, projecting into the water, at the distance of forty miles, the fells of Westmoreland ...

And he continues to describe the full panorama of distant mountains, from Cumberland to Carnarvonshire, with the Isle of Man breaking the western horizon when weather and time of day allowed.[19]

This kind of description became a commonplace of propagandist presentations of Blackpool, combining as it did elements of the fashion for the picturesque and the sublime which helped to make shorelines appealing rather than threatening (or appealing *because* threatening) across Europe in these years.[20] The vastness of Blackpool's sea even diverted the prosaic Butterworth from his task of chronicling, if only for a sentence: 'The most prominent and striking object here is the Irish Sea which is seen in all its terrific grandeur.'[21] Granville drew an arresting analogy between the crowded sands at low tide and the 'desert of Suez with the parted waters of the Red Sea', evoking the area's relationship with myth, religion, distant parts and human origins in ways which were also current elsewhere in Europe, although the lack of shells, seaweed and visibly interesting geological formations at Blackpool made popular science as a recreation less attractive here than at some rival resorts.[22]

Blackpool was undoubtedly a beneficiary of the new, positive ways of responding to the sea and its environs which Alain Corbin has identified as a widespread European phenomenon in the later eighteenth century and afterwards. It is interesting to see this theme in evidence in such a relatively unintellectual and down-market setting.[23] The ways of seeing and experiencing which Corbin discusses had clearly become part of a provincial middle-class culture which had learned to find the sea attractive and interesting as well as healthy. But we over-intellectualise the sea's attractions at our peril. The court portrait painter Samuel Finney, who was certainly no provincial hobbledehoy, wrote a letter describing Blackpool in 1789, but all he had to say about the sea and bathing was that, 'I shared not further in it than dipping my finger into the sea and tasting the delicious drop that hung upon it.'[24] But even this trivial level of response might have been unthinkable without the wholesale sea-change in attitudes to the marine environment which Corbin chronicles, and which formed an essential element in the making of Blackpool.

Perhaps the best description of the distinctiveness of Blackpool's attractions in these early days, in terms of sea and situation, comes from the surgeon John Roberton, whose letters home from a therapeutic visit in August 1842 offer a delightfully informal and unclinical account. He began with a jaundiced attitude to the whole place, complaining of noise, wind and rain as well as general *malaise,* and insisting, 'Climate of Lancashire all alike bad'. But two days later he provided a fuller and friendlier appraisal:

> I fear that this keen sea air (and no air can be more bracing) is not doing me good. I find many, however, who say it tries them in the outset, though afterwards they are strong and full of life ... The worst thing is the *weariness* and languor in spite of even this most blessed air. In truth every face, save mine, wears a rosy hue and smile of happiness; and the gait of every young one I meet is elastic. I am almost certain the place would suit *you,* for it is neither like the Isle of Man nor like any other sea-bathing place you ever saw – a headland on which the sea beats and rages incessantly ... the character of the air and of the sea depends on this – that there is no bay, nor *bend* in the line of coast, for a distance of 18 miles; consequently, no sheltered nook, no hills, no projecting tongue of land to give you a stormy or calm side at your option. The sea and the wind beat upon the shore alike at all points ... It is the most open, naked, bleak, unsheltered shore, with the deepest sea and highest tides, of any place in these parts; so, if sea air be the object, no where can it be found in greater perfection. Then, as regards bathing, know that there are no rocks – not one, but only an immense sandy beach over which the tide, driven generally by a south-wester, comes tumbling in majestically. But at all times, unless it blows very hard, you may bathe even at neap tides within 300 yards of the shore. And, such is the character of the strand, that whether at high or at low water, the bather is in perfect safety ... It is this smoothness of the beach, this absence of rocks and consequently of deep holes, this perfect exposure to the sea breezes, this sufficient depth of water for bathing, quite near the shore, that gives Blackpool the pre-eminence over, I am told, any other bathing place in the Kingdom, even over Brighton. Then again, there being no hilly region near, the clouds pass inland, leaving the climate comparatively dry; which is a great thing to people from the interior of so moist a climate as that of Lancashire and the West Riding – the regions whence come nearly all the bathers.[25]

This encapsulates the natural advantages and drawbacks of Blackpool, including the absence of nearby picturesque scenery apart from the compelling seascapes. Other commentators remarked on the complete absence of trees, and antiquarians bemoaned the lack of places of historic interest, which was due to the district having been (as Butterworth put it) 'too remote and obscure to have been the scene of any important occurrences'.[26] But what the place had to offer in climatic and sea-bathing terms was unique; and Roberton makes it clear that it combined a sense of the majesty and playfulness of the sea with a feeling of complete safety. Notions of the untamed majesty of the vasty deep could be enjoyed, but without real risk to the contemplative bather and promenader.

In its own small way, however, Blackpool was also developing the artificial and sociable amenities without which no resort could grow very far: they were essential to the enjoyment of the more worldly and prosaic visitors who made the consumer and entertainment markets work, and with whom Blackpool's future was to lie. Samuel Finney in 1789 found good company and interesting conversation, and seems to have wanted little else: 'Some of the other houses admit Gaities [sic], as card playing, and sometimes Balls, but we did very well at ours, without these ...'[27] Hutton revealed that by this time Blackpool boasted a grassy promenade for display and flirtation, a coffee house, 'diminutive' bowling greens, sailing, archery, dancing and even a theatre, 'if *that* will bear the name which during nine months of the year is only the threshing-floor of a barn'.[27] There were also fortnightly fairs for 'the lads and lasses from the adjacent country', where 'the young men practice their little diversions; the old women wish to dispose of their fruit, and the young of their hearts'.[28]

Half a century later the pace of development of artificial attractions was only just beginning to quicken. Butterworth listed the 'public institutions' in 1835, pointing out that there was still no 'public building of sufficient magnitude to merit notice in a county history'. However, he listed 'a Library and News Room, Assembly Rooms at [four of the] Hotels, several Billiard Rooms, an occasional Theatre, warm and vapour baths, which are attached to every Hotel'. This was a significant advance on 1788, but unremarkable: what was offered would have paled into insignificance on the south coast, at Scarborough or even at nearby Southport. Meanwhile, recent measures had been taken to improve Blackpool's reputation for moral restraint and respectability: the horse races on the sands, which had been a feature of the summer for many years, had been suppressed in the early 1830s, while the Sunday fairs, which Hutton had viewed in such a relaxed way, were said to have 'fallen into desuetude, the old women and their gingerbread baskets being banished, together with the gangs of wicked brutal company'.[29] It would be interesting to know more about the roots of these disappearances. Blackpool, like Southport, was trying to clean up its image at this stage, but it is not clear whether the changed portrayal of the fairs since Hutton's time reflected the demeanour of the fairgoers or the changing attitude of the observers, in the light of the Evangelical revival and increasing preoccupation with morality and respectability. Attempts to woo respectable society continued with the opening of the first purpose-built assembly rooms, the Victoria Terrace and Promenade, in 1837. It offered newspapers, billiards and a library, but its long first-floor meeting and dancing room was apparently unsuitable for concerts.[30] At least Blackpool had a church by this time: it had been consecrated in 1821, and had to be enlarged twice during the 1830s, when nonconformist provision was also expanded beyond the original Independent chapel of 1825.[31] We can see that on the eve of the railway age Blackpool was beginning to make up for lost time in the provision of basic amenities for polite society at the seaside, but it lagged behind larger and more prestigious resorts elsewhere, especially within London's orbit. It was certainly not a centre for competitive consumer spending in its own right, as Bath and the county towns had long been, along with London's West End.[32] Rather than promoting the values of a notional consumer society, it offered at best a pallid and intermittent reflection of them for the few fleeting weeks of its summer season.

Shaping Blackpool: landownership and local government

Blackpool's development before the creation of a Local Board of Health in 1851 was achieved with a minimum of intervention from large landowners or local government. Hutton tells us that in the 1780s the visitors regulated their own bathing, with times set apart for men and women and a fine of a bottle of wine for transgressors; and the shared values of (relatively) polite society continued to sustain a measure of civility and decorum among the 'better-class' visitors.[33] But formal local government was based on village institutions. Overseers of the poor and surveyors of highways were chosen at township meetings, while the manorial court was still holding sessions in 1835, at which constables, by-law enforcers and wreck examiners were appointed. The by-laws in question dealt with such issues as turf-cutting rights and the maintenance of drainage ditches.[34] The Lords of the Manor lived outside it and owned little land within the township. The 'respectable yeomen', in Butterworth's words, who held the freehold properties which predominated were able to develop their own plots of land, or let them remain agricultural, in a piecemeal way as they saw fit. The tithe award of 1837 shows that land in Layton-with-Warbreck was highly sub-divided. Not only was two-thirds of it held by owners of less than 100 acres: nearly one-third was held by owners of less than 50 acres, and most individual property-owners held two or three separate parcels of land. Most of the 24 estates of more than 25 acres were away from the sea-front: only five such estates, of between 26 and 44 acres, were to be built up before the 1890s. Matters might have been different: the Forshaw brothers had built up an extensive estate which covered much of what was to become northern and central Blackpool from the later eighteenth century, but their lands were subjected to a forced sale by mortgage holders in 1832 before they could be developed, and the estate was broken up.[35]

This fragmented landownership and lack of overall control made for piecemeal, unplanned development, and any possibility of going up-market was checked by developers' inability to predict what would happen on adjoining land. An ambitious crescent could quite easily have found itself next door to hovels and pigsties. So Sir Peter Hesketh-Fleetwood, Lord of the Manor in the mid-1830s, preferred to develop a new town bearing his name at the mouth of the River Wyre a few miles to the north, rather than set an example to his Blackpool neighbours by planned development on his 8 acres of prime central sea-front land. The Cliftons of Lytham, a prominent nearby gentry family, began to consolidate a Blackpool estate from about 1832, buying up a substantial portion of the Forshaw estate, but again preferred to concentrate their planned villa-building operations on their core estate at Lytham itself, a few miles to the south, when they saw what neighbouring developers were doing at Blackpool.[36] Butterworth acutely observed that the predominance of freehold tenures and the lack of manorial controls probably freed Blackpool to grow faster than it would otherwise have done, although such a perception was very much in tune with his own (and his employer's) belief in Free Trade as a social cure-all.[37] The down-market nature of Blackpool's eventual destiny was certainly bound up with its pattern of landholding and lack of manorial control. The aesthetic results of this freedom received a mixed press in the 1830s. Several contemporaries felt obliged to apologise for the absence of regularity and overall plan on the preferred Georgian model; but others espoused an alternative set of values which could find enjoyment in a scattering of rustic cottages interspersed with slightly more pretentious buildings.[38] As befitted an unplanned and isolated village, the access roads were still a source of complaint: Butterworth summed up the consensus by describing them as 'provokingly circuitous', and there were still no milestones.[39] Blackpool's accelerating growth in the 1820s and especially the 1830s was achieved in spite of continuing difficulty of access.

Popular sea-bathing: the 'Padjamers'

Despite this, what really made Blackpool distinctive during these years was the unusually large number of sea-bathers from the lower orders of Lancashire society who made an annual pilgrimage to the village. Hutton noted their presence in 1788, but it was no new thing in the late eighteenth century, and may have gone back a very long way without finding its way into the written record. Hutton was told that in about 1760 the 'people who then frequented Blackpool were chiefly of the lower orders', and he himself mentioned 'an inferior class, whose sole motive for visiting this airy region is health'. Indeed, he interviewed a Lancaster shoemaker who fell squarely into this category.[40] At the dawn of the railway age the June census of 1841 found half a dozen skilled workers among a visiting public which was dominated by commerce, manufacturing and people of independent means. There was no similar presence at Margate, the most 'popular' of the resorts serving London at this stage.[41]

Much more spectacular than this, though of little economic moment as yet, were the invasions of the so-called 'Padjamers'. These were artisans and small farmers from inland Lancashire who came in carts, on foot or riding pillion on lumbering horses to bathe and drink the sea-water by the gallon at the August spring tides, sleeping several to a bed or in barns. They came for the 'physic' which was said to be in the sea at this time of year. A quasi-magical belief was current that contact with sea-water would cleanse, purify and protect against misfortune for the coming year. Similar beliefs were current throughout Roman Catholic Western Europe, and this bathing custom was found all along the Lancashire coast (especially Liverpool) and in parts of Wales, above all where Catholic survival was also strong. It has all the hallmarks of an adapted pagan custom with very deep roots and wide currency, and although it only comes into view in Blackpool at the turn of the century, there is every reason to assume a much longer pedigree. Rather than declining with the new century, it actually increased its popularity, and newspaper accounts of the 1820s and 1830s describe cavalcades of hundreds of people, using a motley array of conveyances, passing through Preston to the coast from as far away as the Manchester and Burnley areas. In the early 1840s the 'Bathing Sunday' tradition, as it was called, transferred itself to the railway. Blackpool was easily the most popular destination for these unpretentious bathers, and the custom was strong and resilient enough to have had an important formative influence on the growth of the popular season. It was probably from roots such as these that medical writers derived the fashionable perception of sea-bathing as an aid to health in the early eighteenth century: an example of fashions moving up the social scale before being passed downwards again, which complicates assumptions about the 'trickling down' of fashion through society by a process of emulation or 'aping one's betters'. The processes were more complicated than that.[42]

On the eve of the railway's arrival, then, Blackpool was already accelerating its growth as an unpretentious provincial seaside resort with a mainly regional, middle-class visiting public. On the Butler/Goodall model of resort growth which was discussed in Chapter 1, it can be placed at a point of transition between the second stage, where local initiatives are beginning to undertake development and exploitation of natural resources to attract and keep visitor patronage, and the third stage, where the involvement of outside capital boosts the pace and scale of growth, and indeed its sophistication. This third stage was to be ushered in by the arrival of the railway in the 1840s.

CHAPTER THREE

Blackpool in the early railway age, 1840–1870

I T IS IMPOSSIBLE TO IMAGINE Blackpool matching the scale of the growth it experienced under Victorian conditions without railway access, especially if we assume that its competitors were thus equipped. Railways permitted much greater volumes of passenger traffic than hitherto, at faster speeds and lower fares which in turn cut the cost of leisure travel in time as well as money, thus helping to boost demand for seaside visits. But we should not assume that seaside resorts, or attractive sites which showed a potential for resort development, automatically attracted the interest of railway promoters in their own right. This was palpably not the case: the seasonality of resort traffic, and its vulnerability to changes in fashion, both increased capital expenditure requirements relative to receipts and heightened the level of risk. Significantly, hardly any resorts were established by purpose-built railways on virgin sites, and the clearest example, Silloth on the Solway Firth in Cumberland, was far from being a roaring success. Many resorts did grow from very small beginnings along rail routes which skirted shorelines but were built for other purposes, but this was a less clearly marked pattern of railway influence. The impact of railways on the resorts they served was variable in extent and timing, and railway policies towards resorts ranged from eager promotion and invest-ment to apathy. They were quite capable of changing over time, especially when the lines themselves were transferred from one company to another. The influence of the railway on Blackpool itself was far from straight-forward, as this introduction to the issues suggests; and although it made a significant difference to the resort's fortunes right from the start, its full impact was delayed for a generation and depended on interplay with several other influences to become effective.[1]

Arrival of the railway

When the railway came within easy reach of Blackpool for the first time in July 1840, its arrival owed little to the promoters' perceptions of the actual and potential holiday traffic. The Preston and Wyre Railway, which provided a convenient railhead for Blackpool 4 miles away at Poulton-le-Fylde, was part of a broader scheme to develop a commercial port and planned town on a virgin site at the mouth of the River Wyre, a few miles north of Blackpool itself. The new town of Fleetwood was named after its founder, Sir Peter Hesketh-Fleetwood, and was intended as the railhead for Scotland, Ireland and the Isle of Man, as well as becoming a high-class seaside resort in its own right, with grandiose terraces and crescents by the fashionable architect Decimus Burton. So the new railway was apparently a threat to Blackpool as well as an opportunity, and the traffic projections envisaged in the prospectus which had been issued in 1834 gave little weight to the Blackpool market. 'Passengers for commerce and to Blackpool', put together, were expected to amount to only 4,000 annually, bringing in 12 per cent of the expected passenger receipts and less than 3 per cent of the anticipated total revenue. Blackpool was incidental to the Preston and Wyre's plans, and its moving spirit sold his land there, investing instead in the venture at Fleetwood which was to bankrupt him.[2]

Two Blackpool freeholders who had been prominent in early building activity, Henry and Robert Banks, took a different view of the possibilities, for they appeared on the list of proprietors when the railway company obtained the necessary Act of Parliament to build the line in July 1835.[3] They were proved right, for they made money both out of the railway and its consequences. When the newly completed line opened in 1840 the summer broke all records in Blackpool. Not only were new middle-class visitors attracted: the directors' decision to run third-class carriages in pursuit of the Bathing Sunday traffic was vindicated by events, while carts from east Lancashire continued to bring large numbers of 'Padjamers'. This was no flash in the pan, and the building of a branch line over the flat and easy terrain from Poulton was soon undertaken: it had the great and tangible merit of cheapness. Blackpool itself was connected to what was rapidly becoming a national railway system in April 1846.[4]

The opening of the branch line brought Blackpool into direct contact with Preston, Bolton, Manchester and more distant towns on the Manchester and Leeds line, and with the West Coast main line to London. Within four years extensions to the system added almost all of the substantial industrial towns of Lancashire and the West Riding to the list, and through traffic was eased when in 1849 the Preston and Wyre line was leased jointly by the Lancashire and Yorkshire and London and North Western companies, the former taking two-thirds of the receipts. The scope for increasing the holiday traffic was now immense, and Fleetwood's brief domination of the excursion market had been swiftly terminated by the opening of the Blackpool branch. Fleetwood apart, Blackpool had a head start over most of its regional competitors in obtaining railway access, and the Lancashire and Yorkshire, especially, was eager to exploit the possibilities. Cheap excursions multiplied during the season, as the railways ran their own trips and also offered facilities to organisations such as Sunday Schools. Accommodation was far from palatial, and in 1856 the Lancashire and Yorkshire had to borrow cattle trucks from neighbouring companies when its own were all in use on Sunday School trips at the height of the season; but the important thing was that, from as far away as Manchester, fares were fixed at less than a day's wage for a man. The Lancashire and Yorkshire line was renowned neither for speed nor for punctuality, but it was keen on promoting excursion traffic (to a unique extent), and indeed it offered more encouragement to trippers than to the seasonal commuters from the comfortably-off middle classes who were a less numerous but potentially lucrative market. Under the auspices of the railway Blackpool's middle-class visiting public certainly increased in numbers, fortified by first-class rail fares at little more than one-third of the stage-coach rates; but the distinctive and remarkable changes involved working-class visitors. The new opportunities for coastal visits became available just as an economic upturn began to raise the purchasing power of wages for skilled workers in urban Lancashire, and it was easier to take holidays in better times without worrying about the response of employers who needed to keep their workpeople. Cheap rail fares extended the Bathing Sunday traffic to weekends throughout the summer, including the great Lancashire Whitsuntide holidays; and where 1,000 might have been thought an unusual influx of 'Padjamers' in pre-rail days, by the early 1850s up to 12,000 might arrive at a time, many of whom would use cheap weekend tickets to stay over from Saturday to Monday in cottage lodgings. The sheer scale of this phenomenon was unique to Blackpool, and it posed severe problems for the resort's rulers in the short term. So the arrival of the railway brought social problems as well as economic opportunities.[5]

Coping with the trippers

The greatly expanded numbers of working-class trippers in the early railway age proved indigestible to the mainstream middle-class visiting and business public. Some of their behaviour offended against canons of order and decency which were becoming dominant in the public discourse of 'respect-able' society, if not always in the actual behaviour of middle-class people. The excursionists seem to have been drawn mainly from people at the crest of the 'poverty cycle', young men and women who were wage-earners but did not yet have family responsibilities, and perhaps older people whose children were now self-supporting, although it was the younger people (especially the men) who were more visible to censorious contemporary commentators. The quiet, sedate norms of the middle-class family, already centred on the bucket and spade and the newspaper or the novel, were challenged by some of the trippers, who sought to enjoy their limited leisure to the full, arriving early and departing late, shouting, singing, drinking, dancing, and bathing without recourse to bathing-machines or heed to conventions about modesty. Their dress offended, as did their defective personal hygiene. Chokers, clay pipes and clogs were not deemed suitable holiday attire by the 'better classes', whose own priorities on holiday embraced the display of fashionable outfits and elegant manners. As a Bolton dialect writer remarked, the railways were open to both saints and sinners. Cheap trips promoted sociability, education and a broader understanding of the world; but people could and did also use them 'for nowt but a spree', to get 'so bloind drunk as to be thoroughly unable to see any oth beauties uv naytur'. Comment in mid-century Blackpool tended to emphasise the latter at the expense of the former.[6]

Criticism was directed especially against the Sunday day-trips which were run by the Lancashire and Yorkshire Railway, at fares as little as 1s. 6d. (7.5p), well within the pocket of an employed labourer without family ties even as early as the late 1840s. In 1849 a press correspondent denounced 'railway mammon' for destroying the pristine solemnity of the local Sabbath by importing flashily dressed 'barbers' apprentices and shoeblacks' who were 'ignorant of the decencies of society' and set the 'bewildered' policemen at defiance. The trippers themselves were only part of the problem, for in their wake came expanded numbers of hawkers and donkey drivers, who blocked the way to the beach, swore and shouted when people declined their custom, and sometimes fought among themselves, especially in 1852 when a band of Southport donkey-men invaded Blackpool in search of a share of the local spoils and were eventually driven away by the home team after a pitched battle. There were also public health difficulties, not only from sewage on the beach but also from the congregations of donkeys, whose accumulated droppings were an added health hazard for those who followed tradition by drinking the sea-water in copious quantities.[7]

This crisis of the early railway age was short-lived but telling in its long-term impact, although Blackpool's rival Southport experienced similar public order problems at the same time without compromising its ultimate career as a high-class residential resort. Middle-class visitors, after all, were quite capable of (for example) setting the bathing regulations at defiance on their own account. But, significantly, just as Southport and other resorts were coming under the tightening control of landed estates with an interest in promoting planned, high-class development during the 1840s, it was at this very time that the influences in this direction at Blackpool were withdrawn in direct response to the new working-class presence. The Clifton family of Lytham, who might have used their strategically-placed estate (which included the direct route between the new railway station and the sea) to promote an opulent development of villa residences, chose not to do so. Instead, they concentrated this kind of activity into their main estate at Lytham, a few miles to the south-east, where they could control their surroundings and exert a strong influence on local government.[8]

Development and drainage

This outcome was not inevitable. Thomas Clifton had been systematically acquiring land at Blackpool during the 1830s, and by 1844 he had accumulated a substantial estate on the north side of the emergent resort. For several years Clifton and his agent, James Fair, toyed with the idea of constructing an impressive main approach from the railway station to the sea, which might have encouraged similar ambitions elsewhere. A Liverpool architect was brought in and produced an estate plan which featured spacious villas set in extensive gardens, but as the crowds of trippers began to throng across the estate towards the sea Clifton heeded his comment that the whole estate was 'liable to be built closely upon by property of an inferior description'. He decided to sell and take his profit, on the assumption that land values had peaked in 1847 with the boom which accompanied the coming of the railway. The land was developed piecemeal with small terraced houses and no architectural embellishment, just as were the surrounding small estates. Despite the new sources of capital and expertise which the railway had theoretically made available, Blackpool continued to grow in its original unplanned way, with narrow streets and no scope for ambitious planning. Every developer was vulnerable to the inferior ambitions and lust for quick profit of his neighbour. The accelerated building activity of the railway decade did nothing to raise Blackpool's social tone.[9]

What the problems of the later 1840s and early 1850s exposed was a lack of local government institutions to keep order and regulate development, in the absence of an active Lord of the Manor or other dominant landowner as was the case at Southport, Lytham or, further afield, Eastbourne. Such a lack of civic control was a common feature of early Victorian towns, but it had special potential to damage an emergent resort which depended on a reputation for providing a healthy and secure environment for visitors and residents. Blackpool's Lancashire rivals were already setting up Improvement Commissions to provide basic public health and public order machinery, and even as the railway arrived in 1846 the first such proposals were being debated in the little town. As things stood, everything except the barest essentials of road repair and poor relief was left to individual initiative. Drainage was the most noticeable problem. Cesspools and ditches were the only means of sewage disposal, and unpleasant smells resulted, especially at the height of the season when warm weather coincided with additional pressures on the system. Contemporary belief in the miasmatic theory of disease made the stenches seem life-threatening as well as disgusting. A visiting land agent commented in 1846:

The nuisance is intolerable ... when the wind is from the sea which should be the best the stench is past bearing even in the Houses if the

Doors and Windows are open . . . It is impossible for Blackpool to maintain its position if these nuisances are not removed . . .[10]

Four years later a government inspector found that 45 sewers and open
drains trickled prettily across the beach at Blackpool and its neighbouring
satellite settlement of South Shore. The Spen Dyke, the original 'Black
Pool', took the brunt of the sewage, which spread itself 'in large stagnant
pools upon the sands'. At the same time Blackpool had 421 houses but as
many as 181 pigsties. Water supply was deficient, with many of the town's
wells polluted and charges being levied for access to pumps. The absence
of street lighting was beginning to be felt, and the roads were undrained
and inadequately made up. To all this the emergent public order problems
had to be added.[11]

Introducing local government

In 1845–6 a group of leading citizens and property-owners responded to
the situation by proposing an Improvement Bill to set up Commissioners
with power to levy a rate or property tax to pave, light and sewer that part
of the township which was expected to become building land, and to
control the donkey drivers, cabmen and others who catered for the summer
visitors. The Bill's supporters included the Manchester banker Sir Benjamin
Heywood, who had some claim to being Blackpool's leading citizen, as
well as the Cliftons' agent, James Fair, and several central landowners and
property developers. But their initiative came to grief in the face of intran-
sigent opposition from outlying landowners who saw no benefit to
themselves in the proposals, and were adamantly opposed to paying rates
in support of the better-placed building speculators at the seaside.[12] They
were, perhaps understandably, unable to look ahead to a time when their
land might also reap the benefits. This was the prototype of a kind of
conflict which, in various guises, was to be an enduring theme in seaside
resorts in general, and in Blackpool in particular.

As pressure for intervention mounted, the Public Health Act of 1848
provided a less-controversial route to establishing urban local government,
after the same opponents had successfully obstructed a second Improvement Bill proposal. The 1848 Act was cheap to adopt, and the doubters
were reassured by the limited powers of central oversight which it turned
out to provide. It was the visiting inspector under this Act who pointed
out the town's sanitary defects in such graphic detail, and he concluded
that they were 'not only very inconvenient to the inhabitants, but . . . in
many cases they inflict pecuniary injury upon them by driving visitors
away from the town'.[13] The Act was adopted in 1851 and a Local Board of
Health with nine members was duly elected. What the Public Health Act
did not do, however, was provide powers for policing, public order and

the regulation of the streets and foreshore; and these had been at least as high on the agenda as the public health issues. The barrister and Staffordshire county magistrate John Bill, for example, had been rather intimidated by aspects of his reception at the new railway station in August 1846: 'The terminus at Blackpool, though very large and lofty for the place, was very uncomfortably crowded with spectators, eager expectants, and idle people, of all sorts and sizes, some of them, perhaps, "indifferent honest", as Hamlet has it ...'.[14]

Bill was worried about his luggage, took care to stow it safely on an omnibus, but then found that he had lost a portmanteau, which was later restored to him under very suspicious circumstances on payment of 2s. 6d. (12.5p) 'reward'. This was just the kind of reputation a nascent resort could not afford to acquire, and worries about the security of visitors combined with the need to control the trippers and their hangers-on to make further local legislation necessary. The Improvement Act of 1853 enabled by-laws to be established to license trades which were plied in public places and to impose minimum approved standards of behaviour on the visitors. It also allowed the Local Board, as an Improvement Commission, to buy up the market and the new gasworks. The by-laws received official approval from central government in October 1853, enabling the Local Board to license donkeys, bathing-machines, boats and cabs, and to deny access to these trades to the opportunistic outsiders who had been a source of much complaint among the locals. Severe restrictions on Sunday trading were imposed, and bathing was strictly regulated, the sexes being separated by fifty yards, while men were required to wear drawers. Bathing without using a machine was prohibited.[15]

This new regime, which in the name of morality effectively 'privatised' the use of the beach for certain purposes, restored enough order and decorum to the streets and foreshore to enable Blackpool to keep the 'better-class' market on which it still depended: the trippers' visits were too brief and their spending power too limited to make it thinkable to try to base the town's economy on them. A spate of fines at the start of the 1854 season effectively drove home the new authority's determination to make the changes stick, and the Improvement Act enabled the local authority to pay the county police to supply extra constables during the season, a necessary practice which had hitherto had to be guaranteed by private citizens. The restabilisation of the 'respectable' season was completed when in 1856 the Lancashire and Yorkshire Railway withdrew its controversial Sunday excursions, after which, significantly, the Sunday observance by-laws were enforced less strictly. They had arisen less from genuine religious sentiment than from a desire to restrict the behaviour of the cheap trippers and to make Blackpool less attractive to them.[16]

The Local Board of Health and Improvement Commission, united in the same hands, ushered in a period of stable growth on more or less conventional middle-class lines, although Blackpool continued to be remarkable for its unusually numerous working-class presence on summer weekends. The long saga of local government involvement in providing necessary services and amenities began in the 1850s. It started jerkily and was slow to gather momentum, under the auspices of yeomen and small tradesmen who operated under the jealous gaze of outlying proprietors who were keen to keep local taxation to a minimum, in a climate of opinion which was deeply suspicious of public expenditure. Such attitudes were reinforced by the lack of expertise of officials who were part-time and readily corruptible, in the absence as yet of a professional culture of municipal service. It is not surprising that Blackpool, like other Local Boards, began its work timidly and made early mistakes, confining its early activity to the provision of essential services in which private enterprise was unwilling to invest or unable to operate at an attractive prospective rate of return, and for which individuals were unwilling to band together collaboratively on a voluntary basis. By the mid-1860s, however, as we shall see, the Local Board was growing in confidence and winning widespread assent for more positive policies. The opening of an impressive new promenade in 1870, with associated sea defence works, was to set the seal on this important new trend and helped to underpin its continuation.

The Local Board and urban improvement

The Local Board began by tackling the sewerage problem, which had been attracting so much damaging comment; but it also moved swiftly into gas manufacture and the purchase of a market which had been set up by a local syndicate. This last was a more dubious priority, for it was owned by members of the Local Board who had campaigned for the power to transfer it to the new authority by purchase. They proceeded to sell the market to the Local Board at considerably more than the current value of their shares in what was obviously an ailing concern, in a clear conflict of interest. The market, once acquired, was allowed to languish. This was the first of many similar scandals in Blackpool's local government. The sewerage scheme also got off to a bad start. There was insufficient gradient in the early sewers, which was worsened by the absence of a piped water supply to flush them out, making leaks and blockages more likely. Incompetent surveyors and contractors added to the difficulties, and the saga culminated in a political row in which a Ratepayers' Association mounted a successful electoral *coup* against the original Board. After this, however, the sewerage proceeded more smoothly, to be completed during 1856–7, although advice to have the sewage treated was ignored. Blackpool, like most other seaside resorts, preferred localised pollution of the sea to the problems and expense of finding a site for a sewage treatment works, at a time when such technologies were admittedly unproven; and this was to prove an enduring embarrassment as the resort and its visiting population grew.[17]

While this was going on the Local Board gave Blackpool an unexpectedly pioneering role in the municipal ownership and operation of gasworks. In 1851–2 a so-called Vegetable Gas Company had set up a gasworks close to the sea-front on Bonny's Estate, an area of cottage property at the back of the future Golden Mile, the heart of the sea-front. This was an outside speculation, promoted from Hull, and using a system which had already been outflanked by coal gas. In striking contrast to the market purchase, the Local Board made no attempt to buy it out after obtaining the power to do so in 1853. The company's technology was flawed and its gas was stratospherically priced, so it is perhaps reasonable that it was allowed to wither on the vine, while the Local Board built its own new coal gas plant further south and began to use it to light the new street lamps as early as September 1853. After a few difficult years the new gasworks was leased out to William Crippin, who also ran the Southport gasworks, for most of the 1860s. Only in 1869 did it revert to municipal operation under the management of John Chew, who was inherited from the Crippin regime and presided over an enduring success story, as cheap prices were combined with high profits to set against local taxation. Blackpool was thus among the pioneers of municipal gas, although a long way behind Manchester, which started in 1817, and indeed a few years behind the rival resorts of Lytham and Southport. Resorts were generally early in the field, as lighting was an important asset in the competition for visitors both in terms of amenity and personal security. Gas and public order were thus inextricably linked.[18]

A good water supply was equally important, and here the local circumstances made dependence on private enterprise inevitable. Blackpool was fortunate to benefit from an initiative from nearby Lytham to set up the Fylde Waterworks Company in 1860. This was promoted by the Clifton Estate and found support from other Fylde landowners in its second incarnation: an earlier initiative in 1853 had failed to gather momentum. The company had a broad geographical remit and most of its capital came from districts outside Blackpool: indeed, in 1863 Lytham people held nearly five times as many shares as the 26 Blackpool investors. The small local shareholders included several tradesmen and lodging-house keepers. It was clear that, whether or not the company made a profit, the indirect benefits to the resorts would be considerable. The company's capital was five times Blackpool's rateable value, which would have made it unthinkable as a purely local or municipal venture, and it provided the only possible access to gathering-grounds in the hills 20 miles to the east, which offered the best hope for a pure and copious supply which was capable of expanding in step with population and visitor numbers. Given the likelihood that any water shortage would coincide with the summer season, it is difficult to see how Blackpool could have sustained its late Victorian growth without the Fylde Water Company's life support system; but this necessary contribution to the town's rise was out of the hands of the locals, and must be counted as an incidental benefit from a scheme designed mainly for other purposes. The parallels with the early arrival of the railway, also promoted by a local landowner for reasons unconnected with and even potentially prejudicial to the fortunes of Blackpool, are vividly apparent.[19]

Blackpool began to receive the Company's water in July 1864, and within three years two-thirds of the houses were supplied. This put Blackpool well ahead of most rivals, and as late as 1879 such prominent health and pleasure resorts as Bournemouth, Folkestone, Llandudno, Hastings and Torquay still had no constant water supply. Fylde water was an important propaganda asset at a time when Blackpool was still predominantly a health resort. Important changes in other respects were just getting under way as the water supply arrived; but before investigating them we need to look a little more closely at what sort of place Blackpool became after its initial adjustment to the arrival of the railway.[20]

Mid-Victorian expansion

The arrival of the railway brought a visible stimulus to Blackpool's urban growth. The population of Layton with Warbreck, which became the Local Board district, increased at 2.3 per cent per year between 1821 and 1831, but the corresponding figures for the following decades were 3.7 per cent, 6.0 per cent (in the first full decade of railway access) and (as the initial boom eased) 4.1 per cent between 1851 and 1861. From 943 in 1831 and 1,378 in 1841 the population grew to 2,564 in 1851 and 3,907 in 1861. The rise of over 86 per cent in Blackpool's population between 1841 and 1851, followed as it was by an increase of a further 52 per cent in the next decade, added up to an impressive growth-rate even in the context of a rapidly urbanising nation, although the low base figures made the performance easier to achieve.[21]

By 1851 Blackpool's mid-Victorian pattern of ways of making a living was already well-established, and subsequent population expansion over the next generation meant basically more of the same. Roughly one in seven of the household heads were professionals, large employers or other substantial earners, or had independent means. One in four were lodging-house keepers or publicans, nearly one in five were in retailing or small-scale manufacturing, and one in seven were in the building trades, the town's most important manufacturing industry. Services and the residential sector were more in evidence than in most towns, and up to this point Blackpool fitted a general resort pattern. Where it diverged was in the role of women in the local economy: it was already accumulating a substantial proportion of female lodging-house keepers, who accounted for 7.9 per cent of all women over ten years old in 1861, although domestic servants were less overwhelmingly predominant among the economically-active female population than in most resorts (though they still accounted for nearly a quarter of the female over-tens in 1861). These figures are drawn from spring censuses which understate the importance of female and seasonal occupations, especially those connected with the holiday trades; and the emergent entertainment industry is hardly visible in this source. But we can already see in 1851 the first symptoms of a distinctive distribution of age-groups and sexes, with women outnumbering men very markedly in all age-groups, especially the twenties, fifties and sixties, suggesting that domestic service and the opportunities presented by lodging-house keeping were important in this pattern. As yet, however, there was no real evidence of Blackpool's population being skewed towards the middle-aged and elderly: this was a thing of the future in most resorts at this stage.[22]

Comers and goers

The local economy still relied overwhelmingly on the middle-class market: families who came for health and relaxation for two or three weeks during the summer, and whose numbers grew as businesses proliferated and professional and white-collar occupations began to multiply in Blackpool's hinterland. The visitors were still drawn from the pre-rail catchment area: there were simply more of them, and their journeys left them with more time and spending power at their destination. Analysis of the visitors' lists in the *Fleetwood Chronicle*, a source which is biased towards longer-stay and 'better-class' visitors, suggests that whether at Whitsuntide or in July and August over four-fifths of the visitors came from Lancashire and Yorkshire, with the overwhelming majority from the former county. Of the holiday weeks sampled in 1851 and 1861, the highest proportion of visitors from beyond the two counties was 18.2 per cent in mid-July 1851; and most of the rest invariably came from Cheshire and the West Midlands. Visitors from beyond this decidedly provincial catchment area never added up to more than 3.6 per cent of the total in any of the weeks sampled.[23]

The inhabitants were similarly drawn from a limited geographical range. Blackpool's growth was fuelled predominantly by migration, but only one-sixth of its inhabitants in 1851 and one-fifth in 1861 came from beyond Lancashire. In both years more than half came from the surrounding agricultural district of the Fylde and the nearest sizeable industrial town, Preston. All this drives home the essentially provincial nature of Blackpool's development in the early railway age, and the overriding importance to its fortunes of Lancashire's industrial prosperity in these formative and transitional years. Without a buoyant economy in its immediate hinterland, Blackpool would not have been able to construct the springboard for future growth which was the product of the crucial decades which spanned the mid-century.[24]

Amusing the visitors

The visitors amused themselves sedately. Contemporary guidebooks have little to say about artificial amusements, although there were occasional visits by touring theatre groups in the 1850s and subscriptions were sometimes collected for bands to play on a regular basis in public places, augmenting the opportunistic itinerant groups of musicians which visited from time to time. Public places of entertainment were in short supply, however, and Blackpool lagged behind its neighbours in this respect. The holiday regime concentrated on bathing, donkey-riding, enjoying the beach, and walking or riding to explore the surrounding countryside. Guidebooks provided helpful lists of the local flora and fauna, marine and otherwise; but the environs of Blackpool lacked the scenic and historic interest of many resorts. The first permanent theatre building opened as late as 1859, and the 1850s saw a series of piecemeal, short-lived and unsatisfactory attempts to construct and repair a marine promenade, as the multiplicity of sea-front proprietors squabbled among themselves over who should take responsibility for what. Access to the growing satellite settlement of South Shore was impeded and made less attractive by this problem. The enduring fragmentation of property ownership, which inhibited planned development, more generally ensured that the extensive new building of this period would be ill-conceived and architecturally unimpressive, as each developer strove to derive the maximum rental from small plots of land with the minimum concern for wider amenity. Public buildings were few and uninspiring. This even applied to the churches which were an important part of a middle-class resort's menu of attractions at this time. Some attempt was made to offer extra church and chapel accommodation to cater for visitors as well as locals, and the number of sittings in Blackpool doubled during the 1850s; but most of the growth came from the expansion of South Shore parish church and Bank Hey Wesleyan chapel, together with the opening in 1857 of the remarkably opulent Holy Trinity Roman Catholic church, the ostentatious gift of a wealthy lady and, in effect, an accidental windfall for the local Catholics in an area with much traditional attachment to the faith.[25]

This apart, in matters religious as in other respects Blackpool was failing to meet the aspirations of its more exacting visitors and residents, even as it continued to grow at a respectable rate during the 1850s. The problems were a long way short of crisis proportions, but they were provoking adverse comment and anxious navel-inspection by the late 1850s. The new decade was to see renewed activity and enterprise on a broad front, however, from entertainments to improved railway communications. It was at this point that, under several different auspices, Blackpool really began to emerge from the provincial shadows and to cultivate a distinctive identity on a wider stage.

Moving up-market

The early 1860s saw two important initiatives for the improvement of Blackpool's layout and building quality: the adoption of building by-laws and the development of a planned estate of high quality on the cliffs to the north of the original village centre. The second of these innovations was probably more important than the first, for the building by-laws were not enforced as assiduously as they might have been. They were adopted in 1861, and followed the standards laid down by central government in all respects except one: the minimum rear air-space for buildings of *any* height was fixed at 150 square feet, whereas the model by-laws made this the base figure for a sliding scale. Revealingly, the clerk to the Local Board explained that the recommended scale was 'inappropriate to so small a place as Blackpool and would restrict building operations and tend to stop the progress and improvement of the town'.[26] This early indication of the power of the building lobby to put the maximisation of letting space for holidaymakers' bedrooms before the amenities of residents and visitors was borne out by the way in which the regulations were often evaded and sometimes defied in practice. The part-time inspector of building plans, who was appointed in 1863 and paid on a piece-rate, is unlikely to have

Lansdowne Crescent, Blackpool's first up-market sea-front development, and until the inter-war years its only crescent, in striking contrast with sea-front architecture elsewhere in England.

been able to keep up with the rapid growth of the town over the following decade. The by-laws may have raised minimum standards by their very existence, but they were not enough to provide Blackpool with planning and building styles appropriate to a high-class resort.[27]

The activities of the Blackpool Land, Building and Hotel Company, on the other hand, made a clear difference to the social tone of the resort as a whole by providing a controlled, quiet enclave with some architectural pretensions on the North Shore, where 'better-class' residents and visitors could keep their distance from the trippers when they so chose. The Company was registered in January 1863 to develop a thin but lengthy strip of coastal land which had been pieced together through various purchases. Five of its promoters came from Blackpool but most of the capital was invested from Manchester. The leading lights were the Galloway family who ran a well-known engineering works and had also invested in Southport. The building of Lansdowne Crescent, Blackpool's first and for many years its only sea-front crescent, was entrusted to a Southport builder rather than a local man. The stone-fronted four-storey houses had their surroundings safeguarded by prohibitions on offensive trades and by the imposition of a penny toll to pass across the greensward between the crescent and the sea. Viewed in the wider context of English resort development this was not an architecturally inspiring initiative, but the Crescent was a cut above anything else in Blackpool at the time; and the area was propelled further

The Imperial Hotel, home of Prime Ministers in the party conference season. The original building of 1867 is on the right: nearest the camera is the extension of 1913.

up-market in 1867 by the opening of the Imperial Hotel, which began its long and continuing reign as the flagship of Blackpool's high-class accommodation industry.[28]

All this confirmed an emergent trend for the North Shore to become the 'best end' of Blackpool, although this relatively elevated status did not extend very far inland, as small terraced houses soon pressed close to the rear of Claremont Park, as the Land Company's estate became known. The rush of early development here was not sustained beyond the 1860s, however, and we shall see that the local authority had to rescue the Land Company by providing expensive sea defences when erosion became a problem towards the turn of the century. Together with the building of relatively up-market terraces of houses at South Shore, at the other end of the sea-front, these North Shore developments helped to sustain Blackpool's middle-class holiday season through the mid-Victorian years when it was still the best-paying proposition for the town. A further contribution to this process was the opening of the North Pier in 1863.

Piers and promenade

The first of Blackpool's three piers was sited where Talbot Road, the direct route from the railway station, met the sea. It lay towards the northern end of the existing built-up area, and helped to confirm the increasingly elevated social tone of this part of town. It made no concessions to the excursionist market: the company's official powers extended only to providing an 'extensive and agreeable promenade' at high tide and offering 'access to and landing from pleasure boats and other machines'. Nine of the eleven original promoters lived in Blackpool, including four shopkeepers and a lodging-house keeper; but respectability was guaranteed by the stern presence of the Rev. C. H. Wainwright, a Church of England Evangelical who would countenance no frivolity or Sabbath-breaking. The timing of the initiative in 1862 probably owed much to fear of competition from Southport, whose pier had opened two years earlier; and the sources of investment were overwhelmingly local and regional. Nearly 30 per cent of the shares were taken by Blackpool people, a further 22 per cent from nearby Preston, and almost all of the rest were purchased by investors from Blackpool's established Lancashire catchment area, with a considerable Manchester presence. Without the recent introduction of limited liability, a speculation of this kind would have been almost unthinkable, immensely popular and successful though the pier proved to be. We see here a combination of locals anxious to enhance the appeal of their resort in a competitive environment, and outsiders who knew Blackpool well and could make an informed assessment of the prospects for its pier. The North Pier, as it soon became known to distinguish it from its first local rival, was a logical but enterprising extension of the existing pattern of Blackpool's

growth as a resort for the middle classes from a well-defined area of burgeoning industrial prosperity.[29]

The pier actually opened in the middle of the Lancashire 'cotton famine' of the early 1860s, which should have been a serious setback to a resort which depended so heavily on custom from the 'cotton towns'. In fact, even the excursionist market was surprisingly buoyant, and the pier soon became uncomfortably crowded with working-class visitors on the great Lancashire holidays of Easter and Whitsuntide and when the weekend trips flowed in during July and August. Railway company figures indicate that 195,287 passengers arrived in Blackpool during the troubled year of 1863, and there is no indication that the problems of cotton Lancashire were passed on to its most popular resort. As the 'cotton famine' ended, however, so resurgent growth in the working-class holiday market became obvious enough to stimulate new investment aimed at the trippers' pennies and sixpences. By 1873, at the climax of the great boom in wages and working-class spending power which had inaugurated the new decade, Blackpool's passenger arrivals had more than quadrupled to 850,000 in the year, and the foundations of the resort's prosperity were beginning to shift in an unprecedented and definitive way.[30]

The North Pier, with the Indian Pavilion which was added in 1878. ('The North Pier', *New Album of Blackpool and St Annes Views* (n.p., n.d., *c.* 1900)

The promotion of a second pier, the South Jetty, was an early response to these pressures and opportunities. So many trippers thronged the original pier from its first year of operation, in spite of its twopenny admission charge, that it was claimed that 'respectable visitors would not go upon the pier during the time that the excursionists were there', and the pier's secretary proposed a second pier to the south as early as 1864, with a view to siphoning off the excursionists who already preferred that part of town, dividing the market and pre-empting possible competition. When this plan was not adopted by the existing company, a splinter group among the shareholders formed a South Jetty Company of their own, aiming primarily at the tripper market. Robert Bickerstaffe of the Wellington Hotel gave a plot of land as an inducement to siting the new pier on his doorstep, and the necessary Act of Parliament was obtained in 1866 in the teeth of opposition from the established company. Most of the South Jetty's promoters were outsiders, with six coming from Manchester, two from Preston and one each from Rochdale and Huddersfield. There was only one Blackpool-based signatory to the Memorandum of Association which launched the company. Similarly, more than half the capital (as at June 1866) came from inland Lancashire, and only one-third from Blackpool, where the investors came overwhelmingly from the southern half of the town. The company did have the support of the Local Board and a large majority of the householders, and its Blackpool-based promoter owned an up-market fancy goods bazaar; but it does seem that the positive initiative for a trippers' pier at this time came from sectional interests within the town. Hitherto, the working-class visitors had been catered for by small-scale entertainments offered by stalls, side-shows and beerhouse proprietors, especially at the south end of the town, where the tightly packed cottages of Bonny's Estate offered cheap accommodation just behind the sea-front on the future Golden Mile. Uncle Tom's Cabin on the northern cliffs, well beyond Claremont Park, was also becoming popular, with its dancing, shooting galleries and other amusements. But the South Jetty, which charged only a penny toll for promenaders, was the first major commitment of resources to pleasing this more plebeian public.[31]

The South Jetty opened in 1868, although it did not begin to flourish until the early 1870s, when Robert Bickerstaffe, nephew of the Wellington's owner, took over the management and put on cheap steamer trips and unpretentious dance bands, which soon generated healthy dividends. We shall see that the Raikes Hall pleasure gardens, which opened soon afterwards and also set its stall out for working-class custom, was a similar success story of the early 1870s. Meanwhile, however, the main thrust of Blackpool's development during the 1860s continued to involve investment in the dominant 'better-class' season, although some of the amenities provided turned out to be transferable to, and indeed an essential basis for, the growth of a more popular market a little later. The Assembly and

Concert Rooms Company and the Prince of Wales Arcade, rival promotions of the late 1860s, offered respectable concert, theatre, shopping and bathing facilities, with Manchester investment prominent alongside local money and initiative. Alongside this secular and profit-orientated investment went an expansion of church facilities, including the distinctive and eccentric Christ Church (now sadly demolished) on the fashionable north side of town, and three Nonconformist chapels. These were clearly aimed at the better-class visitors, and were well filled during the season, making a necessary further contribution to the hitherto inadequate facilities for the mainstream respectable season.[32]

Uncle Tom's Cabin, the ramshackle popular entertainment centre on the northern cliffs, which remained beyond successive town boundaries until after the First World War. ('Uncle Tom's Cabin', *New Album of Blackpool and St Annes Views* (n.p., n.d., *c.* 1900)

But the most important development of the 1860s, in the long run, was probably the Local Board's successful solution of the problem of the sea-front promenade, which had been so intractable during the previous decade. A publicly owned promenade, and the sea defences which went with it, was an essential asset to any ambitious resort, especially with a popular market; and under the local circumstances of property subdivision along the sea-front, the local authority was the only possible guarantor of solid construction, adequate maintenance and free public access. Blackpool had a long history of flawed, temporary and piecemeal efforts to maintain a marine promenade, but a series of committees in the 1840s and 1850s had been unable to do more than raise subscriptions for temporary improvements and resurfacing work. Enlargement and effective protection against erosion were beyond the scope of such bodies, and there was no large property-owner with a strategic interest in putting a plan together. From 1855 onwards the Local Board explored the possibility of intervention, but in 1860 a ratepayers' meeting heavily defeated a motion inviting the Board to buy up the Parade. Attitudes soon began to change as growing visitor numbers crowded the existing facilities uncomfortably, while erosion worsened at South Shore and the 170 frontagers showed no signs of coming to a voluntary agreement among themselves. In December 1863 the Local Board decided to take over the sea-front, and the necessary parliamentary bill went through in 1865.[33]

This more enterprising frame of mind may have owed something to the presence of more substantial businessmen on the Board, but the opposition was itself spearheaded by large property owners such as the Salford engineer James Parrott. The conflicts which gave the scheme a rough passage were not simply a confrontation between parochial, penny-pinching locals and more sophisticated offcomer business interests. The dispute was cross-cut by arguments about how much the frontagers themselves should contribute to improvements which would benefit their property, and how much should be borne by the ratepayers at large. That common bugbear of active mid-Victorian local government, the Ratepayers' Protection Association, struggled to limit maximum expenditure to £17,000, raising the fear that the proposed improvements would lead to a dramatic rise in local property taxes. It was noticeable, however, that even this organisation did not oppose Local Board intervention as a matter of principle: debate by the mid-1860s concerned the manner and scale of the scheme rather than the matter of it.

The opposition had been fierce enough to give the Local Board pause for thought, and legal problems remained in dealing with obdurate frontagers; but in 1867 the first tenders were advertised for the full scheme, and work began in the following year. The Act of 1865 had authorised the spending of £30,000 on the project, far more than the Ratepayers' Protection Association's preferred maximum; but as building went ahead, determination to do a proper job overrode financial caution. Extra borrowing powers were obtained from central government, and the eventual cost was nearly £60,000. What the town obtained was a capacious new 2-mile promenade and carriage drive, which immediately reduced congestion and provided an amenity shared by very few resorts at that time, while also solving the pressing problem of erosion along the route between the North Pier and the future South Pier (still a generation away) at South Shore. As the Ratepayers' Protection Association had feared, the rates soared: they had varied between 1s. 6d. (7.5p) and 2s. 0d. (10p) in the pound since 1863, but in 1871, the year after the new promenade was opened, they reached 4s. 4d. (22p). They remained at a similar order of magnitude thereafter, but few people seemed to mind. The opening ceremony at Easter 1870 had attracted national publicity, and the success of the scheme was immediately apparent in such concrete guises as land values and rentals. Extra local property taxation was seen to be a price worth paying to boost the popularity of the visiting season, and the promenade opening ushered in a new era of municipal enterprise which was to prove a vital element in Blackpool's continuing growth.[34]

The limits to growth

This transformation of local government from a cautious, inefficient, reactive posture to an active and successful promoter of the town's development was not being matched at this stage by the town's railway companies. The Lancashire and Yorkshire, in particular, was an enduringly keen provider of excursion trains, and this was appreciated in the town; but delays at the height of the season were endemic from the early 1850s, and until a minor accident occurred in 1863 the single-line Blackpool branch from Poulton-le-Fylde was worked by verbal instruction, with no formal signalling system. Two years later the line was at last doubled, but it was still inadequate for the summer service; and earlier on the route all the Blackpool traffic had to pass through Preston, which was already a notorious bottleneck. Locomotives and rolling-stock were always in short supply, and commuting was not yet a practicable proposition. The railways had not needed to promote Blackpool's growth in these expansive years in any active way, and in practice they had not kept pace with swelling demand. More important in the long run than the minor changes on the 'main line' was to be the opening of a new line along the coast from Lytham to Blackpool in 1863, although at first it did not link up with the branch line which had joined Lytham to the Preston and Wyre Railway since 1846. Until this connection was made in 1876, providing an alternative through route to Blackpool from industrial Lancashire via Lytham, the new Blackpool and Lytham Railway was of limited value to the town. It was promoted by a similar consortium of Fylde landowners to those who had been responsible for the waterworks, with the Clifton agent James Fair again to the fore, and it was originally more an agricultural than an excursionist line. It soon began to make a difference to Blackpool's central and southern topography, however, because by taking a route parallel to the shore it cut off inland areas from convenient access to the sea, encouraging the development of a lower class of housing. It also set up the future Central Station, originally known less imposingly as Hounds Hill, at the edge of the existing built-up area, where its presence was to promote the development of the future Golden Mile and the imposing lodging-house area around Albert Road when the trippers began to pour in by this route from the mid-1870s. For the time being, it is important to note that here again Blackpool's path to future growth on the grand scale was being eased by the policies and investments of nearby landowners, undertaken for reasons of their own.[35]

Blackpool's rate of population growth picked up during the 1860s. Between the censuses of 1861 and 1871 it averaged 5.8 per cent per year; the off-season population at the 1871 census was 7,092. The town was growing big enough to generate distinctive social areas, with the North Shore taking the cream of the visitors and residents, while disreputable centres of common lodging-houses and overcrowding were to be found in the insanitary cottages of Lark Hill and on Bonny's Estate, at the back of South Beach. The town's growth was being stimulated more by the efforts of entrepreneurs and of the Local Board than by the railways, although it continued to depend on buoyant demand in its hinterland (which contrived to defy the 'cotton famine') and on investment from Lancashire and Yorkshire businessmen. But the continuing importance of Fylde landowners in providing essential services should not be ignored, and this is a further reminder that Blackpool's fortunes were not self-made. Nor was it an easy town in which to live, with a highly seasonal and vulnerable economy which made for caution and economic single-mindedness among its residents. The difficulty of sustaining cultural organisations such as debating societies and libraries is significant here; and in striking contrast to the Lancashire towns from which so many Blackpool residents had migrated, voluntary bodies from trade unions and friendly societies to choirs found it hard to recruit and keep commitment going. This, again, was to be an enduring theme.[36]

The years between 1840 and 1870 in Blackpool were a period of consolidation and adjustment. The arrival of the railway brought in outside capital and thereby helped to introduce a transition to the third stage of the Butler/Goodall model which was mentioned in Chapter 1. But the shift to the overriding importance of external investment took a generation to work its way through, as substantial outside investment in building estates, amenities and entertainments did not begin in a systematic way for a relatively sophisticated market until the 1860s. And the sophistication *was* relative: Blackpool's investors and visitors alike were provincial, drawn above all from the town's industrial hinterland and its capital, Manchester. The distinctively numerous presence of working-class visitors and the *petite bourgeoisie*, though not yet dominating the local economy, reinforced the town's provincial accent and aspect, as did styles of building and layout (featuring a hard red Accrington brick) which recalled the 'cotton towns', though without their fog, damp and smoking factory chimneys. But an infrastructure was being laid down in these years, by local government as well as private enterprise, which would make it possible for Blackpool to respond dynamically to the unleashing of hitherto unthinkable levels of working-class demand in the late nineteenth century, and to dominate this expanding and (in Lancashire's case) lucrative mass market. This theme will provide the organising principle for the next chapter.

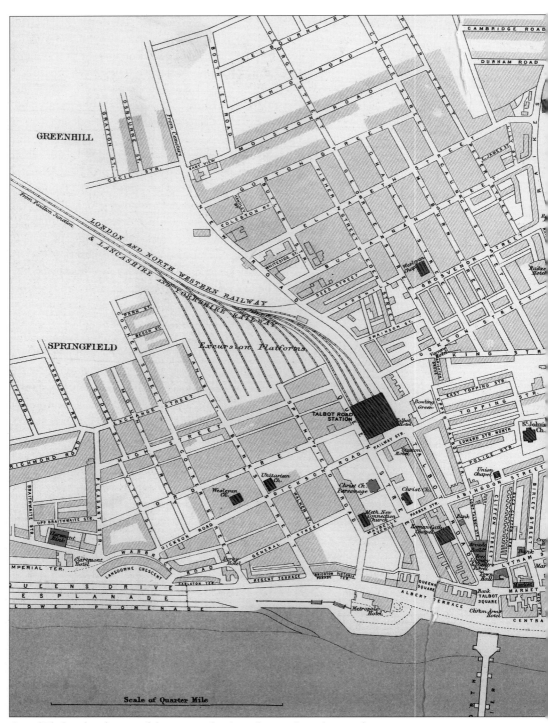

Central Blackpool at the turn of the century, showing railway stations, the central entertainment district and two of the three piers.

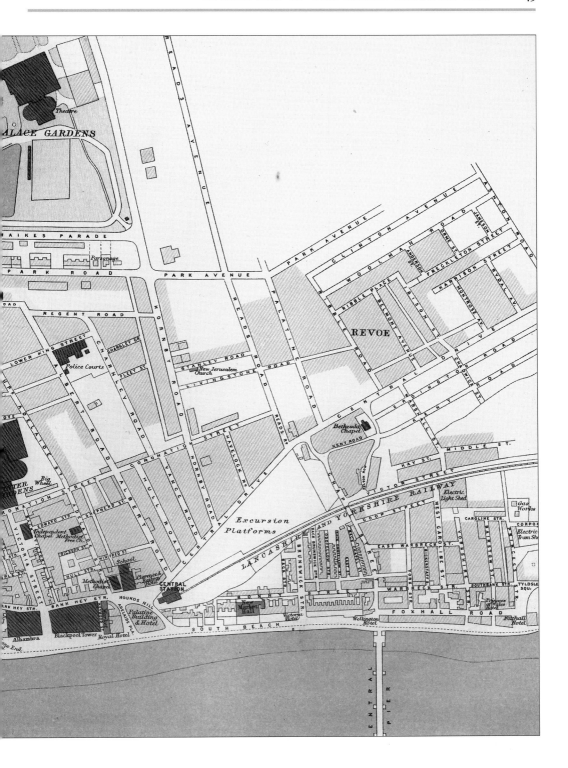

CHAPTER FOUR

The making of working-class Blackpool, 1870–1914

THE YEARS between the early 1870s and the outbreak of the First World War saw Blackpool's metamorphosis into one of the world's leading leisure towns, with an unchallengeable claim to the status of the world's first working-class seaside resort. The unprecedented expansion of the town's working-class visiting public fuelled population growth which easily outpaced that of other towns in England and Wales which had been of comparable size at the start of the period. In each of the last three decades of the nineteenth century Blackpool's resident population grew at more than 5 per cent per year. Even during the relatively difficult years between the 1881 and 1891 censuses, which was a decade of transition in the local holiday industry and of recurrent slack trade in Blackpool's industrial hinterland, the population rose by 70 per cent in ten years. During the previous decade the corresponding figure had been 83 per cent, and in the spectacularly buoyant and innovative years between 1891 and 1901 it was 115 per cent, as Blackpool more than doubled in size from a base figure of well over 20,000.[1] In the new century growth eased off to 23 per cent during 1901–11, but this was still enough to add over 11,000 people to Blackpool's resident population, taking it to 58,371 and pulling the town into the ranks of the county boroughs, with their special status and powers in local government.[2]

Blackpool on the national stage

Moreover, this late Victorian and Edwardian expansion was sufficient to promote Blackpool into the very highest level of the resort population league. In 1881 it ranked twentieth among British seaside resorts on this measure, below Whitby and Weymouth and just above Weston-super-Mare. By 1911 it was fifth, having become the largest seaside resort away from the south coast, although this claim to fame was partly an artefact of where boundaries were drawn: Southport would have risen above its Lancashire rival if adjoining Birkdale, with its 18,000 inhabitants and separate local government system, had been brought within its municipal area. Blackpool, in turn, had Bispham on its doorstep, which was also beginning its path to urbanisation, but at this stage it was puny by comparison.

Taking the boundaries as we find them, Blackpool grew faster in terms of numbers of residents than any other resort except Bournemouth and Southend between 1881 and 1911, with a net increase of 45,382; and only eight resorts outpaced it in percentage terms, most of them having the mathematical advantage of starting from much smaller base figures in 1881.[3]

Blackpool was one of a cluster of fast-growing Lancashire resorts during this period; but it was becoming increasingly distinctive in its visitor profile and in the sheer numbers of holidaymakers it attracted. It was this that enabled it to outpace its regional competitors and make such a strong showing nationally. Calculations based on multiplying passenger train arrivals during the season by contemporary estimates of the number of passengers per train, at a time when practically all visitors came by rail, suggest that visitor numbers increased by more than 350 per cent between 1873 and 1913, from up to 850,000 in the former year to 3,850,000 in the last full season before the First World War. The most expansive decades were 1873–83, which showed a 54 per cent rise, and 1893–1903, which included the boom years at the end of the century and saw an increase of 60 per cent. These figures are very approximate indeed, but they can be trusted for trends and broad orders of magnitude, and it is abundantly clear that Blackpool was already catering for far more visitors than the most popular of its rivals in Britain. Only New York's Coney Island, which was much more strongly dominated by day-trippers, rivalled it on the world stage. During the years between 1873 and 1893 just under one-third of the arrivals came by special excursion trains, suggesting visits of short duration, a figure which fell to less than a quarter in 1903 but rose again to nearly 30 per cent ten years later as Blackpool extended its catchment area into more distant parts.[4] By the turn of the century growing numbers of visitors from the Lancashire cotton towns were staying for a full week, and a specialised accommodation industry composed of the celebrated 'Blackpool landladies' was flourishing on a novel and unique scale to cater for this demand.[5]

The nature of the holiday industry

The growth of the distinctive lodging-house districts around the railway stations, especially the tall houses in Albert Road and the neighbouring streets adjoining Central Station, with their displays of fiery Accrington brick, elaborate bargeboards and bulging bay windows displaying cakestands and curtains, was only one of the novelties of the new Blackpool of the last quarter of the nineteenth century. There were the great pleasure palaces, on a scale which was cumulatively unmatched elsewhere at the British seaside, from the pioneering Raikes Hall pleasure gardens and the Winter Gardens of the 1870s to the Tower of 1894, the ultimate enduring symbol of the popular holiday industry, and the Alhambra next door whose fame lies primarily in the annals of great investment disasters, although it made a lasting contribution to Blackpool's popular entertainment menu. There were the three piers, two of which were multiplying entertainments in exotic buildings by the turn of the century, and there was the Pleasure Beach at the southern extremity of the promenade, which brought the latest in American roller-coaster and other amusement technology from Coney Island and added a distinctive flavour of its own. There was also the unofficial fairground which appeared on the beach between the two original piers, transplanting the joys of the Lancashire Wakes holidays to this seaside setting, and pullulating and proliferating to such an extent that it frightened the Corporation into draconian schemes of regulation and suppression at the turn of the century, from which it had to retreat in the face of a popular outcry. Meanwhile phrenologists and fortune-tellers, oyster-sellers and steam roundabout proprietors had moved across the promenade into the front gardens of once-respectable boarding-houses at South Beach to form the nucleus of the future Golden Mile, alongside the waxworks which had been founded by Elias Fletcher a few years earlier. Beyond all this there were theatres, baths, music-halls and pubs without end. This panorama of popular entertainment was unmatched in any rival resort, and indeed anywhere in Britain, by the 1880s; and the developments of the next decade left Blackpool far in front.[6]

It should be emphasised, however, that Blackpool achieved this transition to catering for the masses on an unprecedented scale without losing touch with a more respectable and affluent visiting and indeed residential public. The North Shore remained a protected enclave, safeguarded by the Corporation from unseemly development and behaviour as well as from the erosion of its cliffs; and it continued to attract 'better-class' visitors, retired residents and a few industrialists who commuted to their businesses inland. Meanwhile, the decades at the turn of the century saw South Shore, at the other end of the promenade and along the inland tramway route via Lytham Road, attracting superior clerks and commercial travellers to semi-detached villas which also became retirement havens. This part of Blackpool developed more features in common with nearby St Annes and Lytham than with the down-market liveliness of the central entertainment district, and Blackpool's own professional and business middle class also began to settle here, despite the controversy provoked by the nearby development of the Pleasure Beach at the turn of the century. An inland district eastward of the packed streets of holiday accommodation near Central Station also became a favoured residential area for the local elite, as the big houses and long gardens at the far end of Hornby Road were supplemented in the new century by residential development on the site of the Raikes Hall pleasure grounds, whose original purposes had been supplanted by rival enterprises nearer to the stations and the sea. By the 1890s, in fact, Blackpool was big enough to have developed its own system of social zoning for visitors and residents, making it easier for it to satisfy a variety of markets and to grow on a broad front. It had become a complex urban organism; but the heart that circulated most of its life-blood was still located between the North and Central Piers and within the orbit of the Tower and Winter Gardens.[7]

An analysis of Blackpool's remarkable and unprecedented growth during these years must therefore begin with the new visiting public. This was a consumer town, in the crucial sense that it lived by those who bought into the image it disseminated, and who came to consume it and the myriad of sights, experiences, flavours and excitements which its shore, streets and businesses offered to those who chose to try them out. Who were these people, where did they come from, and why were their seaside visits so overwhelmingly channelled into Blackpool rather than accessible alternative destinations such as Southport, Morecambe or Scarborough?

Working-class playground

The great expansion of Blackpool's holiday industry in the late nineteenth and early twentieth century was fuelled, above all, by the working classes of the Lancashire cotton-spinning and weaving towns, supplemented increasingly from the textile towns of the West Riding of Yorkshire and, towards the turn of the century, from the Staffordshire Potteries and the West Midlands. More distant sources of working-class visitors, especially in the East Midlands around Nottingham and Leicester and in south Yorkshire around Sheffield, were also being tapped on a smaller scale, as Blackpool Corporation's advertising posters appeared on the hoardings in these new territories. From the 1870s onwards working people from the Lancashire cotton towns were stretching their summer holidays to three days beyond the weekend, and by the 1890s the full-scale 'Wakes Weeks' were beginning to appear, with their Saturday-to-Saturday rhythm. At the beginning of the new century some of the cotton towns were acquiring short September holidays as well as the main summer ones, and these were also being used for seaside visits. Holiday extensions came later in Yorkshire and the Midlands, but here, too, enthusiasm for Blackpool was running high by the turn of the century, as seaside enjoyments gradually complemented or replaced local fairgrounds and festivities in the affections of the workpeople.[8]

By the turn of the century the local press was recording the places of origin of railway excursions to Blackpool. This makes possible a quantitative treatment of the origins of short-stay visitors, although many also arrived on the ordinary trains, especially from the resort's now-traditional Lancashire catchment area. Only at Easter did Lancashire dominate the excursion traffic, and the proportion of Easter Monday excursions originating within the county fell from 81.7 per cent in 1897 to just over 60 per cent in 1907 and 1912. The great Lancashire holiday of Whitsuntide saw around half of the cheap trips coming from Lancashire throughout this period, and the figure for mid-July actually recovered from less than 40 per cent in 1902 to around 55 per cent in 1907 and 1912. A similar pattern is discernible for the end of August. At the first weekend in August, however, which had become August Bank Holiday in 1871, Lancashire's share of the tripper traffic hovered around 40 per cent. This was an important holiday in parts of the Midlands, but not in Lancashire or the West Riding, where traditional holidays spread through the summer had become the basis for seaside visits, and this was reflected in the growing importance of the East and West Midlands, which accounted for 22.8 per cent of the Bank Holiday special trains in 1906 and 27.8 in 1912. Meanwhile the West Riding's share of the excursion market in this particularly busy week fell from just over 40 per cent in 1902 to just over 20 per cent in 1912. This week apart, Lancashire and the West Riding almost always accounted for more than three-quarters of the 'specials', and arrivals from beyond these industrial counties and the Midlands (extending as far south as Leicestershire and Worcestershire) rarely accounted for more than 2 per cent of these trains at the turn of the century, although they were picking up to between 5 and 10 per cent in July and August by 1907 and 1912, indicating a significant if still small extension of Blackpool's sphere of influence.[9] Blackpool continued to depend on its densely populated immediate industrial hinterland for most of its visitors: in 1884 the Lancashire and Yorkshire Railway's traffic manager submitted evidence to a parliamentary enquiry that 80 per cent of the Blackpool traffic originated within a 55-mile radius of the resort. Significantly, almost all of these visitors came from Manchester and the textile towns: Blackpool recruited relatively sparsely from Liverpool or the mining and heavy industry districts of Merseyside around Widnes and St Helens. Industrial towns in the north of the county, with little waged work for women and children, also sent few working-class people on resort holidays, although here the sea was more accessible on a local and informal basis.[10] Blackpool was still very much a provincial resort, but it was achieving almost saturation coverage within its grimy fiefdoms in the northern textile districts, and it was stretching its tentacles further into areas which might have been expected to develop stronger holiday loyalties in North Wales or on the Yorkshire and Lincolnshire coasts. These phenomena will need to be explained.

The new working-class visitors were recognisably different in dress and demeanour from the middle-class families who had hitherto provided Blackpool's bread and butter, but who were pushed outwards to protected enclaves to north and south as the trippers and those who catered for them invaded the town centre and the most popular and accessible stretch of beach between the two original piers. The working-class visitors clustered at the high points of the poverty cycle. The most prominent groups were young wage-earners who had disposable income after paying their parents for their upkeep, and who had as yet no other family responsibilities; and older people whose children were self-supporting but who still commanded a reasonable family income. This contrasted with the middle-class families with young children who had previously predominated, and elements of high spirits among the younger, unattached visitors made coexistence difficult. It was just as well that Blackpool's extensive beach offered plenty of room for seekers after quiet as well as pursuers of excitement and boisterous fun. A range of sets of preferences could be satisfied.[11]

By the early twentieth century, after a difficult transitional period in the 1880s, Blackpool was dominating the holiday habits of its Lancashire hinterland and penetrating deeply into local lifestyles, habits and customs. Its influence was particularly powerful in the weaving settlements around Blackburn and eastwards to the late-developing and relatively prosperous towns of Nelson and Colne: the area from which the 'Padjamers' had come in the early nineteenth century. At Darwen, south of Blackburn, Blackpool took two-thirds of the holiday bookings in 1881, requiring a separate temporary booking office during the holiday period. At Blackburn itself, 65 of the 126 excursions at the main summer holiday in 1912 went to Blackpool, with only 11 heading for its Lancashire rival Southport and 9 going to Morecambe. Four trips went to Scotland, three to Bournemouth and one to Paris, but Blackpool's absolute dominance remained clear, and this was the case throughout the cotton and especially the weaving district.[12]

Blackpool's was the major share of a rapidly growing market. By the 1890s the exodus to the coast at the Wakes holidays was such that some Lancashire towns were acquiring a deserted appearance. Not only were many shops closing for at least part of the holiday, but churches and chapels had to hold combined services and local newspapers were put on sale at Blackpool, which became 'Oldham by sea', or whichever towns had their holidays in that week. At Burnley's Peterstide fair in July 1899 more than 60,000 holidaymakers left the town for a day or more at the seaside, three-quarters of the population, and as usual the bulk went to Blackpool.[13] This was an unusually widespread willingness to allocate time and money to a seaside trip rather than to other uses, and the cotton-spinning towns to the south were less universally captured by the lure of the sea. Male wages accounted for a higher proportion of what were often smaller family incomes here; Bill Naughton, whose parents were not badly off by the standards of the Bolton working class in the early twentieth century, regarded the numerous Blackpool holidaymakers as enjoying a lifestyle which was beyond his family's reach. He was to reach Blackpool for the first time by bicycle in his teens, finding it alien to the point of incomprehensibility.[14] And Rochdale, close to the border with Yorkshire and perhaps sharing some characteristics of the Pennine woollen manufacturing economy, sent at most one-third of its population to coast and country in a good year, with a much smaller number of excursion trains than was usual in either Blackburn or Bolton.[15] Everywhere within the cotton-working district, and especially in the metropolitan environments of Manchester and Salford with their casual labour markets, sweated trades and higher levels of structural unemployment, there were pockets of poverty which effectively excluded the rise of the Blackpool habit, as Robert Roberts's memories of growing up in Salford and Andy Davies's oral history work confirm.[16]

So there were, as we should expect, exclusions from the Blackpool paradise (as it was coming to be seen); and there were also voluntary exiles, the serious-minded workpeople of nonconformist religion and often so-cialist cast of mind, mainly skilled and white-collar, who despised Blackpool's commercial artificiality and high-pressure amusements and preferred the breezy pleasures of rambling and cycling, spiced with natural history, geology and songs round the camp-fire.[17] There is also the question of whether 'working-class' is the best label for the people who made up Blackpool's new mass market. Patrick Joyce would prefer to see them as drawn from a popular or populist set of groupings which pulled together manual and white-collar workers with tradespeople, and which derived its identity from a shared culture and set of attitudes rather than a way of making a living. These were, in Lancashire dialect parlance, the self-styled (at least through dialect literature) 'gradely folk', honest, open, cheerful, good-humoured and unpretentious, and in broad terms respectable, but with no inclination to look up to or be patronised by their 'betters': a rough-hewn (Oldhamers celebrated themselves as 'roughyeds'), take-us-as-you-find-us democracy at play.[18] There is something in this, although it has the defect of taking a literary celebration of such a culture, which was not always produced within it, at its own valuation: there was an aggressive, outspoken, hedonistic and intolerant downside to this culture which some-times surfaced at the seaside. Moreover, there is no disputing that the great majority of the new visitors came from the ranks of wage labour, and manual labour at that; and we have seen that a growing minority, and sometimes apparently a majority, came from cultures other than that of the Lancashire cotton towns. 'Working-class' remains the best shorthand label for the phenomenon we are witnessing.

Blackpool and the 'cotton towns'

Why did the cotton towns of Lancashire pioneer the development of the working-class seaside holiday? And why was so much of this demand chan-nelled into Blackpool? In the first place, we can point to several distinguishing features which may help to explain the spending power of working-class people in this distinctive economy, and their preference for seaside holidays rather than, or as well as, alternative means of gratification.

During the sustained fall in the prices of basic daily necessities which helped to fuel the rise of working-class Blackpool in the late nineteenth century, the wage-earners of the Lancashire cotton towns were able to build on existing advantages to achieve a higher material standard of living than anywhere else in Britain. Where the male breadwinner wage was the norm, and when living standards were boosted by increased money wages, the extra income was liable to be siphoned off into drink and related masculine amusements, as was clearly visible in the boom of 1870–3 with its high level of drunkenness convictions. But where, as in the cotton towns after the mid-1870s, falling prices were the motor of improvement, the increased purchasing power of wives spread resources more evenly around the family. And paid employment for women was itself becoming more general, especially in the weaving districts, where a capable four-loom weaver was right at the top of the female earnings league table. Children, too, were better paid than elsewhere at an earlier age, as the widespread working-class support for the half-time system, decried as it was by educationalists, made clear. So Blackpool's visitor heartland was an area of relatively high and rising family incomes. They were also relatively reliable, with fewer and less damaging seasonal fluctuations than in most wage-earning settings, and trade union agreements for sliding scale wage settlements and the minimisation of set-piece disputes added to the sense of security. Trade depressions increasingly brought limited, controlled wage cuts and short time rather than catastrophic unemployment, and major strikes and lock-outs became rare, although this is not to suggest that industrial relations had become conflict-free.[19] This workforce was developing a capacity to consume while it saved; and it had an established and developing system of voluntary organisations based on workplace and neighbourhood which made savings for predictable consumer goals all the easier. The Friendly Societies, popular insurance organisations which were particularly strong in the cotton towns, had accustomed people to making regular weekly payments to sustain a regular entitlement to benefit. This principle was readily transferable to the holiday savings clubs which proliferated in these years, set up by churches, pubs, workplaces and street committees, to enable people to save to take holidays which were, in almost all cases, still unpaid and therefore required careful budgeting through the rest of the year. The dividend payments of the Co-operative societies, which were also achieving mass movement status in these years, also offered lump sums which could be assigned to holiday spending, including new clothes and shoes for the occasion. Significantly, all these elements of what has been called 'social capital' were much more in evidence in the cotton towns than in other industrial settings. And such bodies not only acted as vehicles for saving for enjoyment as well as for a rainy day: they also organised excursions to the seaside themselves, which helped to familiarise members and friends with the attractions of an environment which might otherwise have seemed threateningly different.[20]

There were contemporary debates over whether seaside holidays, along with the other accessible enjoyments and little luxuries which were emerging in cotton town society during these years, were an unalloyed benefit. They could be argued to plunge working people into 'secondary poverty' for most of the year, as they economised on 'essentials' to pay for the holiday; and (especially in their Blackpool form) to represent a descent into high-pressure hedonism, sensuality and extravagance which ruined health and undermined morals, as people played even harder than they worked, rather than reinforcing them for the rest of the year. Children were dispatched into the mill at the earliest opportunity, it was claimed, to help to pay for this irrational binge. Such practices could be blamed on a culture of emulation, a pattern of 'keeping up with the Joneses' which sucked people into spending patterns they could not really afford.[21] Early socialists like Bolton's Allen Clarke were among the critics.[22] But such comments were unsympathetic to the pressures under which families lived, and to their capacity to make their own leisure on their own terms from the (admittedly restricted) menu on offer. Enjoying seaside holidays was increasingly part of a shared culture, in which people participated in a common grammar of consumption and pooled their experiences in a shared array of expectations and stories; and Blackpool benefited from this because a holiday there became part of this common culture, whereas trips to more exalted destinations smacked of aspirations above one's station. Emulation is far too simple an expression of what was happening.[23] It is time to pursue these issues further as part of wider explanations for the increasingly common choice of the seaside in general, and Blackpool in particular, as an outlet for the new popular consumer spending and an expression of the new commercialised leisure culture, alongside football, the music-hall, gambling, and domestic consumer durables, from pianos and sheet music to curtains and linoleum.

The contribution of the railways

It is tempting to begin with the railways, as before. The sheer scale of Blackpool's growth would have been unthinkable without their capacity for cheapening travel in time and distance and expanding the capacity of the transport system, but they brought the coast nearer and made it easier to reach without providing, in themselves, sufficient reasons or motives for the avalanche of visitors. The lag of around thirty years between the railways' arrival and the great expansion of the popular holiday market demonstrates that explanations also need to be found in the developments inland which have just been discussed; but we shall see that the resorts in general, and Blackpool in particular, were also the authors of their own success. And nor did the railways provide Blackpool with sustained or demonstrable advantages over its competitors. The joint railways were slow to respond to the pressure of demand for additional services and facilities which was snowballing during the 1870s and 1880s. The Lancashire and Yorkshire had been favourable to excursions in principle but dilatory in investing in additional sidings and improved station accommodation, and there were sustained complaints from Blackpool about the perceived superiority of its Southport services. Meanwhile the London and North Western had more attractive options on the North Wales coast, where it owned the access route from Birmingham and many West Midlands industrial towns throughout. The joint railways' most important contribution was to buy up the Blackpool and Lytham line, opening a second through route to Blackpool's Central Station, conveniently sited between the piers, in 1874, and diverting large numbers of excursion trains to the new line two years later. But the 1870s saw the Lancashire and Yorkshire's abandonment of three-day and eight-day tickets from Manchester and the West Riding, and when they were restored in 1880 some of the Yorkshire traffic had been lost to east coast competitors. At this point the Lancashire and Yorkshire was the most notorious main-line railway in the country for antediluvian locomotives, exquisitely uncomfortable rolling stock, slow schedules and unpunctuality: it became, literally, a music-hall joke. To make matters even worse, all services had to negotiate Preston station, which had become an infamous bottleneck, and the physical discomfort of two-hour delays on non-corridor services was only too apparent. At the point where Blackpool began its crucial transition to the mass market, the railway companies gave it little positive help. They were, at best, belatedly reactive.[24]

By the early 1880s the situation was so bad that Blackpool tried to promote a railway of its own, in partnership with the Manchester, Sheffield and Lincolnshire Company. This eventually came to nothing, but the threat of competition galvanised the existing companies into action, with improved ticket systems and extended summer services. At the turn of the century large-scale investment in terminal facilities and excursion sidings at both the main stations was followed by the opening of a new cut-off line from Kirkham to South Shore and the quadrupling of the track between South Shore and Central Station. Enlargement of Preston station in 1902–4, with dedicated lines for the Fylde Coast traffic, also helped matters, although criticism was never completely disarmed and new proposals for competing lines still surfaced in the twentieth century. But all this enabled the ever-increasing volume of holiday traffic to be handled, while improvements elsewhere on the system eased the flow of long-distance traffic, especially from the East Midlands. Access from Liverpool and district was still difficult in the absence of a bridge and direct line across the Ribble below Preston, and traffic from north-eastern England still had to take long and roundabout routes to Blackpool. These influences of railway geography affected the catchment area enduringly. What is clear is that the railway kept pace with

Blackpool's expansion, but it neither caused it nor actively encouraged it. The key stimuli came from elsewhere.[25]

Blackpool's attractions

Another logical place to begin an explanation might be the distinctive natural attributes of Blackpool. Its lack of picturesque or dramatic scenery, and of places of historic interest, limited its potential appeal for holiday-makers who espoused the 'romantic gaze', solitary and individualistic, and searching for satisfactions mediated through formal literary and artistic culture. Any hope of lasting success, or at least sustained expansion, had to be founded on adherents of the 'collective gaze' who shared their appreciation of objects and experiences whose essence lay in being common property. Very distant views of Snowdonia and the Lake District were part of the advertising currency of relatively up-market sea-front boarding-houses, and the 'furnace fires of Barrow' on the other side of Morecambe Bay might even be incorporated as a nocturnal emblem of the sublime, but these were minority tastes.[26] But the two suggested ways of seeing came together in responses to the sea in boisterous mood. Blackpool's publicity always emphasized the way in which the sea came right up to the prome-nade, washing the whole of the beach twice every twenty-four hours; and this recognised asset was compounded when it provided a free spectacle of waves transgressing boundaries, breaking spectacularly over the sea defences and encouraging people to indulge in games of chasing and dodging with the water, playing with sensations of fear and perceptions of the sublime while feeling secure behind ultimately stable man-made barriers. Special trains were put on when this kind of experience was on offer, and it was an acknowledged feature of Blackpool which was not shared by its regional rivals.[27] Attempts were also made to claim distinctive climatic advantages for Blackpool. The Medical Officer of Health even produced a guide-book at the turn of the century which hoped (among other things) to promote a winter season, although this initiative never passed beyond the conventional pieties to which all resorts necessarily subscribed.[28] A more popular discourse which emphasized the invigorating qualities of Blackpool's sea air, continuing commentaries which went back to the resort's earliest days, was more important in elevating it above its rivals, and these popular perceptions of Blackpool's distinctive attributes undoubtedly helped to single it out as a favourite destination.[29]

These attitudes to Blackpool are closely related to another of its advant-ages: the popular tradition of seaside visits at the August spring tides which had brought the 'Padjamers' and which was built upon rather than being superseded in the railway age. Bathing in itself became less important over time, although belief in the therapeutic virtues of local sea-water was commercially exploited by the Blackpool Sea Water Company from 1872,

A contemporary celebration of rough seas at Blackpool, showing waves breaking over the Promenade at South Shore during a storm. ('South Shore during a Storm', *New Album of Blackpool and St Annes Views* (n.p., n.d., c. 1900)

and right up to the First World War Blackpool's busiest holiday period remained mid-August, the old Bathing Sunday period, rather than August Bank Holiday week at the beginning of the month, as was the case almost everywhere else.[30] More obviously important was the survival and development of the Lancashire Wakes holidays. These were inherited from the feast days which commemorated the dedications of parish churches and their subordinate chapels, or from medieval fairs. Their numbers were augmented by new creations in the nineteenth century, sometimes speculations by publicans, sometimes (as in Blackburn and Bolton) negotiated summer holidays in places which lacked an older custom on which to build. These local holidays were scattered through the summer months, from early July to early September, and although the older ones were eroded in the early decades and depressed years of the first half of the nineteenth century, they survived to be extended again in better times, often as a result of employees voting with their feet and failing to return on the official day. As the popular seaside holiday developed, the balance of these festivals tilted from local observance to increasingly extended seaside visits. It was on this holiday pattern that the Blackpool season was based, with particular weeks being consecrated to particular towns and behaviour being constrained within tacitly agreed limits by the knowledge that family, friends and neighbours were ever-present in the familiar crowd. The Wakes thus provided a core of self-policing visitors who were spread through the summer to form the basis for a viable working-class season. The mixture of work and leisure discipline which enabled holidays to be negotiated, savings to be accumulated and exuberance to be confined within

conventional limits offered a unique mixture of mutually reinforcing attributes to the resort which was its chief beneficiary.[31] In many ways the
popular Blackpool seaside holiday was a tradition invented in the late
nineteenth and early twentieth century; but much older patterns of popular
behaviour and belief were cornerstones of Blackpool's dominance of its
Lancashire hinterland.[32]

Once the working-class visitors had arrived, the Blackpool of the 1870s
and onwards was increasingly attractive to them, both in itself and by
comparison with the alternatives. This was an 'open' resort, historically
free of many of the constraints on and channellings of development which
were imposed in many other places, both by landed estates (who preferred
the apparent security of a 'better-class' market and found the aesthetics of
decorous planning more in keeping with their sense of their own prestige)
and local government (which often followed landowners' preferences even
if it contended with them over the exercise of power within the
resort).[33] As a freehold town whose rulers were unwilling to interfere with
private property rights under most circumstances, Blackpool was able to
acquire a formidable array of pubs and beerhouses in its central entertainment area, and stalls and fairgrounds offering cheap alfresco food and
entertainment multiplied in front gardens, on vacant lots, and on the beach
itself. Streets continued to spread piecemeal and without an overall plan

A classic back-street
view in Victorian
Blackpool, showing
the cramped layouts
which resulted from
neglect of the
building by-laws.

on the small estates which were developed on a cellular principle. A survey of the practices of the Corporation's Building Plans Committee between 1887 and 1892 showed that as many as 57 per cent of the plans which were actually *passed* infringed at least one of the authority's own by-laws. Over one-third had unsatisfactory drainage arrangements and more than a quarter had insufficient yard space.[34] But this regime produced a holiday environment which was attractive rather than otherwise to working-class visitors. It allowed lodging-houses to maximise the number of bedrooms on a site, and thereby helped to keep prices to a minimum for the many visitors who could only just afford a seaside holiday. The unpretentious buildings in which visitors stayed were similar in architectural idiom to the streets of their home towns, writ only slightly larger; and many central streets were paved with stone setts, in the same noisy and workaday style as the industrial towns. Visitors were not frightened off by formal, symmetrical, sterilised, alien layouts, and they were also able to enjoy the kind of fairground and street entertainments which were associated with popular festivals inland. Indeed, many of the showmen on the fairground circuits began to migrate to Blackpool for the season.[35] Blackpool became positively welcoming to working-class visitors who might have been repelled by a planned resort environment aimed at the mainstream middle-class market of these years.

Building a popular resort

All this was in striking contrast with Blackpool's neighbours and immediate competitors for the Lancashire and Pennine market, Southport, Lytham and St Annes (which was not developed until the 1870s). Southport's development was controlled by two large landed estates which, from the 1840s, were concerned in their different ways to generate secure income and capital appreciation by imposing minimum standards, discouraging down-market and visible entertainments, and relegating insalubrious but necessary activities to a safe distance from the sea-front. The Hesketh and Scarisbrick estates leased building land under strict conditions which (although flexible in some respects) were clear about the undesirability of (for example) pubs and stalls in front gardens. The environment they created was attractive to affluent industrialists who chose to commute from and retire to Southport, and whose dominant role in local government reinforced the policies of the landed estates. These trends took time to become established, but they were really taking hold in the mid-1870s, at exactly the point where Blackpool's path diverged in a firmly populist direction.[36] Lytham followed a similar path, with its local landed family, the Cliftons, taking a firm grip on development in the 1840s, even as they retreated from their villa-building proposals near Blackpool railway station; and nearby St Annes was a decorous, up-market conception from the beginning, promoted by a land company on virgin sand-dunes.[37] Further north, Morecambe lacked the overall controls which were imposed in these resorts, but its local government developed more up-market aspirations than Blackpool's and it lacked direct rail access from the towns whose appetite for popular seaside holidays grew fastest, depending more heavily on more respectable supervisory and clerical strata from the Leeds and Bradford area.[38] The examples of Windermere and Grange-over-Sands, which did depend heavily on Lancashire markets, illustrate that divided landownership and a lack of formal development controls in formative years did not necessarily open the floodgates to the working class; but their distinctive place-identities reflected the obvious marketability of scenery and climate to the comfortably-off and increasingly the elderly, while they lacked Blackpool's accessibility and the popular and traditional pulling power of its boisterous sea. Moreover, the building of Windermere was dominated by a single family firm, the Pattinsons, who imposed their own architectural unity on the emergent resort.[39] Blackpool's combination of openness and accessibility remained unique.

The town continued to develop in piecemeal fashion. In the process it settled out into specialised zones with marked social characteristics, which enabled it to assimilate the new working-class visitors without needing to depend on them to the exclusion of all else. This was a necessary condition for continuing rapid growth, especially in the light of the uncertain permanence of the popular seaside holiday as a trend, which was the basis for worried comment in the 1870s and 1880s. Exploring these developments is a necessary step towards understanding the enthusiastic success of Blackpool's embrace of the working-class market, and the important point that it was not the whole story.

The emergence of a social zoning system followed patterns which were already emerging in the mid-Victorian years, when (as we saw in Chapter 3) the North Shore coastal strip was becoming the town's most genteel and architecturally pretentious district. The Claremont Park area and points north continued to cater for the 'better classes' throughout the dynamic and transitional years between the 1870s and the First World War, despite a difficult period towards the turn of the century when the Corporation had to step in to save the estate itself from erosion. It was then obliged to buy up the adjoining area to the north, around what became Gynn Square, in order to obtain filling-up materials for the coastal defence works, and took the opportunity to forbid stalls and fairgrounds, and impose minimum planning and development standards, as building spread from a fully developed Claremont Park into this new area in the early twentieth century. From 1899 onwards development in this area, and further north along the coast at Bispham, was fuelled by the Blackpool and Fleetwood inter-urban tramway, which also ended the isolation of Claremont Park by penetrating its peaceful sea-front and terminating the access toll. Controversy raged

Early up-market development at South Shore: 50 Dean Street, a detached villa dating from the mid-nineteenth century.

on these issues in the later 1890s, but the result was not the social disaster some had feared.[40]

Meanwhile, better-class' housing was also spreading at South Shore, the southern satellite settlement which was now growing apace and becoming linked to Blackpool itself by a continuous line of sea-front terraces. The extension of the built-up area on all sides of the old village core featured substantial three-storeyed terraced or semi-detached houses, with a few detached villas, rated at between £20 and £40 per year in the early 1890s, and accommodating commuters and retired people as well as respectable 'company-houses'. Between 1871 and 1891 Blackpool's two southernmost wards increased their population eightfold, to more than 8,400, while the town as a whole trebled its numbers; and South Shore continued to be the most dynamic part of the borough, acquiring its own specialised shopping district around Church (later Bond) Street. There were some unpretentious terraces inland, east of Lytham Road, but most of the new housing was, by Blackpool's standards, up-market. Sea-front development, especially, was boosted by the opening of the promenade tramway in 1885, although there were vociferous complaints from neighbours when its terminal stimulated the growth of fairgrounds on vacant lots in the 1890s, followed by the development of the Pleasure Beach on an altogether larger scale. Trams could be a two-edged sword. But this was a local difficulty within a wider panorama of rapid colonisation of suburban land by lower and middling strata of the middle classes, who set the tone for South Shore as a whole.[41]

These seaside suburbs at either end of the town were mainly inhabited by incomers. They, and their beaches, also provided a sedate setting for 'better-class' family holidays. Beyond all this, during the last quarter of the nineteenth century Blackpool's own local elite was becoming sufficiently numerous and affluent to generate a suburb of its own, a haven for the commercial and professional middle classes at a safe distance from the shore and the lively visitor economy from which they made their living. This distinctive district grew up on and around Enoch Read's 48-acre Bonny's Farm Estate, to the south-east of the town centre and beyond the most affluent of the lodging-house areas. Plans and elevations had to be approved, materials were specified, minimum rentals, heights and widths required, and a wide range of activities were prohibited. On Hornby Road, conditions were even stricter, with all non-residential uses proscribed and a minimum area of lawn required at the front of the houses. Rateable values were considerably higher than at South Shore, and there were some very substantial detached houses in extensive grounds. This was where Blackpool's successful entertainment promoters, doctors, lawyers and real estate speculators found the peace and comfort to enjoy the fruits of their labours, their good fortune and their eye to the main chance.[42]

The results of these processes can be assessed from the rate-book of 1910, which listed householders' occupations for the 'better-class' parts of town. A comparison of sample groups of streets shows clear differences in social structure between North and South Shores, with the Hornby Road area having a profile of its own. At North Shore the affluent sea-front districts of Claremont Park and the Gynn Estate had a high proportion of female householders, more than 40 per cent of the total. These were women of mature years with private means, sometimes augmented by keeping high-class boarding-houses. Gentlemen of independent means accounted for nearly one-fifth of the households, and commuters and commercial travellers for one in nine. The rest were divided fairly evenly between tradesmen, white-collar workers and professional and managerial groups. The Lytham Road South area of South Shore was much more a haven for commuters and commercial travellers, who picked up the best Manchester expresses which went from Central and South stations: they accounted for nearly one-quarter of the householders in this sample district. This was, above all, a development which followed the rail service improvements at the turn of the century, and the opening of a tramway along Lytham Road itself. Professional and managerial groups, some of whom would also be commuters, accounted for just over 11 per cent, and were nearly as numerous as white-collar workers and tradesmen combined. More than 22 per cent had private means, and just over 30 per cent were women of similar standing. So here there was a strongly defined social profile which combined commuters and the comfortably-off retired. The local elite area around Hornby Road contained fewer female householders (just over a quarter of the sample) but plenty of men of independent means (24 per cent). Otherwise it was dominated by professionals (nearly 22 per cent) and substantial tradesmen (nearly 19 per cent), with very small numbers of commuters and commercial travellers despite the proximity of Central Station. By the Edwardian years, middle-class Blackpool was itself a sub-divided and sophisticated social system, with different habitats for different sorts of people. The same applied lower down the social scale.[43]

Blackpool was capable of catering for the 'better classes'; but it also had slum areas which were becoming more sharply etched on the late Victorian map. The first of these dated from the beginning of the railway age, when Sir Peter Hesketh-Fleetwood, desperate to reduce the debts he had incurred in developing Fleetwood itself, sold off his sea-front estate at Blackpool to the local yeoman farmer and slate merchant John Bonny in 1841. This was to become a prime site, between the North and Central Piers and close to the future Central Station; but at the time it was low-lying, ill-drained and subject to flooding at spring tides. Bonny erected three-storey lodging-

The last surviving original houses from Bonny's Estate, where Brunswick Street meets what is now the Golden Mile, photographed in 1972.

houses for visitors, with long front gardens and sea views, at the front of the estate; but behind this façade a different story unfolded. Building took the form of four-roomed cottages on a haphazard plan with no attempt to secure sea views; and beerhouses and pigstyes added their own distinctive flavour. In the 1850s and 1860s the area was already being colonised by building workers and other labourers, and it provided cheap, overcrowded lodgings for seasonal workers. In 1863 the building of the Blackpool and Lytham Railway across the back of the estate turned it into a cul-de-sac, and gave travellers arriving at Central Station an unenticing first impression of the town. It remained 'the Whitechapel of Blackpool', in a phrase of 1901, until slum clearance in 1964. It was opposite Bonny's Estate that the beach became most densely occupied during the 1870s by stallholders and fairground activities, which came ashore to the unpoliced front gardens on the seaward side of the district at the turn of the century, as we shall see. Already, then, at the core of the resort lay what was, by the 1870s, an established slum; and although it provided cheap, convenient accommodation for essential workers, its presence posed enduring problems for the local authority and for all who would have preferred to propel Blackpool up-market.[44]

The other dubious districts were more peripheral. The first of them arose to the south and south-east of North Station from the 1850s, close to sidings and coalyards, on land owned by the Lytham Charities, whose well-connected trustees chose not to hold back development by insisting on onerous conditions and increasingly neglected to enforce those which were originally in place. The Lark Hill district, as it became known, was developed on 99-year leases, and prohibitions were enforced on back-to-backs, cellar dwellings, beerhouses and offensive trades; but the ground plan was haphazard and cottages, workshops and warehouses were put up cheek by jowl. From the 1880s the area became a haven for tramps and itinerant hawkers, as a large common lodging-house in Seed Street opened the door to similar establishments when the restrictive covenants proved unworkable, and a marine store dealer also moved in. Sanitary conditions were also poor. Some of the houses had been built on 'made land' where brickmakers' excavations had been filled with ashpit refuse, and in the 1880s and 1890s Lark Hill was a centre for infantile diarrhoea and other illnesses. The Corporation, acutely aware of the potential threat to the holiday season from epidemics, stepped in to flag and concrete yards and cellars in the 1890s, but this remained a problematic area until (again) demolition in the 1960s.[45]

The other problem areas were more peripheral still. Indeed, Lark Hill shaded off into an extensive area of respectable artisan housing to the south, in which working-class holidaymakers found cheap accommodation during the season. Queenstown was altogether more isolated. It was built up from the 1870s by small local speculators on pastures and brickfields half a mile inland of North Station, and its grid of four-roomed cottages, let at low rents, soon attracted 'all the immigrants of the lowest possible character', as Alderman Henry Hall described them in 1880. Common lodging-houses proliferated, and the streets were enlivened by fighting on Saturday nights. Missions, temperance work and the withdrawal of off-licence facilities made little impression, and poverty continued to find expression in barefoot, breakfastless schoolchildren and high death-rates from infantile diarrhoea and related illnesses. Queenstown acquired a similar but less notorious neighbour at Green Hill in the 1880s, closer to the railway line, and cottage property also appeared on the other side of the railway. The whole area, which lacked influential advocates, became a repository of industries and services which the town needed but which most districts preferred to repel. The cemetery at Layton predated Queenstown, opening in 1872; but between 1880 and 1905 this area acquired the infectious diseases hospital, the Corporation abattoirs, William Smith's extensive marine stores and Catterall and Swarbrick's brewery. If this part of Blackpool had not existed, it would have been necessary to invent it. It was essential to the functioning of the resort, including its need for cheap and seasonal labour; but it needed to be at a safe distance from the spaces which were consecrated to health and enjoyment.[46]

Much the same applied to the Revoe district, which was closer to the sea-front but came to share many similar characteristics. It originated when local speculators took advantage of an anomaly in the local authority boundary, which came quite close to the shore at a point a little way inland from the core of the resort area. Revoe was downwind of the gasworks, and later of the locomotive depot and municipal refuse destructor, which were all between it and the sea; and the boundary alignment freed early developers from Blackpool's municipal building and sanitary regulations and enabled them to avoid urban property taxes. The land around Ibbison Street, the core of the settlement, soon became a maze of piggeries, stables and scattered houses; and its position made it an ideal location for the seasonal floating population of donkey drivers (with their donkeys) and 'hundreds of travelling musicians and itinerant vendors of all kinds', who were able to keep their children at work in defiance of Blackpool's School Attendance Officer. In 1879 Blackpool Corporation used Revoe's reputation for bad sanitation and contaminated well water to annex the area by Act of Parliament, as part of the local Improvement Act of that year, and when building revived in the early 1890s the new streets, although down-market, were more conventional. Three cottage property magnates, two of whom also became leading local politicians, took on most of the development alongside their grocery and brickmaking businesses. James Cardwell and the brothers Thomas and Henry Brown had enough influence to secure the systematic relaxation of the building by-laws, and in 1901 the Ibbison Street and Ribble Road areas had the highest population density

in Blackpool, at 131 per acre. This was outside the holiday season. Revoe had the same public health defects as the other problem areas, although it lacked formally-defined common lodging-houses and provided holiday accommodation for the most impecunious of the visitors. It retained an unsavoury local reputation, but here again the cheap accommodation it provided for casual and migrant workers was necessary to the trajectory of Blackpool's development in these years.[47]

Henry Brown's original grocer's shop at 1 Ibbison Street, Revoe, shortly before demolition.

Accommodating the visitors

All this reminds us that Blackpool was an industrial town, and needed to house its army of casual, seasonal and sweated workers, preferably at a safe distance from most of its customers. Part of its plant also consisted of the lodging or 'company'-houses (the contemporary term for respectable houses which took in summer visitors) in which the visitors stayed, for the handful of sizeable hotels could accommodate only a diminishing fraction of the swelling visiting public. Another, and in many ways the most visible and necessary, feature of Blackpool's growth in the late nineteenth and early twentieth century was the rise of the specialised company-house districts, which were crucial to the success of the popular season because they catered cheaply and welcomingly for the throngs of working-class visitors. This process also began in earnest in the 1870s, although its origins can be found in the spread of lodging-house listings in some of the back streets close to North Station at the end of the previous decade. It was pushed all the harder by the commercialisation of the original town centre, which had hitherto been largely given over to holiday accommodation, but was now being converted or redeveloped for shopping, entertainment and later office purposes. It was, in fact, becoming a fully-fledged central business and entertainment district, which came to be surrounded by the streets of company-houses which accommodated its (and their) customers. These were, by turns, consumers of bedrooms, sitting-rooms, meals, shops, entertainments and the marine environment, as part of the overarching process by which they consumed Blackpool.[48]

The first specialised company-house districts which provided purpose-built premises for working-class visitors began to radiate from the newly upgraded Hounds Hill station, soon to be renamed Central and greatly expanded to cope with its new long-distance excursion traffic, and from the new South Jetty (the future Central Pier) from the early 1870s. The Central Station area saw particularly imposing developments, close as it was to the new entertainment centres of the 1870s (especially Raikes Hall and the Winter Gardens, of which more anon). The immediate beneficiary

The distinctive boarding-house frontages of Albert Road, looking eastwards from the site of Central Station.

was Hull's Estate, 15 acres of low-lying but gently rising land to the south and east of the station. Ironically, its then owner, Rev. Edward Hull, had opposed the siting of the station in 1861 because it would cut his land off from the sea. What it actually did was to separate Hull's land from the mean streets of Bonny's Estate to the west, while generating a market for accommodation on a scale Hull could never have imagined even in the previous decade. Hull, Vance and Albert Roads became the core of Blackpool's most extensive and most famous company-house area, dominated by three- and four-storey lodgings. These distinctive buildings, with tall bay windows, red-brick or stucco fronts and sometimes ornate bargeboards, had long extensions at the rear which ate up yard and washing space, but offered bedrooms in abundance to shelter the crowds of holidaymakers who practically fell across their thresholds from the nearby station entrance. Their salient characteristics were echoed on a smaller scale around York, Yorkshire and Bairstow Streets, whose development was stimulated by the completion of the Central Pier and Promenade between 1868 and 1870. The houses here were less homogeneous and imposing in appearance, though perhaps more 'homely'; and the proximity of the gasworks and of fairground activities reduced their selectness in an area which quickly shaded off into smaller cottage property away from the sea.[49]

Further popular company-house areas developed on the northern and eastern fringes of the built-up area of the 1870s, although they were less distinctive in their architecture and suggested family economies which had a more even balance between catering for visitors and other kinds of wage-based or trading income. They were much closer to, and gave place almost imperceptibly to, artisan terraces of a much more familiar kind, with two or three bedrooms which might find room for the odd visiting family in the most crowded part of the season. This was the mainstream housing stock of late Victorian and Edwardian Blackpool, and the distinctive social areas described above were like islands, some of them quite large, in a sea of small to middling red-brick terraces. This was a familiar kind of landscape for working-class visitors, in contrast with much of Southport, Lytham or indeed Llandudno or Scarborough. It was, in an important word, homely.[50]

This was a key aspect of Blackpool's attractiveness to working-class visitors. Accommodation could be found in a familiar setting writ large; and the landladies who ran the company-houses tended to come from the manufacturing towns from which the visitors were drawn. They were recruited largely from skilled working-class people who had saved enough to accumulate the limited capital necessary to buy into a company-house, under conventions whereby the business and its goodwill were bought but the house itself was rented; and where savings were not enough, credit might be forthcoming, if only from family and friends. Bookings could often be made on the basis of direct contact or personal recommendation, and origins and lack of pretension were advertised immediately by accent and house name. There was no fear of being patronised or humiliated, and prices were kept low by a mixture of convention, fierce competition and the knowledge that many visitors could not afford more than a bare minimum. To this end houses were crammed to the rafters, costly amenities were kept to a minimum and the apartments system enabled visitors to buy or bring their own food for the landlady to cook at a very small charge. Attempts were sometimes made to charge extra for such items as use of the cruet, and these passed into popular folklore; but they tended to be counter-productive in a setting where landladies sought to acquire a 'connexion' of visitors who returned regularly to the same place, and where visitors who sought to replicate the secure rhythms of domesticity were content to do so. Where whole towns went on holiday at the same time, colonising the same streets for their holiday week and going back to the same core of amusements even as they sampled the novelties with avid delight, this accommodation system was a considerable asset. Blackpool was able to cater for working-class visitors in a manner which did not intimidate, to which they rapidly became accustomed, and to which they were happy to return.[51]

The policing of pleasures

A further attractive aspect of Blackpool was the limited extent to which local government interfered with popular pleasures in the areas which were taken over by working-class visitors. The establishment of a Borough Corporation in 1876, with its Charter, additional powers and weight of ceremonial and imposing titles, was part of a drive to gain greater control over the regulation of streets, public places, popular pleasures and petty crime, but in the end the new powers were deployed with a light touch. Policing was carried out with tolerance and flexibility provided that a generously defined grammar of popular acceptability was not transgressed. The establishment of Blackpool's own borough force in 1887, ending dependence on the county, ensured the continuation of this policy. The inauguration of a borough magistrates' court in 1899, using local Justices of the Peace, increased local autonomy further in dealing with these issues. This did not mean complete permissiveness: far from it. The aim was to provide a town centre in which all the visitors could mingle without people, property or sensibilities being outraged or threatened, and in which the broad working-class preference for sensation, variety, noise and bustle, for an experience not unlike the fairgrounds of their home towns, could be accommodated without running riot and damaging other interests. Lancashire working people on pleasure bent liked street vendors, cheapjack auctioneers, quack doctors selling patent medicines, swingboats and 'whirly-gorounds'. They enjoyed haggling with hawkers and bandying words with showmen, and they did not mind being accosted in the street by touts extolling the virtues of a company-house, eating-house, emporium or show. Nor did they have inhibitions about throwing down handbills in the street or on the beach. Policing policy in a popular resort had to work with the grain of these preferences or risk alienating the affections of those who held them.[52]

The regulation of popular consumption of streets and entertainments was aimed directly at the providers of goods and services rather than the users of them: at traders rather than trippers. This emphasis was very important: it made it less likely that visitors would be restrained, reprimanded or prosecuted, and kept up an atmosphere of holiday freedom as they experienced it. So, for example, where national legal frameworks strictly applied might have been intrusive to the point of generating riotous resistance, the practice was increasingly to use them sparingly. Convictions for drunkenness illustrate this point. The rate for local inhabitants followed the national trend by declining steadily from a peak reached in 1875, while convictions of visitors declined absolutely between 1887 and 1914, despite the enormous increase in visitor numbers. Blackpool had no shortage of pubs: the number of hotels, pubs and beerhouses nearly doubled from 42 to 80 between 1868 and 1880, and although it subsequently became harder to obtain new licences, existing provision was concentrated in the older and more 'popular' areas of the town. Drink was not hard to find, and for many men (especially) it was an essential element in a Blackpool visit, as part of the general atmosphere of escapist enjoyment. It is hard to imagine that the incidence of drunkenness, somehow measured on constant criteria from some point in the 1870s and 1880s, actually declined. Much more plausible is the notion that police and fellow-holidaymakers increasingly took a more relaxed and tolerant attitude, under circumstances where drinking culture expressed itself through singing, laughing and (at worst) staggering rather than through abuse or violence. Tolerance was all the easier as the town separated out into distinct social areas; and the unthreatening nature of most mild inebriation opens out issues which deserve further research into changing notions of what it was to be drunk, and of how people who had taken drink behaved.[53]

Sunday observance, in the context of a society in which this was a live issue and a touchstone of important definitions of public and private respectability, is a similar issue. Significantly, the Local Board of Health's by-laws, which supplemented national legislation in specific instances, were enforced less and less during the 1860s, after the threat of the Sunday railway excursions was removed, and boating and bathing were tacitly allowed, while the North Pier acquired a Sunday band and Sunday steamers. Donkeys were still discouraged but cabs plied discreetly. None of this was a problem, except to a few staunch Sabbatarians, until the influx of working-class visitors began in earnest. There was then a brief campaign for a stricter

Sunday, with support from the local press, to emulate the more 'respectable' regime at Southport, which was held to be attracting a better class of visitor. Very little came of this, however, and it was soon engulfed in a steady expansion of Sunday trading and entertainments, including the opening of the Aquarium and Winter Gardens, as business interests sought to profit from the new visitors. By the early 1880s Sunday provision extended to omnibuses, oyster stalls and, from 1883, 'sacred concerts' at the Winter Gardens; and when the new Chief Constable, J. C. Derham, prosecuted a batch of Sunday traders in 1887 he found local magistrates unwilling to impose penalties, and gave up the struggle. During the 1880s predominant local opinion had shifted against Sabbatarianism when Sunday trading was found to pay, and only the serious Nonconformists continued a principled resistance. For them, the opening of the municipally run promenade tramway on Sundays in 1896 was the last straw, and the Free Methodist minister J. S. Balmer was moved to write a pamphlet, *Blackpool, Paris and Sodom*, in which he claimed that every sin in the other places had its counterpart in Blackpool, and feared a divine judgement on the town. This did not happen, and the 'continental Sunday' continued to make headway against vociferous but unavailing opposition. In 1906 Derham explained his conversion to Sunday trading for shops selling food and refreshments to short-stay visitors, as well as services such as photographers, and unobtrusive back-street shops selling essentials in 'the working-class neighbourhood'. By 1913, when Sunday evening cinema shows were allowed, Blackpool could claim to have the brightest, most open Sunday, with the most opportunities for entertainment, of 39 towns whose policies were surveyed for the Chief Constable. This policy, like the relaxed attitude to drink, proved to be a winner in attracting and keeping the loyalty of working-class visitors who were rarely shackled by Sabbatarian inhibitions. In any case, there were never enough church sittings to accommodate all the visitors, and the fashionable and comfortably-off set a bad example by beginning their ostentatious 'church parade' on the North Pier before the services had actually ended: a reminder that strict Sabbatarianism was a minority taste among Blackpool's middle-class clientele as well as among the working-class visitors.[54]

All this was symptomatic of a relaxed attitude to public morality in general. The strictest line taken was on sexual behaviour, and this was in keeping with the values of a visiting public which could enjoy a bawdy joke but was censorious about extra-marital sexual relations. Prostitution was kept out of sight as far as possible. The first specific instructions to the new borough police force in 1887 enjoined 'particular attention' to suppressing 'any house of ill fame'. This reflected growing concern during the 1870s and 1880s, and in 1880 a local councillor broke a taboo by mentioning the question in open debate at the start of the season. After this, the issue faded into the twilight. The silence was punctuated by regular low-key prosecutions, which probably represented occasional efforts to admonish and deter, directed against unusually overt activities or responding to complaints from neighbours. The fiercest local campaign was directed against the 'singing saloons' of some of the town centre pubs, which were held to promote immorality by attracting young girls into an environment which combined drink and sexual temptation. Chief Constable Derham was particularly assiduous on this issue, and the music and singing licences were withdrawn in 1900 as the culmination of a campaign he had waged since 1889. They were not restored, and the only remaining 'singing saloon' was at Uncle Tom's Cabin on the northern cliffs, which lay beyond the borough boundary. This unusually restrictive action may well have been connected with Blackpool's developing, and officially unwanted, image as a place for flirtation and casual sexual encounters. This was a growing feature of popular media treatments of the resort, just as was the case with Brighton, a similar 'place on the margin' where everyday social restraints were held to be suspended. In practice, Brighton's more cosmopolitan visiting public lent more credence to such allegations, whereas Blackpool's visitors, as we have seen, brought their own social constraints and censorious collective gaze with them to keep excess within consensually acceptable bounds.[55]

Municipal intervention was also directed against exhibitions, postcards and penny-in-the-slot machines with sexual overtones. Crusades against the sale of 'indecent prints' and the display of 'obscene pictures' in the 1880s were followed in the next decade by action against the slot machines, culminating in 1899 with the closure of several 'mutoscope' parlours which

Lancashire women were able to enjoy themselves assertively at Blackpool, walking arm in arm several abreast along the promenade and enjoying banter with passing males.

The Promenade, South Shore, Blackpool.

exhibited moving pictures involving women in various stages of undress. The postcard craze, which emerged in 1903 as a seaside phenomenon, soon generated comic and 'continental' varieties of card, some of which were deemed to be suggestive and obscene. In 1906 a Chapel Street dealer was fined the vast sum (in context) of £12 10s. (£12.50), and the police were able to suppress the 'continental' cards. The comic ones were more resilient, in spite of a personal vendetta against their vulgarity by Councillor Sharples, who objected to their allusions to bedbugs and other unmentionables as well as to sexual innuendo. In 1912 a new Chief Constable set up a Censorship Committee which brought together dealers and local tradesmen in successful pursuit of consensus about the threshold of unacceptability, and the issue faded from the public eye. There was ample scope for ridicule when a popular resort with a free-and-easy reputation began to navigate these waters, but the campaigns produced relatively little adverse publicity on either side, and the concern to dampen down the direct public expression of sexual interest (as opposed to the more diffuse and pervasive culture of allusion and innuendo) went with the grain of the broader culture from which visitors were drawn. Relative strictness on this issue was not a problem.[56]

All this was in tune with the expectations of most visitors of all classes; and the focus on regulating and disciplining providers rather than consumers of services made it all the more palatable. As the *Blackpool Gazette* commented in 1887, expressing a new decisiveness on these issues after some heart-searching during the decade, 'The inhabitants of Blackpool are not the moral preceptors of their visitors, and have no right to dictate morality to them, the duty of the Corporation being merely to protect the best and largest number of visitors from discomfiture by having their moral instincts shocked.'[57] The regulation of street trading of less controversial kinds was undertaken in similar spirit, but a more permissive line could be taken with hawkers, touters, street musicians and stallholders, except when their sheer numbers or exuberance threatened to get out of hand. Hawkers were particularly problematic. They became numerous in the central streets from the mid-1860s, offering everything from hatguards to bootlaces, and from 1865 onwards they were controlled with increasing severity through by-laws and licensing. No attempt was made to suppress hawking altogether, and even in 1889, after ten years of licensing, the 105 local men who were privileged to work the streets were augmented by 60 itinerants with national pedlars' licences, and a further 200 unlicensed men who regarded the occasional small fine as an acceptable local tax. Central government forbade further tightening of the rules, which kept numbers in check and (from 1887) forbade noise and persistent pestering; and even John Bickerstaffe, normally a defender of Blackpool's free and easy image, complained of visitors being 'pestered to death' in 1893.[58] There were renewed complaints to the Home Office about seasonal influxes of disreputable hawkers in 1914, and there is no doubt that, given a free hand, Blackpool's officials and councillors alike would have been much more repressive.[59] The problem remained that hawkers (annoying as they were in their guise as tax-dodging competitors of local tradesmen) were part of Blackpool's attractions to many visitors, even as they irritated others; and under these circumstances, and with limited support from central government, the local authorities had to live with them even if they could not love them.

Touting in the streets, which involved the assertive personal advertising of shows, restaurants and accommodation by buttonholing passers-by, was an even more equivocal matter. It was a source of annoyance and, it was suggested, of unfair competition; but it also provided the only means of advertisement for small lodging-houses and other businesses away from the main thoroughfares. It was endemic in the larger eighteenth-century resorts, and first attracted media attention in Blackpool in the mid-1860s, when new areas of back-street company-houses were appearing, and railway by-laws were used to ban touts from the station. By the 1880s and 1890s touts and their sometimes picturesquely expressed rivalries were an inescapable part of the Blackpool experience, despite the introduction of by-laws offering fines of up to £2 in 1882. But legal problems about touting from private land, and practical problems about getting witnesses to attend, made the legislation difficult to enforce; and, as with the hawkers, sympathetic magistrates often imposed nominal fines. Persistent campaigns for strict enforcement from the Company-House Keepers' Association were given short shrift, and Corporation and magistrates alike recognised by the early twentieth century that if touting were suppressed entirely 'the whole business of the town would be stopped'. The practice might offend respectable visitors and established traders, but it was part of the town's picaresque image and fulfilled a useful function in the local economy. Here again, the overall tone of municipal policy was in tune with popular attitudes, and the overriding concern was to regulate but not to suppress.[60]

A similar ambivalence arose regarding stalls and entertainers in the streets and on the beach. Forecourt stalls enabled shopkeepers to extend display areas to offer items of small value for the enticement and enjoyment of casual passers-by, but they could be regarded as an eyesore and an obstruction as well as an opportunity, according to taste, and their proliferation during the 1890s across much of the central business district precipitated efforts at control. By 1901 an estimated 700 stalls lined the streets as far inland as North Station, selling garden produce, fish, oysters, ice-cream, crockery and even bibles. This was an unacceptable extension of a problem which had for many years been confined to South Beach, the core of the future 'Golden Mile', where front gardens had been going over to oyster stalls, phrenologists, fortune-telling booths and fairground attractions since the late 1860s, taking advantage of the huge volume of trippers flowing past towards the Central Pier. Attempts at thoroughgoing regulation through the Improvement Act of 1901 were thwarted in Parliament, where the interests of small proprietors were regarded as paramount, but the spread of new stalls was halted by the granting of additional planning powers. By this time, South Beach was a lost cause, but here above all the attractiveness of the fairground in the front gardens to working-class visitors was such that suppression would have been counter-productive. The vested interests of the shopkeepers were in line with the cultural preferences of enough of the visitors to turn the stalls into an asset in this and similar settings, but they could not be allowed to colonise areas where different standards prevailed.[61]

Singers, musicians and minstrel troupes in the streets brought out similar tensions. As in other resorts, street musicians began to provoke complaint in the 1850s. Most were a cut above the hawkers, and tended to stay for the whole summer, varying in character from the usual organ-grinders and German bands to an 'itinerant Scottish bagpiper'. Noise and obstruction were the main complaints, the former encompassing cultured objections to the standard of tunes and musicianship: 'not always the best adapted to the tastes of the visitors of a fashionable watering-place', as an optimist commented in 1856.[62] The volume of complaint and the number of itinerants increased with visitor numbers in the 1870s and 1880s, and the Corporation again felt constrained to intervene, banishing 'nigger minstrels' in 1877 and making the street musicians subject to being moved on by householders under a by-law of 1881. But alongside regular complaints from householders, including landladies, the street entertainers also had their defenders. Correspondents to the local press threatened to transfer their affections to the Isle of Man if they were not restored: 'Blackpool is getting too grand. Perhaps you will get a better class of company. Much good may it do you.' Such sentiments were widespread enough, and threatening enough, to lead to a relaxation of the policy of 'extermination' (as the *Blackpool Gazette* had put it) during the 1880s, and only the most persistent and irritating offenders were being prosecuted by mid-decade, with limited fines being levied by the magistrates. Here again a *modus vivendi* was achieved, as Blackpool's working-class visitors rapidly became important enough in the town's economy for their preferences to affect local public order policies in a relaxing way.[63]

Controlling the beach

The most difficult and symbolically important problems of achieving a balance between freedom and control involved the regulation of the central area of beach between the North and Central Piers. This was fitting, given the importance of beaches to resort identities and their status as liminal zones where property ownership and legal powers were uncertain and codes of behaviour were likely to be relaxed.[64] From the earliest stages of formal resort development beaches were controlled by whatever local authorities were available, to prevent observers from being shocked by bodily exposure and by uninhibited behaviour which transgressed dominant assumptions about propriety and decency; and there was a widespread tendency to exclude or discourage plebeian locals or visitors from frequenting fashionable parts of the shoreline.[65] Blackpool's regulatory regime was less demanding than many. The bathing regulations introduced under the 1853 Improvement Act, requiring the use of bathing-machines (those dank and inelegant horse-drawn boxes on wheels which protected modesty and onlookers' susceptibilities) and dividing the beach between the sexes, were absolutely typical of Victorian England. They were increasingly evaded at low tide, when the long shoreline was difficult to police; but continuing aspirations to control on the 'better-class' northern and southern beaches were expressed in official instructions to policemen and, in 1884, in the issuing of a telescope to the foreshore inspector to extend the long gaze of the law.[66] By the end of the nineteenth century, however, bathing on the old therapeutic model from the machines was already in decline, as the five-year average numbers of licensed machines peaked at between 108 and 111 between 1876 and 1895 before falling back to 54 in 1901–5 and 46 in 1911–14.[67]

These statistics are particularly striking at a time when visitor numbers were still growing impressively; but the machines could never have coped with the holiday crowds of the later nineteenth century, and they were too expensive to have been part of the mainstream working-class holiday experience. 'Mackintosh bathing', involving changing in lodgings and removing outer garments on the beach, was apparently on the increase, but for most people contact with the waves increasingly took the form of paddling rather than plunging, and this lay outside the regulatory regime. The beach was well frequented: indeed, contemporary photographs bear out press descriptions of the central section as crowded to saturation point on busy days. But most of the occupants, who made increasing use of deck-chairs from the turn of the century, were fully-clothed and sedentary, with most women wearing hats and most men keeping their jackets on. What attracted them was sea air and a comfortable temperature (sun-bathing remained a fashion of the future), and the entertainments that the beach increasingly provided. Here, rather than in the regulation of bathing, was where the local authority encountered problems, in contrast to the balance of priorities of most resorts at this time.[68]

The part of the beach opposite Bonny's Estate, with its cheap accommodation just behind the sea-front, and its increasingly nodal position between the stations and the popular pier after 1870, was an obvious area for fairground attractions to congregate, especially as it was the last section of shoreline to be covered at high tide and therefore gave traders and showmen the longest money-making period. From the 1850s onwards fairground activities had colonised gardens and vacant building lots in this area, and when building occupied these sites in the 1870s the swingboats, shooting galleries and other attractions migrated to the beach, where they joined an existing array of stallholders, whose life had just been made easier by a legal verdict in 1869 that the local authority's power to regulate and levy rents extended only to high water mark, a mere 40 or 50 feet from the promenade. There was now nothing to impede the growth of a great fairground between the piers. As well as musicians and vendors of everything from oysters and Blackpool rock to books, there were traditional components of every Lancashire town fair: quack doctors, cheapjack auctioneers, itinerant corn-cutters and Blackpool's own specialities, phrenologists and gipsy fortune-tellers. The local authority worried about disorder and loss of amenity, but further attempts to clear the area in 1873 and 1880 proved legally unenforceable, despite the securing of additional powers in 1879. A period of truce followed, as the popular season gathered momentum, and the fairground became firmly entrenched. By the mid-1890s it had become one of Blackpool's established attractions, having extended its range to embrace performing dogs, 'men of wonderful memory', and socialist orators. A return compiled by the Town Clerk in 1895 counted 316 people with 'standings on the foreshore'. The laborious and pedantic enumeration included 62 fruit vendors, 57 selling toys, general goods and jewellery, 52 ice-cream vendors, 47 sellers of sweets and refreshments and 21 of oysters and prawns. There were 36 photographers and exhibitors of 'phonographs, kinetoscopes, picture views, stereoscopes and telescopes', 24 ventriloquists and phrenologists (an understatement, according to the British Phrenological Association's figures), 6 quack doctors, 6 musicians and 5 conjurors. There was enough free entertainment at the 'carnival of the sands' to keep an army of trippers happy for a week, with a spectacular array of innovative technology and alternative science. It was at this point that a Corporation containing (as we shall see) a strong representation from the big entertainment companies decided to step in and cut this alfresco entertainment down to size, pleading the fear of disorder and immorality in this lawless zone beyond their official jurisdiction.[69]

The Corporation's legal armoury had been strengthened in 1887 by the purchase of the foreshore from the Duchy of Lancaster, and the 1893 Improvement Act secured new, specific powers to control all types of show, cart, van and temporary building. With its new legal mastery of the beach to low water mark, the Corporation began to license the stalls and impose minimum distances between them. In 1896 140 licences were issued, to local ratepayers only, with pitches allocated by the Chief Constable. But a year later the decision was taken to clear the sands entirely.[70] This was greeted with surprise and dismay. Press comment over recent years had emphasised the popularity of the fairground, which appealed to long-stay visitors – who were amused by the showmen – as well as to trippers. Media response was typified by the *Bradford Observer*, which suggested that more Blackpool visitors would be annoyed than pleased at this 'curious freak of exotically delicate sentiment', which seemed to be aimed at attracting an improbable constituency of 'quiet-loving holidaymakers'. The outcry from the excursionist interest was such that the Corporation had to retreat, despite support for the policy from shopkeepers' organisations and from those who catered for the 'better classes'. A policy of licensing stalls was reintroduced, with only those who were deemed to be fraudulent, offensive or providing unfair competition for ratepayers being excluded. This meant the removal of activities such as palmistry, phrenology and alfresco chiropody, although two particularly popular practitioners were subsequently reinstated, and some of the controversial performers merely returned to the forecourts of houses on South Beach, encouraging the further development of what was to become the 'Golden Mile'. Voting on the issue in Council meetings pitted entertainment company directors and advocates of respectability in unholy alliance against small back-street tradesmen in poor areas and South Beach property-owners, who clearly felt that they benefited from the crowds attracted by the fairground. The reprieve of the fairground, which persisted in its cleaned-up and regulated form, with pitches being auctioned from 1902 to pacify ratepayer interests, was a telling indicator of the more general transition in Blackpool's holiday season. It had become impolitic and economically threatening to suppress activities which a generation earlier had been regarded as a danger to respectability and therefore prosperity. In some important respects, the prevailing values and economic expectations had been turned inside out. The survival of the 'carnival of the sands' might be controversial and contested, but by the mid-1890s it had become inescapable. The fairground on the sands had become an essential part, indeed a symbol, of Blackpool's new dominant identity.[71]

In the medium term, however, the proponents of respectability won the day. By 1914 the overwhelming majority (68) of the 94 remaining stalls sold ice-cream, and a further 11 offered oysters. Only 6 'entertainers' remained, along with two blind musicians. The most lucrative pitches, for which up to £100 and even £145 might be paid for a season's rent, all sold ice-cream. Entertainers paid from £4 to £31. In 1904 a local newspaper had commented on the 'well dressed and respectable' appearance of most of the bidders at the annual auction, and this applied to many of the Italians who dominated the ice-cream trade, although some of their addresses were in unprepossessing areas of Bonny's Estate. So the sands remained animated and full of commercial activity; but they had lost the participatory and anarchic quality which had so endeared them to an earlier generation of visitors. Survival had been conditional on taming and a reduction of species diversity.[72]

Fairgrounds on the beach and foreshore were not unique to Blackpool, and there were similar problems of regulation at (for example) places as far apart as New Brighton, Weston-super-Mare and Brighton itself.[73] Blackpool ultimately adopted a more open and tolerant regime than its rivals, but only after sustained conflict and fierce resistance to an attempt at repression. This matches the pattern which has emerged in looking at the other issues arising from the regulation and control of holidaymakers and those who catered for them, from Sunday observance and drinking practices to street entertainment and bathing. An early instinct for strictness, severity and tidiness was foiled by the rapid growth of working-class holiday-making and its local supporters, and by the difficulty of legislating effectively in face of the rising tide of popular practice. Conflict brought compromise, and in practical terms the results invariably favoured the free-and-easy popular ethos, without going beyond it into license. The survival of the fair on the sands symbolised the general triumph of this outcome by the turn of the century. The rise of the Pleasure Beach, which provided an additional outdoor entertainment experience at hitherto-sedate South Shore and also had to contend with opposition from local government in its early years, was to set the seal on these developments, as we shall see.

Meanwhile, contemporaries' use of the word 'carnival' to describe the seashore fairground and other aspects of the Blackpool season should not be confused with cultural historians' adoption of the term, borrowing from the usage of Rabelais as celebrated and developed by anthropologists.[74] The seaside holiday at Blackpool might make the working-class consumer king for the week or the day, and enable restraints on eating, drinking and relations between the sexes to be relaxed in a setting which sometimes celebrated the grotesque, the vulgar and the usually hidden aspects of bodies and their functions. The emergent *genre* of the comic postcard certainly did this, as did (for example) some of the public practitioners of alternative medicine on the beach (feeling bumps, cutting corns). But authority was challenged implicitly rather than directly, and only up to consensually accepted points of tolerance. People brought a knowledge of the limits of acceptable behaviour on special occasions with them, and in Blackpool (if not in Brighton) their workmates and neighbours came too. Part of the fun, for example, was 'picking up' with a member of the opposite sex; but the whole structure of the holiday industry militated against even the most restrained form of public physical contact, and provided little opportunity for matters to be taken further in private. Postcard humour might be viewed as a safe outlet for resulting repressions; and what the seaside was popularly supposed to lead to was courtship and marriage.[75] The liveliness of Blackpool's popular culture was distinctive and impressive, but it was also (as middle-class contemporaries noted) contained and kept within bounds, to the extent that company-house mealtimes imposed an almost factory-like leisure discipline on many of the holiday throng.[76]

Blackpool was fun, but it was no Rabelaisian carnival; and this is why the local authorities' tolerance of exuberance was, in context, possible.

The Corporation and the holiday industry

The influence of local government on Blackpool's development extended far beyond allowing the development of a relaxed atmosphere in which working-class visitors were able to enjoy themselves, unselfconsciously and without fear of shared freedoms being turned into threatening license. Increasingly, it took an active part in encouraging the popular holiday industry. Above all, it went in for advertising, and for promenade extension, widening and reinforcement; but it also became heavily involved in the operation of utilities which provided a necessary infrastructure for a holiday economy, such as gas, electricity and especially tramways. The world's first public electric tramway opened along Blackpool's promenade in 1885, and seven years later the Corporation took over its operation, subsequently developing an extensive suburban network which helped to encourage the town's residential growth.[77] It was the Corporation's electricity department, one of the first to be established in 1893, which provided the expertise and resources to set up the autumn Illuminations which were introduced for the first time in 1912, and were to prove such an enormous success in extending the season and enhancing the distinctiveness of Blackpool's reputation and image. Electric lighting along the promenade had been introduced with a fanfare of publicity as early as 1879, rescuing the last weeks of an otherwise disastrous season.[78] Gas had been a municipal responsibility since 1853, and water came under the municipal umbrella when in 1897–9 the local authorities which were served by the Fylde Water-works Company took it over after two decades of complaints about quality and volume of service in the summer, including the occasional eel wriggling through household taps. Moreover, Blackpool's local authority took on a pioneering role in certain public health measures, such as the compulsory testing of domestic drains and the control of infectious diseases, as well as stepping up refuse disposal activities and the concreting of yards. The pressures of the season rapidly accumulated potential health and amenity problems, and the Corporation was eager to sustain a reputation for a healthy urban environment.[79]

On the other hand, there were significant areas of activity in which Blackpool's Corporation was less than prominent. Its concern for the town's reputation for health did not extend to the treatment of sewage, which continued to be discharged direct into the sea through a steadily extended outfall pipe a little way to the south of the South Jetty or Central Pier. It was screened from 1909, but remained untreated. The sea was regarded as an inexhaustible source of purification, despite occasional visual evidence to the contrary. This frame of mind even survived the revelation in 1896 that the mussels on the pier were spreading enteric fever because of sewage pollution, and were unfit to eat. The cost of treatment was seen as prohibitive, especially as technologies were still being disputed and the siting of any proposed sewage farm would generate inevitable conflict between threatened parts of the borough. Nor was the local authority terribly concerned with cultural provision or the development of parks and other green spaces for the locals (or even for the visitors). The beach was regarded as sufficient public open space, and the sea air, westerly winds and lack of smoke removed the usual justifications for park provision in more conventional industrial towns. Landowners sometimes offered land for public park use, but such proposals were invariably designed to enhance the amenity of building land nearby, and conflicts between different parts of town over priority in such investments were strong enough to impede provision in any particular area. Parks were not yet seen as attractions for visitors, and would in any case distract them from commercial entertainments. In similar vein, Blackpool had been keen to adopt the Free Libraries Act in 1879, regarding a public library as an attraction for 'better-class' visitors; but when this proved not to be the case it was neglected, and when a Carnegie gift of £15,000 was offered to endow a new Central Library in 1906 the Corporation proved most unwilling to pay for the site. Councillor Theophilus Hodgkinson described libraries as 'machines to grind away the public money'. Eventually the money was found from the gasworks profits, but it had been touch and go.[80]

Meanwhile the local working class received short shrift, with no public baths or wash-houses, and a grudging attitude to popular schooling and poor relief, although religious provision of schools kept a School Board at bay by meeting basic numerical provision of places until 1899, and a secondary school with some scholarship access was established in 1907.[81] There was no hint of municipal housing. Even the new Town Hall at the turn of the century was an unpretentious structure, with many departments having to be farmed out to other premises. The market remained on its cramped and insanitary site of 1844 for nearly fifty years. Wherever the need to attract visitors was not a central issue, the drive to municipal economy prevailed, assisted by the setting of gas prices at a high enough level to assure regular large profits to set against local taxation, although the efficiency of the gas undertaking helped to keep prices to the consumer at an acceptable level. Despite high expenditure on sea defences and promenades, and a unique level of municipal spending on advertising the town, Blackpool's local taxation levels were consistently among the lowest in England. It had an unusually interventionist local council, as did many seaside resorts; but the intervention was directed towards supporting the holiday industry by which most local people lived, in the knowledge that visitors consumed the town as a whole and that its prosperity depended on the collective provision of order and amenities. This was a frame of mind which was later christened 'municipal conservatism', as opposed to municipal socialism: the collective operation of utilities and provision of amenities which were necessary to enable the multitude of tourist businesses to thrive, and to promote the town as a whole in competition with rival resorts. The analogy between the seaside resort and the limited company, with the townspeople as shareholders, was popular and apposite here.[82]

Advertising Blackpool

The Corporation's role in advertising the town was particularly distinctive and important. As in other resorts, advertising of the town as a whole (as opposed to particular entertainment or other enterprises within it) was the responsibility of railway companies or voluntary committees of trades-people, raising money as best they could, for most of the nineteenth century. In 1879, however, the Blackpool Improvement Act incorporated a clause allowing the Corporation to levy a rate or property tax of twopence (0.83p) in the pound for advertising and providing a town's band to entertain the visitors. This was a unique concession from central government, which was generally hostile to such measures, denying the legitimacy of advertising as a local government activity. How it came about remains unclear: the relevant letter-book in the Public Record Office has been lost. No rival resort was allowed these powers, and Blackpool became the only British town which could plan and develop an advertising campaign from year to year and employ an advertising manager, secure in the knowledge that available revenue would expand in step with the rateable value of the town. In 1879 £500 per year was available, and by 1914 the sum had grown to well over £4,000. The Advertising Committee which the Corporation set up after the Improvement Act had two main aims: to extend the short summer season at either end by attracting 'better-class' visitors who could choose when to go on holiday and who tended to be crowded out by the swelling plebeian throng of July and August; and to expand the volume of the popular season still further by tightening Blackpool's grip on its established Lancashire and West Riding catchment areas and extending its range into new territories further afield. The second project gathered momentum a little later than the first, but was successful more obviously and more quickly; but the first began to make headway in the new century, and especially just before the First World War.[83]

The Advertising Committee's first act was to commission a lavish official guidebook to the town, which was distributed to railway waiting rooms, clubs, libraries, hotels and similar outlets. The Committee also continued an existing policy of putting on fêtes to extend the season and attract publicity in up-market media, as in the three-day festival to mark the opening of the Winter Gardens in 1878, which included fireworks and a torchlight procession and brought mayors, town clerks, newspaper editors and railway traffic managers to Blackpool as the Corporation's guests. These latter activities were funded from the gas profits even when the advertising rate became available, but they did not achieve the central goal of extending the season, and they became occasional rather than annual events after 1882. What took their place was an increasing concentration on poster advertising to extend the mass market, a change of posture which reflected the growing influence of the entertainment companies and their allies on the Committee after changes to its composition in 1881. At this point 20,000 colour posters were produced for display at main-line stations across Lancashire and the West Riding, and also in Birmingham and the Black Country. This was a much more 'open', indeed proletarian, advertising system, and in 1885 a new poster, known as the 'mustard plaster' because of the exaggerated colour of the beach, extended it as far as the East Midlands (including Lincoln and Northampton) and the Welsh borders. By 1902 posting stations included Southampton, Dover, Aberystwyth, Cambridge, Paisley, Glasgow and Dublin. The aim was to extend Blackpool's fame and catchment area as a popular resort on to a national stage. But in the early twentieth century posters were also appearing in more up-market venues, including the Waterloo battlefield, Paris and the transatlantic termini. This activity was probably more successful in generating publicity for Blackpool's enterprise and cheek than in actually attracting (for example) American visitors, and Blackpool's first advertising manager, Charles Noden, became famous for his skill in setting up publicity stunts. But the early twentieth century also saw a renewed commitment to extending the season. The popular poster policy had attracted criticism from advocates of catering for the 'better classes', and with additional revenue available it could be supplemented by more up-market activities in spring and autumn, including fêtes, a musical festival, motor racing along the promenade, and in 1909 the first aviation meeting in Britain. By this time efforts were being concentrated into September and October, and the policy was beginning to bear fruit. What clinched it was the introduction of electrical 'Illuminations' in 1912, with illuminated trams and festoons of coloured lights paid for out of the electricity budget, which was thus also enlisted to support the holiday industry. This was a spectacular success, and it was accompanied by more modest and limited attempts to promote a winter season. There is no doubt that much of Blackpool's comparative success in attracting not only an ever-expanding working-class market, but also a pleasure-seeking middle-class public outside the main season, was due to this advertising policy.[84]

Widening the promenade

The other particularly impressive feature of the Corporation's direct support for the holiday industry was the high continuing investment in the promenade and sea defences, following the success of the original scheme which had been completed in 1870. In the mid-1890s more than £60,000 was spent in providing sea defences and public walks at Claremont Park, the up-market district of North Shore, after the Land, Building and Hotel Company which owned the sea-front had professed itself unable to act against continuing erosion. The imperative to intervene was strong enough to overcome opposition from the other end of town, where there were complaints of unfair subsidy to competitors. In the process the Corporation acquired land at Gynn Square in order to gain access to filling-up material, and used its hard-won ownership (acquired under suspicious circumstances from a syndicate drawn from the Council's own inner circle) to control the development of a key area, safeguarding open spaces while keeping fairgrounds at bay. Meanwhile, as the crowds of visitors continued to grow, widening the whole promenade was increasingly discussed, and in 1899 a poll of the ratepayers sanctioned a seaward extension of 100 feet. The work was completed in 1905, at a cost of £350,000.[85] These and earlier efforts were not completely successful, one by-product being a tendency for sand to be scoured away from the beach, exposing the underlying clay;[86] but the importance of combating erosion and flooding, and providing sufficient space for the visitors to enjoy the sea-front, was generally apparent. As the *Blackpool Gazette* remarked, 'We can well afford to sink a third of a million in perfecting our sea-front. It is our principal market-place, and must ever be our greatest attraction.' The wonder is that similar attitudes did not prevail with regard to the sea itself.[87]

Blackpool's rulers

The Corporation thus played a very important part in building Blackpool's success as a popular resort and in sustaining its growth. The composition of its membership helps to explain its policies and to illustrate the nature of local politics. The Local Board of Health had itself experienced a trans-ition in the mid-1860s, from being dominated by parsimonious farmers and petty tradesmen to finding increasing room for professionals, retired residents from inland and prospering shopkeepers with a growing stake in the 'better-class' holiday industry, a more ambitious outlook and a more businesslike philosophy. This was reflected in the building of the new promenade. This membership pattern was perpetuated by the new Cor-poration which was elected in 1876, although the identity of the people concerned changed owing to a short-lived politicisation of elections on national party lines, which brought in a clean sweep of Conservatives. But over the next twenty years the balance of the Corporation tilted steadily in favour of the popular holiday industry, at the expense of the professionals and retired businessmen. More than a quarter of new entrants in this transitional period, when the popular holiday industry really took hold, depended directly on the holiday industry for their living. If we add in people who had directorships in entertainment companies or sea-front hotels, the holiday interest rises to 36 per cent; and if we add shareholders in local entertainment companies, it passes 50 per cent. The other great interests were building, which helps to account for the lax attitude to enforcing the building by-laws, and drink, which may help to explain the low level of prosecutions for alcohol-related offences, especially as the drink interest exercised considerable leverage on the Watch Committee which oversaw these matters. Over 20 per cent of new entrants between 1877 and 1897 were in the building trades, and more than half of the councillors were involved in building development and property speculation, some on the grand scale. In similar vein, a broadly defined drink interest, embracing owners of licensed property, former publicans, off-licence holders and directors of hotel companies, accounted for two-fifths of the original Council in 1876 and more than a quarter of the subsequent new entrants. The leaders of the ruling cliques had their origins in the local yeomanry, and built up their businesses in step with the town's expansion. Freemasonry and friendship helped to pull together these entwined economic interest-groups still further, and there was little room for the Nonconformist conscience. A passive, vaguely defined Anglicanism founded on minimum attendance was the norm. Women, in spite of their importance in the local economy, and trade unionists were completely excluded until the inter-war years, and even the minority of tradesmen and professionals with an interest in the 'better-class' market was increasingly marginalised. It was under these auspices that the late Victorian Corporation pursued the popular holiday market with growing single-mindedness and success. No other seaside resort had a local authority whose composition and dominant values geared it up so directly to this goal.[88]

Towards the turn of the century the ruling groups over-reached themselves at the height of a local building boom, when too many local politicians were seen to be identified with land syndicates who sought to sell to the Corporation for development purposes at inflated prices. A campaign for municipal morality, financial and otherwise, developed, with considerable input from Nonconformists and Co-operators. There was also increasing disquiet at the apparent influence of the drink interest on the Watch Committee, and anger at the lack of representation of lesser tradespeople such as company-house keepers and small shopkeepers, who were developing their own organisations. These pressures brought about the doubling of council membership from 24 to 48 in 1898, with a consequent dilution of the dominant interest-groups. The new council after the municipal general election of 1898 was still overwhelmingly run by building and holiday interests, although company-house keepers and other small tradespeople were more prominent in their ranks; and new entrants between 1899 and 1913 were dominated by retailing and crafts (just over 45 per cent), and professionals and the retired (11 per cent each), with the holiday and building industries falling to one-third of the membership. Under these auspices the advertising campaign moved over to give greater emphasis to season extension (although 40 per cent of expenditure still went on posters on the eve of the First World War), and the town's official guides interestingly switched their emphasis away from celebrating the fun-loving holiday throng towards highlighting 'rational recreations' and 'formality and decorum'.[89] The drink interest was kept on a tighter rein, while for the time being there were no more complaints about 'rings' of councillors engaged in corrupt land speculation. But by this time the transition to the working-class market had been well and truly completed.[90]

In Blackpool as elsewhere, municipal politics was endemically conflict-ridden, although the divisions were based on competition between interest-groups and districts within the town rather than orthodox party politics, which became important only at election times when there seemed some possibility of dethroning the Conservatives, who were the majority party throughout the period. The public virtues and successes of the Corporation were founded largely in the indulgence of private vices and the pursuit of particular interests, but outcomes favoured the unique expansion of the popular holiday season. The overriding power and influence of a few leading figures spanned most of the period. They included Alderman Heap, restaurateur and financial expert, and the long-serving Town Clerk T. H. Loftos and Chief Constable J. C. Derham, who provided important continuities of outlook and experience. But the key figures were drawn from the entertainment companies: John and Tom Bickerstaffe of the Central Pier, Passenger Steamboat and Tower Companies (among others), Thomas Sergenson of the Grand Theatre, and an assortment of their cronies. At an earlier stage a similar circle had W. H. Cocker at its centre, the town's leading citizen at the time of incorporation and the promoter of the Aquarium, the Sea Water Company and the Winter Gardens during the 1870s. In 1907, on the other hand, W. G. Bean of the newly emergent Pleasure Beach began a long spell on the council, bringing a sustained note of conflict between this new southern interest within the town and the established central entertainments of the Tower and Winter Gardens. The symbiotic relationship between the activities of the Corporation and the rise of the entertainment companies is more readily understood if such close and enduring links are borne in mind. And the entertainment companies themselves had a crucial part to play in Blackpool's rise and transformation, and its ability to attract the lion's share of the working-class market. Private enterprise worked alongside public investment, helping to create Blackpool's attractive image in the outside world; and the unique success of the entertainment industry in Blackpool helped in turn to reduce the Corporation's liabilities, preventing it from having to intervene to provide entertainments and bail out or take over ailing companies as happened in most rival resorts. This is another theme of central importance.[91]

The pleasure palaces

The late nineteenth century saw a widespread development of large-scale seaside entertainment companies whose imposing 'pleasure palaces' featured a distinctive maritime architecture of pleasure, with frivolous use of ornamental ironwork, colour and eclectic borrowings from oriental and other cultures.[92] Blackpool was well to the fore in this respect by the end of the 1870s, and took a commanding lead during the 1890s, after an interim decade of uncertainty and taking stock. The rise of Blackpool's entertainment companies had been foreshadowed by investment in the piers during the 1860s, and by the development of popular entertainment on the South Jetty from 1870. Robert Bickerstaffe of the Wellington Hotel, whose eye to new opportunities had propelled the new pier swiftly down-market, saw its monthly takings quadruple in a short time, and by 1875 the pier's social standing could be celebrated by the dialect writer Ben Brierley, who compared the upturned noses, fashionable clothes and aloofness of the North Pier with its unpretentious southern neighbour, where 'th' bacca reech smells stronger, an' th' women are leauder abeaut th' meauth ...'. Dancing began with the arrival of the first excursion trains at dawn, and continued energetically through the day. Over the next fifteen years annual admissions more than doubled to 988,000, and in 1891 shops and a dancing platform were added. A Grotto Railway followed in the new century, when the pier was festooned with advertisements for such indelicate products as corsetry. Its basic pleasures were still accessible for a penny, compared with twopence

The imaginatively named Royal Palace Gardens, Raikes Hall, presented in misleadingly formal and sanitised guise. ('Royal Palace Gardens', *New Album of Blackpool and St Annes Views* (n.p., n.d., *c.* 1900)

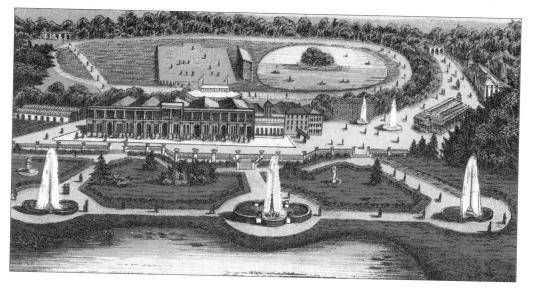

for the sedate North Pier and a shilling for the Manx pleasure gardens where dancing was also the main attraction.[93]

The South Jetty was joined in catering primarily for the rapidly-expanding working-class market by the Raikes Hall pleasure gardens, which opened for its first full season in 1872. This was a venture in the tradition of the eighteenth-century London pleasure gardens and of Manchester's Belle Vue. It occupied an extensive site (51 acres in all) half a mile from the sea, and it provided parks and conservatories, open-air dancing and popular spectacles involving acrobats, tightrope-walkers, fireworks and battle re-enactments. Early attempts to appease 'respectable' opinion by putting on morning promenade concerts were soon abandoned, and when a liquor licence covering the whole of the grounds was obtained in 1874 the whole enterprise careered cheerfully down-market. Prostitutes and pickpockets in abundance posed problems but demonstrated popularity. Innovations were eagerly adopted, including at various times mechanical racehorses, roller-skating and a tricycle track, and handsome dividends were paid to the shareholders, who came from Blackpool itself (half the shareholders and 40 per cent of the shares), inland Lancashire and Halifax (which accounted for nearly a quarter of the shares). At the turn of the century the directors abandoned the site to the builders, recognising the impossi-bility of sustaining competition with new enterprises on the sea-front and taking a tempting profit while the going was good; but for a quarter of a century Raikes Hall had pioneered large-scale catering for sensation-seekers in Blackpool, with a judicious mix of old and new, and its popularity was central to the emergence of Blackpool's raffish and open-handed image.[94]

Raikes Hall's success for its first decade and a half owed much to lack of competition in its chosen niche. The Winter Gardens, the other great entertainment complex of the 1870s, began by continuing the pursuit of the 'better classes', and the two enterprises divided the market in much the same way as the two piers. The company's flotation in 1875 was a response to a similar venture at Southport, as Blackpool continued to keep an eye on its competitors, and the first directors were all local men, with no overlap with the Raikes Hall directorate. It occupied the site of W. H. Cocker's house at Bank Hey, in the original centre of the town, and Blackpool's leading citizen of the time joined the Board when this decision was made. His colleagues were local publicans, tradesmen and property speculators. The Winter Gardens offered indoor promenades among orna-mental plants (hence the name, which reflected unavailing aspirations to a high-class winter season), a concert hall and a roller-skating rink (which catered for a middle-class fashion of the time). It was Blackpool's first all-weather entertainment centre. Tensions soon arose because working-class trippers mingled with the 'better classes', and the two constituencies wanted mutually incompatible entertainments, as was made audibly clear

The Pavilion at the Winter Gardens, emphasizing its role as all-weather promenade rather than popular entertainment centre. ('The Pavilion, Winter Gardens', *New Album of Blackpool and St Annes Views* (n.p., n.d., *c.* 1900)

at some of the concerts. There was also controversy over Sunday opening; but from 1883 onwards the company paid regular dividends. It really took off, however, with the appointment of William Holland as manager in 1887, despite opposition from the more traditionally minded of the directors. Holland had a long London music-hall career behind him, and was clearly selected to turn the Winter Gardens into a trippers' paradise. He more than trebled the receipts in eight years, while the basic admission charge remained at 6d. (2.5p). His innovations included 'ballets' and variety programmes with popular themes such as 'Our Empire', a controversial departure from the classical concerts of the previous regime; but he also presided over the opening of the Opera House in 1889, whose staple fare was Gilbert and Sullivan and West End comedies, leavened with occasional visits from artistes of the calibre of Caruso and Melba, not all of whom took to Lancashire audiences. The Empress Ballroom, a celebration of the Lancashire working-class love of dancing, proved his monument, for he died in 1895 before it was completed. Holland also contributed to Blackpool's welcoming and humorous image in the outside world, telling tall tales about the Winter Gardens' opulence and famously inviting visitors to come and spit on his new 100-guinea carpet, thereby mocking pretentious assumptions about the uncivilised nature of Lancashire folk. His term of office was perfectly timed to turn the Winter Gardens into a lasting emblem of the new Blackpool.[95]

By the end of the 1870s Blackpool's entertainments already outstripped those of much larger resorts, and a period of consolidation followed. Recurrent trade depression made the future of the popular holiday industry seem uncertain. But in the late 1880s and early 1890s, when the resilience of popular spending was becoming apparent and trade depression was becoming more likely to divert investment into mass entertainment than to discourage it, there were renewed speculative stirrings. Developments at the Winter Gardens reflected this, and in more conspicuous style Blackpool acquired the tallest building in England, its own version of the Eiffel Tower: the pleasure palace whose astonishing silhouette became the enduring symbol of the world's biggest and brashest working-class seaside resort. But the making of Blackpool Tower was a complex and contested process. It was promoted late in 1890 by a London-based organisation, the Standard Contract and Debenture Corporation, which was already involved in a similar Eiffel Tower scheme at Douglas, Isle of Man. In February 1891 Standard Contract's offshoot, the Blackpool Tower Company, was incorporated with £150,000 capital in £1 shares, a capital requirement on an altogether novel scale for the town. The share issue included 5,000 founders' shares whose holders would divide half the profits after an 8 per cent dividend. Sixty-two of the subscribers to these shares were from Blackpool, including eleven members of the Bickerstaffe and Nickson families. John Bickerstaffe, a successful businessman from an old Blackpool family who was, at the time, the first Mayor of Blackpool to be a publican, was the only Blackpool representative on the board of directors. This was to be of vital importance.[96]

Early reactions in the town more generally had been sceptical, and the *Gazette*, the voice of the local establishment, commented that 'An Eiffel Tower in the centre of the Blackpool promenade is hardly feasible.' By September 1891 only 8 per cent of the allocated shares were held in Blackpool, despite John Bickerstaffe's £2,000 investment and his ally John Nickson's £1,000. Sixty per cent of the capital came from Lancashire and the West Riding, but for the first time in Blackpool's history districts from beyond the established catchment area made a substantial contribution. Metropolitan interest in Blackpool had probably been sparked by its publicity campaigns and by the work of William Holland over the past decade, as well as by press reports which had increasingly presented Blackpool's orderly working-class crowds in awestruck terms. Henceforth this was to be a lasting theme.[97]

But local scepticism was justified. Standard Contract and Debenture had no intention of seeing the Tower built. It was a shell company, with very little of its capital subscribed, and its aim was to acquire a plot of land, sell it on to the Tower Company at an inflated profit, take on the construction contracts and go into liquidation at an early stage, leaving the project in limbo, with no prospect of constructing a viable business on the over-valued site. This was a common type of fraudulent company promotion at the time, and at Douglas the full scenario was played out, with the Tower remaining an airy vision of temptation. At Blackpool matters worked out differently, in part because of the suspicion of local investors. Standard Contract and Debenture was left with shares on its hands, which allowed an increasingly assertive Bickerstaffe to invoke a clause which reduced to manageable proportions the price the Tower Company had to pay for its site. Enough of the capital had been subscribed for work to begin, and Bickerstaffe was able to reconstruct the company, attract local investment and press on to a successful conclusion. This involved toughness and financial courage (including the purchase of 800 £1 shares at half their nominal value at a point of crisis) as well as perspicacity, and this is an impressive example of an individual making a difference to the history of a town. The Tower made a vital contribution to subsequent developments; and without Bickerstaffe, it would have remained a tantalising phantom.[98]

The Tower opened on Whit Monday, 1894. Its distinctive superstructure became landmark as well as symbol of pleasure and release for all who gazed across the flatness of the Fylde from train and later charabanc, car and coach windows to catch the first familiar glimpse; and it also offered a vertiginous alternative vision of Blackpool itself, its crowds reduced to swarming ants from the crow's-nest viewing platform. But the engine room

The classic view of the central promenade at Blackpool in the 1890s, with the Tower presiding over an animated scene in which sailing vessels feature prominently. ('Central Beach', *New Album of Blackpool and St Annes Views* (n.p., n.d., *c.* 1900)

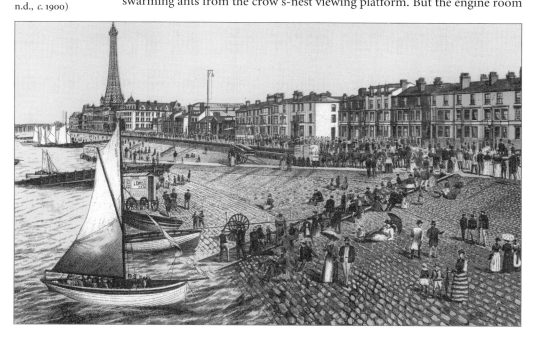

where profits were manufactured was the squared-off brick box below the soaring girders, which contained a ballroom, a concert room, circus, menagerie, aquarium and roof garden, multiplying the trippers' sixpences to impressive effect. But the Tower was inclusive in its embrace: it welcomed curious middle-class pleasure-seekers as well as 'factory folk'. Arthur Laycock's Edwardian novel *Warren of Manchester* was designed to boost Blackpool's cheery egalitarianism as well as to comment adversely on the immoralities of economic competition, but his presentation of the Tower Ballroom, in which 'the mill-girl ... glided cheek by jowl with the factory-master's daughter; the spinner, with the smart city clerk and the stylish salesman', carries conviction, especially as he emphasises the social unease which sometimes accompanied such mixing.[99] The Tower was a democratic place, in which all classes could meet without undue discomfort; and this reflected the town's enduring concern to retain as many middle-class visitors as possible.

The opening of the town's third pier, at South Shore in 1893, showed that investors believed in the future of the 'respectable' season. The pier was promoted from Manchester, with a capital of £60,000, and its shareholders came overwhelmingly from inland Lancashire, which accounted for three-quarters of the shares. A 74-signature petition against the proposal from South Shore residents in 1891, fearing that the company might introduce dancing and stagger down the primrose path of the Central Pier, was outnumbered tenfold by a counter-petition in its support; and the company accepted a clause in its enabling act to prohibit dancing, showing its faith in the viability of the sedate middle-class market. A proposal for a pier at North Shore in 1898 was defeated by residents' opposition, but the success of the South Shore initiative showed the continuing vitality of Blackpool's middle-class season and the resort's ability to accommodate a cross-section of visiting publics.[100]

These initiatives of the early 1890s confirmed Blackpool's status as the English – and indeed European – resort with the greatest array of popular attractions. The all-weather capability of the Tower and Winter Gardens gave visitors added assurance of access to pleasures come rain or shine, and on a scale which could not be matched in contemporary provincial towns or even cities. But this was not the end. In 1896 the Winter Gardens acquired its own hallmark accent on the skyline when a Gigantic Wheel with capacity for 900 passengers opened in its grounds, having attracted purchasers for 50,000 £1 shares, drawn as so often mainly from Lancashire, although the original impetus came from London. A recent study of Manchester Ship Canal has associated that immense scheme with the origins of popular capitalism, but Blackpool's amusement companies must run it close.[101] A year later the Alhambra was promoted on a promenade site next door to the Tower. This was another Manchester venture, with support within Blackpool from the publican, former acrobat and later town councillor Henry Brooks. Its authorised capital was £220,000, nearly half as much again as the Tower's, but belief in Blackpool's limitless potential, at the peak of a building boom, ensured that the issue would be fully subscribed within four months. Inland Lancashire supplied five-sixths of the capital and 60 per cent of the shareholders, while Blackpool put in one-tenth and one-eighth. As far as successful investment went, this was a step too far. The Alhambra's programme was practically a mirror image of the Tower's in its mix of music-hall, variety, dancing, circus and a roof garden. In spite of, or perhaps because of this, it was well-patronised, adding to Blackpool's overall capacity if not to the range of its indoor attractions, but the high cost of site, buildings, decor (which had to be ostentatiously palatial) and artistes proved a crippling financial burden. In 1900 £50,000 of share capital had to be written off, but two years later the Alhambra had to be wound up. In 1904 the Tower Company took over its assets and ran it successfully as the Palace until 1961, showing that the demand for an additional pleasure palace was ample and emphasising that the problems arose from financial mismanagement. Nevertheless, for the first time in Blackpool's financial history fingers were burnt on the grand scale, and this was to be the last of Blackpool's major entertainment companies to be floated on the open market. What is significant in context, however, is how successful most of the great Blackpool entertainment companies were in giving customers what they wanted and reaping impressive returns on investment, in striking contrast to prevailing experiences in highly seasonal popular resort economies elsewhere.[102]

The last of Blackpool's array of popular attractions to be put in place during these formative years was a very different animal. It took the form of a sprawling open-air amusement park, Blackpool's answer to the various similar 'parks' at Coney Island, in contrast with the solidly built, tightly enclosed central 'pleasure palaces'; and it developed on a scale which dwarfed the similar fairgrounds which appeared at such resorts as Southend, Margate and even Southport. The origins of the Pleasure Beach, as it was christened in 1905, came in the early 1890s, when the fortune-telling activities at the gypsy encampment on the South Shore sandhills were augmented by fairground attractions, while the tram terminus at South Shore also attracted a fairground to a nearby vacant lot. When this was purged after protests from neighbours in 1896, its showmen also joined the gypsies on land beyond the promenade which was unsuitable for building until sea defences had been constructed. Here their numbers were augmented by refugees from the clearance of the more disreputable stallholders from South Beach in 1897. The original peepshows, exhibitions (fat bullocks, giantesses and the like), shooting galleries, phrenologists, fortune-tellers and hot pea stalls were soon joined by primitive mechanical rides, and in 1901 the tenancy of 40 acres of sand-dunes was concentrated into the hands of an Anglo-American syndicate which bought the land outright three years later. The front man and manager was W. G. Bean, a Londoner with several years' experience of the American amusement industry; and under his management the fairground flourished, as the syndicate let plots to individual enterprises and negotiated with the Corporation over building plans. A crisis on this issue was successfully negotiated during 1906–8, when a protest movement against the alleged harmful effects of these developments on the 'social tone' of South Shore was beaten off. By this time the fairground had its local supporters as well as opponents, as economic benefits began to be reaped and loss of amenity was found to be highly localised. The Corporation, whose entertainment company interests had shown signs of a hawkish attitude towards this peripheral competitor, was persuaded to regulate rather than suppress, disposing of the gypsies but welcoming the increasingly sophisticated electrical rides. Attitudes were influenced by the Pleasure Beach's growing importances as employer (600 staff in summer by 1914), generator of traffic for the Corporation's trams (up to 100,000 visitors on an ordinary day and 200,000 on a Bank Holiday), and consumer of electricity. By this time investment in the attractions added up to about £200,000, and the pioneering Sir Hiram Maxim Captive Flying Machine of 1904 had been joined by a water-chute, helter-skelter, cakewalk, oscillating staircase, haunted cabin, 'submarine switchback' and Monitor and Merrimac battle show. The Pleasure Beach was the heir to Raikes Hall and much more besides: it celebrated modern technology while appealing to the unexpected and the uninhibited. It was, perhaps, the most genuinely 'carnivalesque' of Blackpool's entertainment complexes, with its encouragement of screaming, flailing, bumping, crashing, vertigo and bodily exposure;

The South Shore gipsy encampment on what was to become the Pleasure Beach site, decorously presented as a tourist attraction in the 1890s. ('Gipsy Encampment', *New Album of Blackpool and St Annes Views* (n.p., n.d., *c.* 1900)

and it was certainly the most American, with its direct links with Coney Island innovations. Its rivals learned to appreciate it, too, as it became apparent that Blackpool's amusements were as much complementary as in competition, and people who were attracted by one aspect of the resort would move on to sample others. There was nothing outside America to match the sheer scale and variety of the Blackpool experience of the early twentieth century.[103]

Beyond all this, of course, Blackpool offered entertainments of a smaller or more usual kind: theatres (including the magnificent Grand of 1894, a

The Grand Theatre.

Frank Matcham masterpiece whose commissioning was Thomas Sergenson's response to competition from the Tower for his circus and variety
entertainments), music-halls, pubs, waxworks, 'art galleries' (featuring such
pictures as 'The Goddess Diana and her hunting party' for the prurient
gaze), and a rapid development of cinemas in the early twentieth century.
Above all, Blackpool became a great provincial theatrical centre, with the
Winter Gardens as well as the Grand regularly attracting star names,
prominent touring companies and prosperous middle-class audiences by
the turn of the century.[104] There was also the fairground on the beach and
its disreputable but engaging appendages on the sea-front between the
piers, where the 'Golden Mile' was coming into being at the turn of the
century (although the official guide-books had nothing to say about
it).[105] There was, literally, something for everyone in this cornucopia of
delights, which celebrated and built on aspects of perceived 'Lancashire'
(or cotton town) character and culture while opening out to new influences
and admitting unpretentious fun-seeking outsiders. This helps to explain
the classless and geographically expansive aspects of Blackpool's popularity
(although an ability to segregate the classes when it mattered was equally
important, and Lancashire versus Yorkshire and other banter was a necessary ingredient).[106] The sheer vitality, distinctiveness and originality of
Blackpool's entertainments was the essential element in its remarkable
growth. Without it, nothing else would have worked.

How the locals lived

Like the contemporary guidebooks, I have left Blackpool's pleasure palaces
and artificial amusements to the last in attempting to account for its
remarkable transformation during the period covered by this chapter. It
will be clear that this strategy is intended to emphasise their importance
rather than downgrade it, for the response of Blackpool's leisure entrepreneurs to perceived opportunities was such as to attract an ever-swelling
stream of new visitors, who were drawn by reputation and by advertising
to a resort which was obviously eager not only to respond to their desires,
but also to create attractive new ones. Without them, the efforts of the
corporation would have been less single-minded and of less avail. What
all this created was a resort with a distinctive social profile, and as a
downside to success as defined in dividends and numbers, it generated a
set of social problems which might be matched in some resorts elsewhere
(especially in Brighton) but were hard to exceed. This chapter concludes
with a discussion of what sort of people lived in Blackpool, and what life
in this unique resort was like for them.

As Blackpool matured and specialised around the turn of the century,
it came to share most of the social and economic features which marked
out the seaside resort as a distinctive kind of town: some modestly, others

to the point of caricature. It was, increasingly, a town of small businesses, which already accounted for well over half of its household heads in 1871, and continued to expand in step with the population. As in most resorts, these were concentrated in retailing, building, transport and accommodation, and in Blackpool's case the enormous number of small shopkeepers and company-houses, aimed primarily at the rapidly expanding working-class market, stood out especially.[107] In 1871, even according to the census (which always understated), nearly one in four of Blackpool's householders were company-house keepers. Evidence from the Medical Officer of Health's reports during the 1880s suggests that the true figure was more than half, and by 1911 the census total of 4,174 was close to one-third of the householders, in a resort whose residential population had expanded greatly over the past decade. Blackpool was far ahead of all rival resorts in this regard, and in 1911 its location quotient of 21.20 for coffee- and eating-house, lodging- and boarding-house keepers compared impressively with nearby Southport (6.65), up-market Bournemouth (5.98) and cockney Southend (5.04).[108] Meanwhile, more than 2,000 shops were open during the 1911 season in Blackpool, of which nearly 1000 sold food, including 238 sweet-shops, 96 fish and chip shops and 60 restaurants. As early as 1903 there had been 201 registered ice-cream dealers. Jewellers and fancy goods dealers were divided into high-class and excursionist trades, and in practice so must many of the 190 drapers, 75 hairdressers and 110 tobacconists. Most of Blackpool's tradespeople looked after the needs of the short-stay visitor in terms of food, drink, trinkets and holiday clothing, and the importance of the season was reflected in the large number of shops which closed down or switched to a different trade outside the summer months.[109] Much of Blackpool's manufacturing (which was unobtrusive but not unimportant) had similar characteristics: almost two-thirds of the 692 factories and workshops which were enumerated in the borough in 1911 made or processed food (including ice-cream and rock) and clothing, and there were 22 jewellery workshops.[110] Blackpool had become, during the late nineteenth and early twentieth centuries, a highly specialised popular resort which had generated its own supporting industries and retail structure. It had also sustained an important professional sector, however, as well as attracting managerial commuters and commercial travellers. Men from these occupational groupings actually increased as a proportion of Blackpool's male over-tens from 8.9 to 10.4 per cent during 1861–1911, partly reflecting Blackpool's hospitality to the legal and medical professions, to accountants, surveyors and estate agents; and although men of independent means fell from 6.6 to 6.0 per cent of their sex, women in this category increased from 2.4 to 4.0. These were not high figures when compared with more up-market resorts, however, and far fewer households kept domestic servants (as opposed to those in hotel or boarding-house service) than in Southport or Lytham St Annes.[111]

At the other end of the scale, Blackpool also developed a pool of im-
poverished casual and seasonal workers who had limited skills to offer in
local labour markets. All trades were affected by an economy based on
'three months' hard labour and nine months' solitary confinement', and
contemporaries observed a great deal of quiet poverty in the back streets
on the margins of the holiday industry, where rents were inflated by
opportunities to take in visitors but extra income often failed to match
expectations. The men who struggled to find work as labourers on building
sites or at the gasworks, or sought a foreman's patronage for work on the
tramways, were particularly vulnerable to the vagaries of seasonal demand;
and many households spliced together several sources of income, combining
the letting of rooms with seasonal work in the holiday industry and winter
work wherever it could be found. Competition from seasonal migrants
kept wages down during the holiday season, when a rush of women flocked
into Blackpool in search of domestic work in the hotels, restaurants and
larger company-houses (the smaller ones depended on family labour).
Despite 'dovetailing' and other survival strategies, which included men
going to work inland for part of the year, relief work and charitable
donations were important to sustaining Blackpool's labour force through
the bleak, blustery, lonely winters. The winter of 1879, after a season marred
by bad weather and trade depression inland, brought the first major charitable intervention, and in 1909–10, the worst of the Edwardian winters,
the Chief Constable's relief fund gave assistance in kind to as many as 15.6
per cent of the town's population. In the next year the peak level of relief
work under the Unemployed Workmen Act of 1905 was reached, with 1,870
men being found employment.[112] Blackpool was no safe haven for a comfortable middle class, although such people could find cosy enclaves within
it: most of its population were working-class by origin and culture, struggling to make ends meet with limited capitals in small businesses, or trying
to survive in a fluctuating and unpredictable labour market which regularly
went out like the tide, leaving them stranded and gasping.

As in the Lancashire cotton towns from which so many of Blackpool's
residents and seasonal workers came, women were central to the town's
economy, although this was not apparent from the composition of the
Council. In 1911 only Southport among the 17 largest Lancashire towns had
a higher ratio of women to men than Blackpool, whose female percentage
of 57.72 was higher than any of the weaving towns where women's work
opportunities boosted the female population. At that same census nearly
40 per cent of women over 10 years old were officially in employment,
though the figure would have been much higher had the census been taken
during the holiday season. Only the specialised cotton-weaving towns had
higher proportions of married women and widows active in the labour
market than Blackpool's 24.8 per cent, and only Morecambe had a higher
proportion of its working women in the cluster of occupations based on

food, tobacco, shopkeeping and (crucially) lodgings than Blackpool's 44.3 per cent. Just over one in five of Blackpool's economically active women were domestic servants (including charring and laundry work, which were especially important here), but the (often sweated) clothing trades were less important, though they still accounted for 8 per cent. Women's contributions to shaky domestic economies were sorely needed, and Blackpool had the highest proportion of widows in paid work among the large Lancashire towns, at just over two in every five. This was a complex economy containing large numbers of women whose labours were exploited or whose independence was dearly bought, though perhaps prized none the less for that.[113]

Most numerous and conspicuous were the famous Blackpool landladies. At least 3,457 women were running Blackpool company-houses by 1911, and their visible control of their businesses helped to further the unease about gender and authority which fuelled the endless jokes in music-hall, dialect literature and comic postcard about their size, strength, cunning and subversive wit.[114] Over 2,000 were widows or spinsters, and the husband was almost invariably a subordinate partner, even where his name was above the door. To a greater extent even than in other resorts, Blackpool's social structure would look utterly different if it were constructed on the basis of female rather than male occupations: it would be dominated by a broad middle layer of small businesswomen, whose husbands' jobs spanned the social spectrum from professional and managerial to unskilled labour. In the big houses on the North Promenade 71 per cent of landladies' husbands (excluding those who described themselves as company-house keepers) were 'gentlemen', professionals or businessmen in 1905; whereas around the stations and in the Central Pier area skilled and semi-skilled labour predominated, in businesses which were accessible to people who had saved from their wages over the years and whose children, if they had them, were old enough to help or off their hands. Single women who had lived frugally as weavers, just about the best-paid female employment of the time, could also afford to set up as company-house keepers, buying the goodwill of an established business and paying the inflated rents which having extra room for visitors entailed; and most houses were held in a woman's name, ranging from nearly two-thirds on the genteel North Shore promenade to 36 per cent around Central Pier and 39 per cent in the big purpose-built houses aimed at working-class visitors near Central Station. This was an urban economy with ample opportunities for women, precarious though they might be, and ironic though it was that most of them involved the practice or supervision of housework on the grand scale, and for very long hours during the season.[115] But this was a women's town, as Arthur Laycock's plain-spoken landlady, Mrs Banks of Homely House, commented:

Blackpool would be a poor place if it depended upon men ... It's we who run this town, but men, especially the Town Council lot, think they do it, but they don't. We run Blackpool all the year round, in summer with the visitors, in winter by our tea-parties, sewing meetings ... and such like. It is we who keep the place alive.

Mr Banks, on the other hand, was a subordinate handyman: 'He'll fix your furniture right and do any odd jobs without filling the place with dust and dirt. I've trained him well. He may as well be here doing something useful as sleeping in the Free Library on Lytham Road ...'.[116]

Population trends

The peculiarities of Blackpool's labour market, shared as they were with other resorts, help to explain aspects of its population structure. The substantial female majorities in most age-groups which were already apparent in 1851 widened further for people in their fifties and sixties by 1881, and a wider gap opened out between the sexes in the forties. Meanwhile the gap narrowed for people in their twenties. All this suggests that women of mature years were being drawn to Blackpool by economic opportunity and by the scope for settling down independently in a healthy setting with attractive amenities, and that this trend outweighed the more usual flow of younger domestic servants which prevailed in the more residential and up-market resorts. Meanwhile young men were migrating outwards in search of work, and children were under-represented as compared to the nation at large. The over-sixties were not yet over-represented compared with national figures; rather, at this stage Blackpool was an unusually middle-aged and female-dominated town. Thirty years later, the 1911 census showed a slight intensification of these distinguishing features, with women becoming noticeably over-represented in the over–60s group as the first hints of a concentration of the elderly became visible. However, this was much more pronounced in more up-market resorts in Sussex and Devon by this time.[117]

As befitted this increasingly lozenge-shaped population structure, Blackpool's birth-rate fell faster than the national trend. The crude average, unadjusted for age-structure, was only just behind the level for England and Wales during 1880–4 at 30.9 as against 33.8 per thousand; but by 1910–14 it had fallen to 15.8 against 24.1. A steady downward trend was only interrupted at the end of the 1890s, when a particularly high level of in-migration sucked in more younger people in childbearing ages than usual.[118] The gap between local and national death-rates (adjusted for age-structure) widened much more slowly: they ran neck and neck in the early 1880s at 18.6 and 18.9 per thousand, and despite a fall to 12.3 per thousand in 1905–9 (compared with 13.4), a rise in 1910–14 (to 12.9, against 13.5) brought the figures closer together. Blackpool did not share the outward and visible signs of healthiness that contemporaries associated with low death-rates in seaside resorts, and here it undoubtedly suffered from the nature of some of its housing stock and its stressful and over-crowded summer seasons.[119]

Infant mortality posed particularly intractable problems in Blackpool. It remained well above the overall England and Wales figure until the early twentieth century, staying at 168 per thousand live births until the turn of the century before falling to 111 (as against 121) for 1910–14. This was a decline of 25 per cent in a decade, coinciding with the appointment of a female health visitor and with a sustained programme of concreting back yards and reducing opportunities for house-flies to breed, along with increased attention to the quality of the milk supply. But even on the eve of the war Blackpool's record was worse than that of the cotton-weaving towns of Nelson and Colne, whose growth trajectory was similar, and for much of the late nineteenth century its infant mortality levels had matched those of more conventional industrial towns. Infant mortality peaked at the height of the season, as did deaths from diseases such as measles, and it is hard to resist the conclusion that this was in part a tribute of infant sacrifice to the demands of the Blackpool season.[120]

Children and migrants

Blackpool's summer economy also had a voracious appetite for child labour, which had a marked effect on schooling. Like the cotton towns, it became a stronghold of the 'half-time' system under which 12- or 13-year-olds could divide their time between work and school, evolving its own distinctive set of practices which recognised that children were likely to be kept out of school during the season. H. M. Richards, the district inspector of elementary schools, explained to a parliamentary committee in 1909 that 12-year-olds could be exempted from school from 1 June to 1 October to contribute to the family economy by street trading, selling programmes and postcards and helping in their parents' company-houses. This system was followed by between half and two-thirds of the children in Blackpool, and Richards was convinced that the 'moral' effects of this were as perni-cious as the educational ones. He concluded that,

> Blackpool depends on the catering for summer visitors, and the children are treated from that point of view. Not only do they get exemption from attendance, but the authority often declines to prosecute when attendances have not been made. The whole life of Blackpool apparently depends on making it simple and easy for visitors to enjoy themselves. Whether these children benefit is another matter.[121]

Children might have been in relatively short supply in Blackpool, but child labour continued to be an essential pillar of the local economy.

Richards also remarked on the difficulty of obtaining hard figures on the proportion of half-timers in the school population, because there was 'such a flux of the population' within a short time.[122] High levels of population mobility were indeed another feature of Blackpool's economy and society, which it shared with other resorts but exhibited to a particularly outstanding degree. By the late nineteenth century the combination of low birth-rates and rapid population growth highlighted migration as the basis for the town's expansion, but even in 1871 only a quarter of Blackpool's household heads were locally born, while nearly one-third came from Lancashire beyond Preston and one-fifth came from further afield. By 1911 just over a quarter of Blackpool's population (including young children who were much more likely to be locally born) came from the town itself, while nearly 40 per cent came from elsewhere in Lancashire, one in seven from Yorkshire, and just over one-fifth from more distant places. Blackpool's proportion of locally-born in the population was lower than in other seaside resorts of comparable size, apart from Bournemouth and Southend, which had grown even more rapidly from smaller beginnings.[123] But census snapshot figures tell only part of the story. This was a very volatile population. Not only did itinerant workers come in for the season for hotel and boarding-house service and the myriad of jobs generated by the catering and entertainment industries: men (especially) also moved out in the winter to take jobs inland, and there were also people who took company-houses for the summer, moving in at Easter to decorate and prepare them and returning inland in the autumn. Even those who settled more firmly in Blackpool often stayed only for a year or two. Only about half the company-house keepers listed in late Victorian and Edwardian trade directories kept going for as long as three years, and about 70 per cent had gone within nine years. Most failed and returned home: only a small minority hung on to make a career of the business, and very few indeed were able to retire on the proceeds. Blackpool offered the illusion of quick money and upward social mobility, but the few who made it were the exceptions who deceived the others. The poet Roy Fuller speculates that

> the whining, frozen-lipped tones of Blackpool which the Boss [his headmaster] tried to eradicate in his pupils were perhaps the dilute results of various Lancashire and Yorkshire accents brought by those who had come to the holiday town in retirement or to make their modest pile in catering or entertainment.

He also accused those who remained in the 'much reduced' out-of-season population of being 'culturally stagnant'.[124] Whatever one might think of that, there is no doubt that Blackpool was a seething and volatile mixture of comers and goers, from all over the north of England and beyond, bubbling uneasily on top of a comparatively small core of established locals.

It was a tolerant place, but a difficult one for outsiders to put down roots and build social networks.

Building a community?

Not that Blackpool was rich in ingredients which were difficult to assimilate. It lacked the conspicuous Irish population which was so prominent in the towns of its visitor catchment area, and its generally prosperous Jewish community was never a source of controversy. The Italians, who were conspicuous in its ice-cream manufacture and among the vendors on the beach by the turn of the century, were the subject of patronising comment from time to time, but the gypsies were the only group to be subjected to anything resembling a 'moral panic'. The three interrelated extended families, which had occupied the South Shore sandhills by the 1870s, were pursued remorselessly by the authorities when their encampment was invaded by the stalls and novelty rides from which the Pleasure Beach developed at the turn of the century. The Pleasure Beach's legal survival was made conditional on removing the gypsies, whose palmistry was penalised by severe fines of ten shillings (50p) and costs, although public health grounds were the ostensible reason for the campaign. This was an unusual display of intolerance in Blackpool, although it mirrored campaigns against gypsies and their way of life elsewhere in Britain, and here as elsewhere there may have been a drive towards cultural uniformity, forcing people into houses and (ironically) 'settled' lifestyles, alongside the other prejudices which were here made visible.[125]

Genuinely settled lifestyles were hard to sustain for those who tried to make a living from Blackpool's seasonal visitor economy. They were condemned to a treadmill of summer hard work and overcrowding (as visitors often pushed members of the family into sheds and other uncomfortable temporary accommodation), alternating all too often with winter poverty. Under the prevailing conditions it was difficult to build up the networks of mutual aid and support, formal and informal, which were strong characteristics of the established industrial towns from which Blackpool drew so much of its working-class and small business population. People were all too often isolated from their families and in competition with their neighbours, while trade unions found the occupational structure and economic fluctuations uncongenial, while employers tended to be abrasive and aggressive in labour relations. The local Trades Council was formed as late as 1891, with strong contributions from printing and building workers; but it never flourished and actually disappeared for a time during 1902–3. Only the Co-operative movement, another late starter, eventually flourished. Blackpool's society was founded in 1885 by railway workers who had to overcome their fears of employer disapproval, and after tentative beginnings its membership approached 2,000 by 1895 and passed 10,000 in 1915, by which time it was on a par with the strongest societies of the industrial towns of Blackpool's hinterland. Migrants to Blackpool brought with them an awareness of the practical benefits the Co-op provided, in terms of fair trading and opportunities to save, and this must help to explain the Co-operation's success in a seasonally fluctuating economy which made it difficult to refuse credit and imperative to extend charity to suffering members.[126] Many of the leading Co-operators were also part of a broader radical associative culture which included the Company-House Keepers' Association, which never organised more than a small minority of these (generally) little businesses but provided winter whist drives and dances as well as financial and legal advice and (generally ineffectual) political lobbying at municipal level.[127] There was also overlap with Primitive Methodism and Spiritualism, but although Blackpool developed a full array of denominational churches during this period, formal religion was not obtrusive in the wider politics and social life of the town. It certainly lacked the architectural riches which Southport or even St Annes acquired through church and chapel endowments from wealthy businessmen in these years: there was no Blackpool equivalent of Southport's magnificent Holy Trinity, and that in turn reflected the more secular tone of Blackpool's middle-class society.[128] Voluntary activities of other kinds might also be hard to sustain. For example, Blackpool's early footballing vitality of the 1880s flagged towards the new century when the town's middle-class supporters viewed professionalism with suspicion, and support was barely sufficient to sustain a presence in the Second Division of the Football League, despite proximity to the great Lancashire forcing-house of the game's development as a spectator sport.[129]Meanwhile the local press prided itself on the town's charitable exertions, with the Ladies' Sick Poor Association, founded in 1891, taking a particularly prominent share of publicity, and firmly directed towards the relief of the deserving, respectable poor in kind rather than in cash.[130] But the winter poverty, and the summer overwork and overcrowding of the back streets, remained intractable.

But these aspects of Blackpool were invisible to most of its visitors, and easily swept under the carpet by its residents. The municipal rhetoric of these years, faithfully amplified by the *Blackpool Gazette* and (usually and when it mattered) by its Liberal Nonconformist rival the *Times*, emphasised unparalleled growth and success on an entirely novel scale. On its own terms, this was undeniably so, and Blackpool became a symbol of all that was reassuring about late Victorian and Edwardian society, with its good-humoured crowds, low rates of recorded crime and peaceful coexistence between the classes. For an earnest, reforming minority it also became a symbol of all that was crass, vulgar and materialist about that society, helping to explain the easy contentment of the working class with an inferior lot, and defusing the sort of political tensions which should, on this reading, have been ever-present.[131] But the optimists dominated the media, and the crowds continued to flow. On the Butler/Goodall model, which has already been discussed, Blackpool had passed through the 'development' phase during the late nineteenth century, to arrive at a position of Edwardian 'consolidation', with external investment on the grand scale, and what was in anyone's language a full-fledged 'mass' holiday market, while population and visitor numbers continued to grow impressively. But would it be possible to sustain this phase, to continue to grow and sustain popularity against competition from new destinations and holiday styles, and to postpone the incipient decline which the model seems to predict? [132] The answer, over the next generation, was firmly in the affirmative; and the next chapter shows how this was achieved.

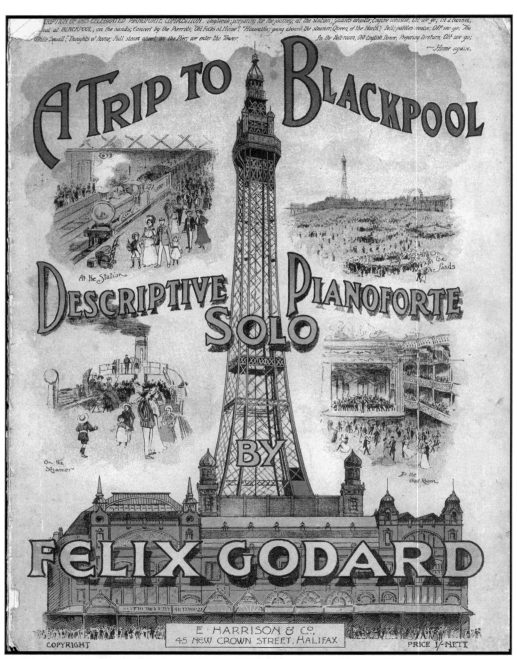

Blackpool's attractions at about the time of the First World War, as presented by a Halifax sheet music publisher

CHAPTER FIVE

War, conflict and renewal: Blackpool from 1914 to 1939

W AR IS ALMOST PROVERBIALLY the enemy of tourism, except in its aftermath, when it creates new heritage sites for post-war pilgrims and cheap transport opportunities using discarded equipment; but Blackpool contrived to prosper during the first global conflict, sustaining its established visiting public and boosting its economy by harbouring refugees, convalescents and troops in training.[1] It then had to cope with a difficult period of post-war adjustment, when record holiday seasons were accompanied by unprecedented social conflict, as strikes in staple industries affected access and services to a greater extent than hitherto, while labour disputes reared their head in Blackpool itself, and in completely unexpected quarters.[2] By the mid-1920s these issues were increasingly being restored in favour of the established order, and Blackpool's generic problems as a resort reverted to type. Corporation, entertainment companies and voluntary bodies alike addressed the problems of how to extend the season and attract new visitors and residents, preferably propelling the resort up-market in the process.[3] But the town also needed to cater for new tastes at a time of growing interest in sunshine, greenery, open spaces and outdoor leisure, an agenda which Blackpool had hitherto failed to pursue. A new-found interest in urban planning, which had been completely absent from local government priorities until now, was one index of these new concerns, as was municipal investment in promenade gardens on the new extensions to north and south, along with the provision of a large park and an outdoor swimming pool of monumental dimensions. Meanwhile, Blackpool's social problems had been exacerbated by the war and the further development of the popular season, and the provision of municipal housing was a particularly contentious issue. But unemployment was also a running sore, and although across Blackpool's expanding catchment area enough people remained in work and benefiting from falling prices to sustain demand throughout the inter-war years, it had serious problems of its own: and not only seasonal ones.[4]

On a more positive note, the continuing development of the residential and retirement sectors strengthened the local taxation base and brought significant changes in the social structure, so that by the 1930s Blackpool was no longer the 'town of landladies' it had been at the birth of the popular holiday season around the turn of the century, despite impressive new boarding-house development on the new southern extension to the promenade.[5] The town was able to sustain an impressive rate of residential population growth in incremental terms. Between 1911 and 1951 Blackpool moved up from sixth to third place among British resorts in population terms, growing by 143 per cent from just over 60,000 (including Bispham) to 147,184, and it also grew fastest in percentage terms among the thirty largest resorts of 1911. This was no mean feat from what was already a substantial population base, and the built-up area spread extensively across the flat expanses behind the sea-front, as well as extending along the shore to north and south. Visitor numbers also grew, reaching perhaps seven million per season during the 1930s, and Blackpool retained and perhaps extended its long lead as Britain's most popular seaside resort (or indeed resort of any kind).[6] Before we develop these themes further, we need to take a closer look at Blackpool's wartime fortunes, which so dramatically defied the fears of contemporaries and the expectations of historians.

The impact of war

The outbreak of the First World War at the beginning of August 1914 caught Blackpool at the height of a holiday season which had promised to replicate the immense success of that of 1913. Disruption was immediate, as visitors tried to return home but found rolling-stock commandeered for troop trains, while within the town there were widespread expectations of economic calamity. These proved unfounded: the full programme of entertainments continued, and by mid-August an atmosphere of 'business as usual' was returning, with cheap excursion trains being revived on a limited scale by the end of the month. As news of deaths in action began to filter through from the front, however, Blackpool's civic and commercial leaders faced a dilemma. The successful season extension campaign of the past few years had made September visitors an important addition to the holiday industry's revenues; but putting on a festive programme in wartime raised issues of taste, morality and popular perception. The September musical festival was abandoned by its voluntary promoters; but the question of the autumn Illuminations proved more contentious. At the beginning of the month the Corporation voted 37–6 to proceed, putting commercial considerations first, and three weeks later the Illuminations were switched on, after an Admiralty request for coastal towns to reduce their sea-front lighting had been evaded by assuming that it only applied to the 'front-line' south and east coasts. Patriotic motifs in the display included Allied flags and an illuminated British crown with a recruiting slogan attached; but reports of visitors expressing shock and anger soon led to a reconsideration of the propriety of continuing with the Illuminations. Some leading local politicians continued to justify the policy, on patriotic grounds of morale-

boosting as well as economic ones; but the overwhelming defeat of Councillor Lawson, the leading proponent of these views, in the November
municipal elections reflected widespread disquiet.[7] The question of the
place of seaside holidays and public leisure in wartime remained a matter
of debate, which affected (for example) professional sport,[8] and the morality
of Blackpool's continuing operation as a leisure town was never universally
accepted; but despite this retreat on a particularly emotive issue, the holiday
industry persisted and thrived throughout the war. The Illuminations were
a step too far, and wartime constraints on resources anyway ensured that
the issue would not recur; but seaside holidays remained firmly on the
wartime menu.

Initial indications were that the war had affected the Blackpool season
adversely. The beach traders, for example, asked for a reduction of their
rents, and when this was refused a campaign of non-payment resulted in
only 23 of 101 stallholders having paid in full by the following March.[9]
More mainstream sectors of the holiday economy, which had been less
exposed to the suspension of the cheap excursion trains, did better. The
accommodation industry benefited, first by the arrival of Belgian refugees
as the season ended, then by the billeting of British troops, 8,600 of whom
arrived in November 1914. At the peak of the 1914–15 winter there were
10,000, along with 2,000 refugees. This provided significant extra income
to counterbalance the loss of revenue from the disruption of the holiday
season, and pressure was taken off the local labour market by the enlistment
of 1,500 men during the first five months of the war, after the instant
departure of the town's German waiters and musicians. These were
palliatives, but they helped to keep many households afloat through the
difficult first winter of wartime, as Blackpool benefited from its distance
from the front line, its unique array of cheap accommodation and its
extensive stretches of beach which could be used for military training.[10]

These advantages came into play increasingly as the war ground onwards.
Blackpool benefited from its geographical position. The bombardment of
Scarborough in the first winter of the war made the east and south coasts
seem risky destinations, especially in the light of invasion fears, although
Brighton also had a prosperous war, benefiting in turn from the inaccessi-
bility of fashionable overseas destinations.[11] The wartime abolition of
steamer services enabled Blackpool to make inroads into the Manx holiday
market, as the island was cut off from its usual visitors from northern
England and Scotland and suffered severe economic distress as a result.[12]
The Clyde estuary resorts, which had also been served by paddle-steamers,
also suffered, and it was at this point that Blackpool really became popular
with Scottish visitors. Meanwhile, travel restrictions kept Blackpool's traditional visitors loyal while encouraging visits from people from northern
England who had hitherto patronised more distant and up-market places;
and these latter were customers who could be retained in later years.

Day-trips were abolished for the duration and beyond, but the Lancashire working classes continued to find their way to Blackpool, even when rail fares were sharply increased in 1917. War or no war, a strong seasonal leisure preference persisted, and visitors were prepared to put together complicated journeys by tram and on foot when trains were not available. A rise in working-class purchasing power as the war continued, brought about by tight labour markets, expanded earning opportunities for women and the need to sustain high levels of production through abundant over-time, all helped to fuel demand; and rationing diverted expenditure from goods which were in short supply to holiday services which continued to be available. Restrictions on the strength and availability of beer made an additional contribution to disposable holiday spending, while reducing public order problems. On top of all this, the continuing demand for billets for the armed forces ensured continuing prosperity for Blackpool's famous landladies, even though rates of pay declined as the war progressed, and by its end there was widespread resistance to having soldiers billeted at the height of the season. Free-spending American and colonial troops brought extra revenue to the entertainment companies, and in October 1915 a large convalescent hospital opened at the south end of the town.

This milling crowd at Central Station in August 1917 shows that, travel restrictions notwithstanding, the urge to get to Blackpool was as strong as ever.

On all available measures, as the local newspapers were not slow to point out, Blackpool's businesses had a prosperous war. The 1918 season was described as 'an enormous success', with entertainment companies paying dividends which surpassed the records of recent summers. The North Pier paid out 18 per cent gross, which remained remarkable even after tax had reduced it to 13 per cent.[13]

Not that prosperity was universal. At the end of 1918 the Chief Constable's Clothing Fund distributed clothing and footwear to nearly 2,000 needy children. The town's endemic seasonal poverty and economic insecurity had not been dispelled by the war, and the low level of allowances for soldiers' dependants and war widows did not help matters, despite the advent of rent controls and rationing in face of wartime inflation and shortages.[14] But the circumstances of wartime did enable groups within Blackpool's labour force, usually cowed and quiescent, to take militant action in unprecedented ways to improve pay and conditions. Arthur Laycock, who had been Blackpool's first socialist councillor for three years during 1906–9, could report little progress for the local labour movement when the Trades Union Congress had its first official Blackpool conference in 1917, chronicling the faltering steps of the local Trades Council since its foundation in 1891 and stressing the hostility of the Corporation to organised labour. But startling new developments occurred in the very next summer, with labour disputes among (for example) bakery workers and electricians, and a successful strike at the core of the holiday industry. Scene-shifters, stagehands and related workers behind the scenes at the Tower and Winter Gardens struck for union recognition and pay rises as the season began in July 1918, and the dispute was quickly resolved in the strikers' favour after arbitration by the mayor, who was a leading employer in the building trades and more accustomed to this kind of conflict than his fellow-aldermen on the boards of the entertainment companies, who were intransigently anti-union. This turning of seasonality to advantage, threatening the companies' takings at their most vulnerable moment, was an important symbolic victory for a disadvantaged and hard-to-organise group, and their spokesmen made great play of the need to pursue fairness in the sharing out of inflated wartime profits. These were novel developments, and most disturbing to those in authority locally.[15]

Peace, prosperity and conflict

The wartime combination of very successful holiday seasons and novel industrial conflict persisted in the immediate post-war years. The new self-confidence of Blackpool's trade unionists also found transient and limited but temporarily exciting additional expression in the election of a Labour (as opposed to independent socialist) councillor to the Corporation for the first time, adding to the worries of the local authorities at a time

when they should have been jubilant at the cheerful ringing of the cash-register. The immediate post-war boom, after all, lived up to all the most sanguine hopes, boosted as it was by a temporary burst of prosperity and full employment in the Lancashire cotton economy, which was still so important to the town.[16] Moreover, it was clear that Blackpool was becoming a truly national resort, no doubt assisted by its role in accommodating troops from all over the country in wartime. The accidentally recorded presence of three South Wales miners at Blackpool in mid-August 1919 was symptomatic of the resort's long-range attractive powers. Such long-distance travellers, who had local resorts of their own available, must have come by the ordinary trains, for train travel was still 'rationed'. Seats were limited and advance booking was required at peak periods in 1919, and this may have helped to spread demand more evenly through the summer, as in the war years. Blackpool was seen as being unusually busy in the normally slack periods between the great popular holidays of Easter and Whitsuntide, and then between Whitsuntide and the start of the unrolling sequence of factory town Wakes holidays in early July. The 1919 season also extended strongly into September, until it was terminated by a rail strike.[17] Despite this slightly premature end, the first post-war season was

This view of Central Station and its surroundings, taken from the Tower in August 1917, also shows the stalls and sideshows of the Golden Mile and the cramped, ill-planned early housing which huddled behind it.

said to be even better than the last wartime summer, and the Tower Company paid a record 10 per cent dividend before tax, with a bonus of 7.5 per cent. The year 1920 was almost as good: the season saw record payouts by holiday savings clubs in Blackpool's immediate hinterland, flooding Blackpool with silver threepenny pieces which were put away during the year and released in a tidal wave at holiday time, as the industrial boom continued; and although there were some reservations in the local press, the overall verdict was again close to euphoria.[18]

All this was achieved without the full excursion train service on which Blackpool had relied in pre-war years. This did not return until after the record-breaking seasons of 1919 and 1920 had given way to less spectacular times. It was possible to cater extensively for the Lancashire and Cheshire miners' demonstration outside the main season, and some excursion trains reappeared in August 1920, but a full pre-war range of services and tickets was not provided until 1921, and then not until the end of July after the effects of the 1921 miners' strike on coal supplies had worked through. At the peak holiday weekend at the beginning of August, however, more special trains ran into Blackpool than ever before: 319, compared with 303 in 1913.[19] The wartime and immediate post-war experience underlined that Blackpool did not depend on cheap trains and cheap trippers for its livelihood; and the post-war years also saw the beginnings of the rise of road transport as a serious alternative, both at the top end of the market through the increasing availability and reliability of the motor-car for longer journeys than hitherto, and at the day-trip end of the spectrum through the cheerful if uncomfortable primitive motor charabancs, which were often converted from army surplus vehicles. This was to have profound consequences. The rapid growth in road traffic of all kinds was a strong post-war theme in Blackpool, raising issues of speed, safety and traffic management. In 1921 the borough council in Preston, through which most of Blackpool's road traffic passed, was already seeking power and finance for a by-pass to relieve the summer congestion in the town centre.[20] Blackpool's own fleet of motor charabancs was diversifying the town's attractions by offering day-trips to the Lake District, which was now within easy reach for the first time, as well as into the Fylde countryside; and this array of additional attractions helped to make up for the terminal decline of the steamer excursions, which never really recovered from the war. As in so many respects, the consequences of war took away with one hand and gave with the other.[21]

The rise of motor transport made calculations of visitor numbers even more difficult, but although the boom conditions of 1919 and 1920 were not fully sustained, Blackpool remained buoyantly popular over what had become a greatly expanded geographical catchment area, which now firmly embraced Glasgow and district and extended to Plymouth as well as South Wales. There was some talk of visitor spending power declining in 1921, as industrial recession and a counter-offensive against the labour movement brought strikes and increasing unemployment; but the holiday imperative remained strong in popular expectations. As pre-war holiday rhythms reasserted themselves, season extension became a problem, especially as government constraints on the use of electricity delayed the revival of the autumn Illuminations until 1925; but the early summer Carnivals of 1923 and 1924, orchestrated by the Corporation, bridged the gap in spectacular style.[22] Meanwhile, building operations had recommenced on the grand scale by the early 1920s, and the local economy had clearly made a successful transition to the post-war regime. This was not achieved without conflict, however.

As in more conventional industrial settings, Blackpool's wartime conflicts over inflation, wages and working conditions persisted into the peace. They were exacerbated in Blackpool's case by problems of unemployment, especially among discharged ex-servicemen, and by a housing shortage which was compounded by the visible existence of large numbers of empty houses whose owners were keeping them vacant in the hope of a rise in prices. There were fierce agitations against rising rents and tram fares, and strikes continued to occur in sectors which were normally impossible to organise.[23] The local authorities were particularly keen to avoid strikes during the holiday season, but there was an obvious logic to presenting demands at this time in the holiday trades. Thus, for example, Blackpool had a bakery workers' strike in August 1919 and a successful catering workers' strike a year later, with pickets, mass meetings on the beach, processions and a 500-strong procession through the town, which generated considerable evidence of support from holidaymakers. There were also strikes in the entertainment industry, which brought unprecedented wage increases for seasonal workers, and despite attempts to agree conciliation procedures to avoid a repetition of the conflict of 1918, there was a musicians' strike in the summer of 1921. All this prompted Ernest Machin of the Trades Council to comment that, 'During the last two or three years, added to the other amusements of the town as a sort of spicey interlude, there had been a strike in Blackpool, and this August was no exception to previous Augusts.' Such militancy could not be sustained far into the new decade, but while it lasted it underlined the turbulent and (some thought) revolutionary quality of these transitional years. Blackpool was an unexpected location for developments of this kind, and this was even more alarming for local (and more distant) upholders of the existing social system.[24]

To make matters worse from this perspective, Blackpool began to show more active socialist stirrings, and organised labour began to make a little political headway. A Labour candidate contested the parliamentary constituency, which was newly defined as a borough, for the first time in the 1918 General Election. Admittedly, Allen Gee of the Textile Workers' Association of Yorkshire came bottom of the poll with less than 10 per cent of the votes cast. He justified his intervention on the grounds that Blackpool had a large number of migrants from industrial towns who were struggling to make a living and ought to be Labour voters.[25] The enduring problem was that they were locked into competition with each other, for work in what was predominantly a casual and seasonal labour market, and for customers in the small businesses which were vital to the survival strategies of so many family economies. They also found it difficult to pull together and sustain the neighbourhood support networks and mutual aid organisations which were so strong in the Lancashire and Yorkshire textile towns.[26]

For the first time, however, the immediate post-war years saw political solidarities being built in the Labour interest on a significant scale. In 1919 J. W. Mitchell, a skilled engineer who also kept a company-house, became Blackpool's first Labour councillor, for the same Foxhall ward which Arthur Laycock had won as a socialist in 1906. Mitchell was a highly respectable figure, a pillar of the Co-operative Society who was already a Justice of the Peace. He had been a councillor in Blackburn before moving to Blackpool, and he benefited from the concentration of gas, tramway and railway workers in a ward whose industries were concentrated just behind the sea-front. But his narrow victory caused disproportionate disquiet among the established parties, who combined fiercely against the Labour candidate when a by-election came up in the same ward in September 1920. Ernest Machin, a tailoring worker and president of the revived Trades Council, was a more outspoken candidate than Mitchell; and the Conservatives and Liberals combined to provide him with a single, 'Independent' opponent who had the backing of both party machines. He was branded as a 'Bolshevik', a 'revolutionary' and an 'extremist', pilloried in the local press, and defeated by a wide margin. This was sufficient to drive Labour back into its shell, and what is remarkable is how little it took to provoke this backlash. Most towns of Blackpool's size had become accustomed to Labour representation on their local authorities, and their rulers soon learned to live with the new opposition. Blackpool's ruling groups were not used to such assertiveness, and even a single Labour representative on the Council was enough to provoke near-apoplexy.[27]

Machin's defeat marked the transition to a new period of eclipse for Blackpool's labour movement, broken only by the strong local support for the General Strike in May 1926. The Trades Council's official history claims that 'not a wheel turned' in Blackpool, where the strike was '99 per cent' effective. This may be overoptimistic, but at the height of the strike only the most basic of municipal services (gas and electricity, but not tramways) were operating, and it may be that many of Blackpool's working people had brought trade union principles with them from inland and were ready to display them when the time was ripe. In Blackpool, however, it seldom was, and after the strike the Trades Council was kept hard at work trying to repel 'victimisation of workers, especially by the larger contractors'. Thus did normality return.[28]

The fears which were aroused by the appearance of industrial conflict and labour politics in Blackpool may have originated in a sense that if seaside resorts were not 'safe' from this contagion, then nowhere was. Blackpool's status as an industrial town was, after all, systematically denied by many of its inhabitants, who preferred to see it as a limited company or even a family business where all pulled together to advance its interests in competition with rivals.[29] Blackpool's special status was articulated with unusual directness and openness by an unidentified Lancashire business-man, quoted by the landscape architect T. H. Mawson (who did a lot of business in Blackpool, as we shall see) in his autobiography. He argued, in the mid-1920s, that working people coped with the workaday round in the smoky industrial towns for as long as they could, but

> once a year they must either burst out or go to Blackpool; and there they go, and after a fortnight they come back quietened down and ready for work again … Blackpool stands between us and revolution. May it long continue as the protector of social order.[30]

Such perceptions of Blackpool as prophylactic against Bolshevism, as a place where anything resembling class conflict was out of place and almost unthinkable, will have made even the gentle stirrings of the years between 1918 and 1921 seem deeply alarming.

It may be no coincidence that Blackpool's local authority made unex-pectedly rapid progress in providing municipal housing, the 'homes for heroes' which, according to Mark Swenarton, were designed to display good intentions towards returning warriors and defuse the threat of revol-ution.[31] The Liberal local newspaper, the *Blackpool Times*, was eager to highlight evidence of foot-dragging in 1919, and expected the worst from a local authority dominated by building interests and with an entrenched opposition to planning. However, by February 1922, 350 of the 616 houses in the three schemes under the Addison Act of 1919, which precipitated the general introduction of municipal housing, had been completed. The whole programme was finished in time to appear in its entirety in the 1923 Rate Book. This was housing on the urban fringe, but it found room for labourers and hawkers in significant numbers, as well as skilled and super-visory workers and the occasional clerk and manager, and the houses themselves were substantial. Meanwhile the Corporation had become converted to town planning, though very much for its own purposes. These were remarkably agile responses to changing circumstances and expectations, and Blackpool's council house record at this stage out-performed most of its Lancashire neighbours. But this was not to last (in 1939 Blackpool's council house numbers had only just reached 1,200, despite the lively start), and it did not solve the established problems of seasonal poverty, overcrowding, pressure of work and unemployment, as we shall see.[32]

Inter-war expansion —→

There was plenty of statistical evidence to fuel continuing optimism among Blackpool's leaders and civic boosters during the inter-war years, however, both in terms of population growth and visitor numbers. Population growth calculations suffer from the lateness in the year of the 1921 census, which was taken on 19 June when the season was getting under way and is therefore not comparable with the April censuses in previous and subsequent decades, and from the impossibility of taking a wartime census in 1941. Blackpool expanded its boundaries in 1918 to take in Bispham, which adjoined it on the northern cliffs, and had 2,244 inhabitants at the 1911 census. It was mainly an extension along the cliffs of the up-market developments at Blackpool's North Shore. With Bispham included, Blackpool's 1911 population was just over 60,000. The 1921 census counted 99,639 people within the same boundaries, and this figure is normally used in published sources; but a subsequent adjustment to take account of visitors and other seasonal arrivals who were not deemed to be regular residents brought this down to 73,800. This was hotly disputed by the Corporation, which claimed that the true figure should have been 85,000 and threatened briefly to organise a census of its own to restore the town's reputation for dynamic gigantism; but what the conflict underlines is the difficulty of defining a notional 'true' population for a highly seasonal resort with a rapid throughput of visitors and temporary residents.[33] When the census reverted to April in 1931, Blackpool's official population reached six figures for the first time, at 101,553, which was a matter for some local self-congratulation; and it is clear that the apparent growth patterns derived from using the original 1921 census figure seriously underestimate the extent of the town's expansion during the 1920s. The population curve between 1911 and 1931 ran much more smoothly upwards than the figures usually cited, which suggest rapid growth before 1921 and stagnation thereafter, seem to indicate.

After 1931 we revert to the Registrar-General's annual estimates for a guide to population trends, and on this measure the town's resident population had grown further to 128,200 by 1939, although this included parts of the Fylde Rural District which contained 4,542 people when transferred to Blackpool in 1934.[34] This level of growth was greater in numerical terms than the spectacular-looking decade of 1891–1901, when the population doubled by adding just over 23,000 people; so Blackpool was clearly maintaining its attractive powers in full measure. The inclusion of the mainly suburban population of the neighbouring Fylde in 1934 was some small compensation for the failure of a grandiose attempt to build a 'Greater Blackpool' six years earlier through the annexation of the substantial small towns of Thornton-Cleveleys and Poulton-le-Fylde, which were firmly in Blackpool's social and economic orbit. Blackpool Corporation's case was that it needed to extend its boundaries to provide improvements to access roads and to plan an overall drainage scheme, but the plan fell foul of increasing official scepticism about the virtues of expanded urban boundaries and was aborted by the House of Lords after an expensive hearing. The estimated additional population would have been nearly 13,000; but even as it was, Blackpool's place among the most dynamic large towns of inter-war Britain was assured.[35]

Blackpool's inter-war growth brought changes in its social structure. Extensions of the built-up area along the coast to north and south, following the promenade extensions of these years, brought new purpose-built boarding-houses and hotels into the holiday market, but the bulk of the building went on inland. This increasingly took the form of three-bedroomed semi-detached houses on private estates, as the Corporation's early activity in building council houses was not sustained. So commuters and retired people became increasingly important in Blackpool's population. A sustained building boom drew in comfortably-off migrants who were escaping from the increasingly shabby and depressed industrial towns of its hinterland. Alongside this trend, however, was a growing influx of unemployed people who came for seasonal work but stayed throughout the year, because their chances of regular employment were no worse than at home and Blackpool was a pleasanter place to live. This ensured that seasonal poverty would remain, and indeed continue to grow, alongside the growth of the prosperous residential sector.[36]

The holiday industry

The holiday industry was still of central importance. The 1931 census, which was taken in April and would exclude almost all seasonal workers, gave Blackpool a location quotient of 17.0 for lodging- and boarding-house work, which was far ahead of other resorts of comparable size: Bournemouth reached 12.0, Brighton 4.6 and Southend a mere 3.0.[37] This was in spite of a fall in the number of company-house keepers recorded in the census. This had reached 5,208 in the June census of 1921 (which would capture migrants who took seasonal lets) but fell back to 3,967 in 1931, which was less than the 1911 figure and accounted for fewer than one in six of the borough's 25,201 houses (it had been 17,455 in 1921 and 13,492 in 1911). If we look at catering and hotel work as a whole, however, Blackpool's insured workers nearly doubled between 1929 and 1939, from 4,751 to 8,741, and accounted for one in six of the workforce in the latter year, although this no doubt reflected a proliferation of restaurants and an increase in demand for domestic work in the larger boarding-houses which were opening in these years.[38] Large hotels were in relatively short supply: the Automobile Association Members' Handbook for 1939 listed two four-star establishments (the Imperial and the Metropole), six with three stars and one with two, compared with Bournemouth's galaxy of five five-star hotels and thirteen with four. Blackpool was outshone even by Southend, as well as by much smaller places such as Torquay, Llandudno and even Sidmouth. It was the thousands of company-houses, which did not need an AA listing, which counted, and which created Blackpool's dominant resort identity.[39]

Employment in entertainment and sport was also increasing markedly: in 1931 Blackpool's location quotient here was 4.9, twice as high as those of Brighton, Llandudno and Sandown and leaving Southend and Bournemouth trailing far in its wake. This was part of a continuing trend, as Blackpool's insured workforce in these fields grew from 1,808 in 1929 to 3,005 ten years later. This was a unique concentration of workers in the leisure industries.[40] Blackpool also had location quotients of two or more in hotel and restaurant service, hairdressing and related activities, and 'other services'; but, significantly, it had a lower representation of private domestic servants than the national average, with a location quotient of 0.8, which compares interestingly with Bournemouth's 2.0 and even Brighton's 1.4. Blackpool's middle-class retirement and residential sector might be growing impressively during the inter-war years, but these were not the sort of people who could afford, or chose to afford, large numbers of domestic servants, unlike their south coast counterparts.[41]

Residential and industrial Blackpool

Even so, the Corporation and the local press rightly made much of the rise of residential Blackpool. The 1931 census found 19 retired or unoccupied men in Blackpool for every hundred in work, compared to 12 nationally and 16 in Brighton (but 24 in Bournemouth).[42] Private house-building proceeded apace throughout the inter-war years, gathering momentum during the 1930s. In 1939 a pamphlet extolling Blackpool's residential virtues for young families as well as retired people claimed that over the past twelve years an average of 1,300 houses per year had been constructed. Despite this rapid growth, the intending resident was assured that not only did the town offer 'abundant health', together with excellent schools and hospital provision, but it was also 'a happy community of warm hearted souls' with a cheerful round of off-season sociability.[43] The Town Clerk admitted that although the new park had attracted 'a high-class residential suburb' to its environs, and the 1934 boundary extension had brought in thickly populated outer suburbs, 'Blackpool's high average rateable value is at the present being "watered down" by the number of the smaller type of residential properties erected in certain of the suburbs'.[44] This unpretentious development for people of limited means who could only just afford to live at the seaside was a distinctive Blackpool feature, and underlined the importance of keeping local taxation levels, and indeed public transport fares, low.

What Blackpool lacked, outside the staple building and brickmaking industries and the municipal utilities, was a manufacturing sector to provide well-paid year-round employment. There were large numbers of work-shops, especially in the food-processing and clothing trades, and in 1939 the Corporation emphasised its eagerness to encourage the development of light industries housed in 'suitable' (presumably smoke-free) premises.[45] But very little had come of this by the outbreak of war. The *Blackpool Times* in 1926 had stressed the leading roles of Sir Lindsay Parkinson's building firm and Catterall and Swarbrick's brewery, while commenting on the rise of the motor industry (which was to take the form, predomin-antly, of coach building); but it concluded that the catering trade would currently see itself as dominant, and 'the members of the Hotel and Apart-ments Association, however, make no secret of the fact that they consider theirs to be the premier industry of the town'.[46] Despite the changes of the inter-war years, this was still the case in 1939, and this means that the development of the visiting season remains central to understanding Blackpool's identity, in this chapter as in the previous one.

The popular holiday season

Blackpool reached a new plateau in terms of visitor numbers in the inter-war years, with a consensus that (day-trippers included) 7 million passed through the town each year by the mid-1930s. There might be half a million visitors at a time on Saturdays at the height of the season. This compared with estimates of 5.5 million visitors per year for Southend, 3 million for Hastings, 2½ million for Rhyl, 2 million each for Bournemouth and South-port and 1 million each for Morecambe and Llandudno. The basis for these figures is uncertain, but it is clear that Blackpool was well ahead of even the most popular of its rivals.[47] Foreign holidays were already growing in popularity among the comfortable middle classes, and Lancashire accents were already easy to find in Belgian seaside resorts by the 1930s, but Blackpool continued to build successfully on old loyalties and create new ones.[48] Despite the advent of severe trade depression in parts of its (by this time) traditional hinterland, especially in the weaving centres around Blackburn in the early 1930s, and the late introduction of paid holidays in the cotton industry, visitors still poured in from the cotton towns, some allegedly returning during the holiday to draw their dole. Beyond this, Blackpool's pull was wide enough for it to benefit from the relative pros-perity of parts of the Midlands, where paid holidays were already spreading before the Holidays with Pay Act of 1938 and Lancashire-style holiday clubs were developing in the engineering plants. Birmingham, for example, sent more excursion trains to Blackpool at August Bank Holiday in the mid-1930s than to all other destinations combined. Urban Scotland was also sending an increasing quota, and Melvyn Bragg's suggestion that adventurous people from Wigton, in north Cumberland, were beginning to forsake their local resort at Silloth for Blackpool's 'holiday crowds and glamour' fits in with wider patterns. London itself was becoming increasingly important as a source of visitors, as was South Wales. Blackpool was becoming a truly national resort.[49]

Blackpool's working-class visiting public continued to be skewed towards the crests of the poverty cycle: young people who did not yet have family responsibilities, and the middle-aged and elderly whose children were contributing to the family budget or had left home. Wage-earners who remained in work during the 1930s benefited from increased spending power as prices fell, and this helps to explain the widespread displacement of the apartments system by full board, a more expensive option, in the company-houses of the time. The availability of full board reinforced the widely held belief that the initiative in organising holidays came from wives rather than husbands, anxious to escape from narrow horizons and daily drudgery.[50] Single people or childless couples on the dole in nearby Lancashire towns might manage a weekend, or even a week, in the cheapest back-street lodgings.[51] Mass-Observation – the anthropological research organisation which discovered Blackpool through its study of Bolton – reckoned that, in 1938, Bolton's holidays would send 'probably 65 per cent of the townspeople ... away for the entire holiday and, counting day trips, perhaps 90 per cent ... at some point in the week'.[52] No basis for this figure is provided, and some would find it optimistic.[53] The people who found it hardest to get away were certainly working-class families with young children. For William Woodruff as a child in Blackburn, Blackpool remained a tantalising paradise, known about but out of reach. His father was a relatively well-paid tackler in the weaving sheds, but there were four young children and both work and expenditure were irregular, so that only once in the mid-1920s did the whole family go to Blackpool, taking their own food and evading paying fares for the children. The only other visit to Blackpool involved mother and youngest child at a time of financial stringency, and seems to have been financed by the mother's part-time work in a brothel, which was certainly an unusual expedient.[54] In an extreme way, this story illustrates the problems some families from one of Blackpool's traditional catchment areas could experience in getting to the 'promised land'.

A distinctive feature of the inter-war years in Blackpool was the growing visibility and importance of young, unattached wage-earners. Increasingly parties of young people, men more often than women, but sometimes including people in their mid- to late teens, would go on holiday together in single-sex groups. They were drawn especially by the dancing, the amusement arcades, the singing booths which became a feature of the promenade in this period, and the scope for promenading and making friendly contact with the opposite sex. Dancing, above all, was immensely popular, and evening excursion trains ran from all over northern England to the late dances at the Tower and Winter Gardens: the 'passion express', as the relevant train was known in Bolton.[55] But the young, for all their increased visibility and spending power, were not yet being identified as a distinctive social problem, although there were worries about the possible consequences of young girls taking too much to drink. Moral panics about teenagers as such were a thing of the future.[56]

The orderly multitude

What impressed contemporaries, indeed, was still the basic orderliness of Blackpool's holiday crowds. D. L. Murray's portrayal, in the novel *Leading Lady*, is unusually detailed but captures a widely-shared set of sentiments:

> Blackpool was already much fuller than when they had arrived a fortnight ago; yet neither the infection of the crowd-spirit, nor the increasingly fantastic headgear of the girls, the louder and louder sports jackets of the youths, nor the exhilaration of a sunny afternoon only slightly freshened by the breeze, could inspire this serene and orderly throng with riotousness. Where it coagulated round tram-stops or the entrances to shows and tea-shops, the personnel, trained, authoritative, and kindly, kept easy order ...

Police were 'almost invisible', and invariably 'as composed as a country constable in a village high street', and the relaxed attitude of the locals, eager to please and to avoid petty restrictions, kept the crowds from frustration.[57]

Outside commentators tended to celebrate the collective virtues of Blackpool's mind-boggling crowds. William Holt's portrayal of the Bank Holiday Monday at the beginning of August 1934, must stand for many others in similar vein:

> 10 a.m.: Three thousand dancing in the tower ballroom, 600 dancing in Winter Gardens, and 'pictures' packed ... Day trippers swarming very near sea. A black fringe all along the water's edge. Signs of clearing up. A murmur of excitement. You can feel the reaction go through the crowds like an electric current. Noon: ... In Albert-road, boarding-house steps crowded, guests sitting or standing out. Melodeon and banjos playing. Footpaths crowded. Greatest congregation of pedestrians between Central Station and Central Pier. Sluggish, gregarious, happiness packed like sardines ... Afternoon: ... Promenade and sands an intensely moving sea of humanity, but without any defined currents. It just appears to be vibrating, and the trams move through it like crowded ships ... Riot of colour and noise increases as the sun nearly breaks through. Infinite confusion. Jazz. Something trying to express itself. Something struggling

to be born out of all their powerful will for life and joy ... Something hatching in the sun. I can no longer watch individuals. I can only watch the crowd with wonder and amazement.[58]

In an earlier article Holt had noticed the tendency of factory workers to keep factory hours, heading for lunch at their boarding-houses at 12.30 and returning to the beach at 1.30 after a pipe and a gossip at the front of their lodgings. He also praised the cotton workers' capacity for song, as they joined in with the latest songs at the 'music bazaars' along the sea-front which promoted them.[59] His account mingles amazement at the crowd as a seemingly self-regulated organism with a sympathetic awareness of the individual lives, choices and preferences which made up the vibrating throng. This compound of awe and sentimentality found its way into local press accounts, but was also paralleled by such external commentators as Charles Graves of the *Daily Mail*, brother of the poet Robert, who also emphasised the overpowering nature of the Blackpool experience and the sheer vitality and methodical determination to pursue enjoyment which its holiday crowds displayed.[60] Mass-Observation was characteristically more astringent. It emphasised the central role of drink in Blackpool pleasures, and the way in which behaviour which would attract censure at home was accepted as part of a general atmosphere of holiday release. There was much staggering and vomiting and singing of bawdy songs around closing time, but the police paid very little attention to it. There was also more bickering in the street, especially between parents and children, than was usual in Bolton; but at the same time dress codes were sustained, and it was rare for formal footwear and even headgear to be discarded, while ties predominated over open-necked shirts. Blackpool was liberating in some respects, but people brought their codes of constraint with them, and the presence of children sharpened the conflicts between hedonism and responsibility.[61]

Mass-Observation also emphasised the ultimate innocence of most Blackpool holiday behaviour, despite an obsessive interest in postcards, shows and souvenirs which celebrated bawdiness and sexual ambiguity, and in the ubiquity of fortune-telling, from gypsy palmists to landladies' readings of tea-leaves. It purported to have shown, by research conducted at night on the beach and sand-dunes, that Blackpool's half-flaunted, half-repudiated reputation for illicit alfresco sex was almost entirely a myth: one of the four cases *in flagrante* to have been identified was participated in by a member of the team of observers, which tarnished its authenticity.[62] The boarding-house, with its self-protective rules and regulations, made indoor activity more difficult. Steve Humphries's oral history research suggested that constraints were more readily evaded than the Mass-Observers supposed, though some allowance should probably be made for retrospective boasting.[63] Much illicit seaside sexual contact probably took place in a workplace context of the harassment of isolated female employees, especially in boarding-houses, which was not a subject for postcard humour and reflected some of the grimmer realities of work in the holiday trades.[64]

Patterns of popular entertainment

Meanwhile, patterns of popular entertainment were changing, in some ways more than in others. The great Victorian pleasure palaces, theatres and music-halls continued to cater for audiences who liked a mixture of the familiar and the innovatively spectacular. In 1937 there were 4 theatres, 5 'pierrot halls', a circus, an ice rink, an Indian Theatre and 19 cinemas, with a combined capacity of 70,000 at two shows per evening.[65] The rapid spread of the wireless during the 1920s and 1930s made some of the shows and star performers into the common currency of the new domestic entertainment, but the prospect of seeing them 'in the flesh' became an added attraction as a result.[66] Mass-Observation characteristically analysed the jokes, which tended towards domestic and sexual embarrassment and the mocking of all kinds of constituted authority, but varied in the mix from show to show, with sexual allusions already featuring most strongly on the South Pier while the North kept its reputation for respectability. The cinema became the great medium of mass entertainment, here as elsewhere, competing successfully alongside the music-hall and other stage shows in which Blackpool's repertoire was unchallenged in the provinces. The manager of the Palladium, with its 1,500 seats, said that his audiences preferred 'mostly blood and thunder and sophisticated comedy', as 'the crowd here doesn't like anything that makes it think'. The great favourites were Lancashire's Gracie Fields and George Formby, whether live or on the screen, and the Mass-Observation team disagreed with J. B. Priestley's strictures about rising American influences, arguing that home-grown material still matched the preferences of Blackpool audiences.[67] What impressed Charles Graves above all, in 1930, was the mixture of cheapness, size, variety and value for money:

> the monetary entertainment unit at Blackpool is 1s. But what you can do with 1s. is incredible. At the Tower, the almost fabulous great red-brick building on the front, you can see for 1s. an aquarium full of Japanese salamanders and other odd fish; you can inspect the menagerie with its lions, monkeys and other animals; you can dance in a ball-room about twice the size of any London palais de danse; you can watch a child's ballet with 150 performers; you can go up to the roof gardens and see the midgets' entertainment.

And so on.[68]

Apart from the rise of the cinema, there were few substantial changes in the main show menu, although dancers wore less as the years passed and innuendo perhaps became more explicit. The North Pier lost its exotic Indian Pavilion to fire, a recurrent seaside hazard, and in 1939 it was replaced by a more utilitarian structure. In 1928 the Tower Company incorporated the Winter Gardens, which had been gathering momentum again after some difficult seasons, and the new management demolished the Gigantic Wheel, which revolved so slowly that only courting couples repeated an experience which was otherwise less exciting than it looked. The Olympia amusement arcade and exhibition hall replaced it on the site, and on the eve of the Second World War a new Opera House opened at the Winter Gardens.[69] But the most impressive innovations wrought by private enterprise in Blackpool's inter-war entertainment menu took place on the Pleasure Beach. Here, the highly profitable post-war seasons encouraged investments in new rides, the most exciting being the Big Dipper of 1923; and during the 1930s investment picked up again under the control of William Bean's son-in-law Leonard Thompson after the founder's untimely death in 1928. Thompson borrowed heavily and suc-ceeded in expanding and modernising the business at a time when many American amusement parks were going to the wall. His mission was to create a clean, modern image for activities which attracted criticism like a magnet, and his use of Joseph Emberton as the Pleasure Beach's chief architect furthered this goal by creating smooth modernist buildings with flowing lines, the antithesis of Victorian elaboration and the epitome of the new international architecture in an unexpected setting. The Casino of 1939, with its air-conditioning and 'magic-eye' doors, was the culmination of this remaking, and of the Pleasure Beach's bid for respectability and recognition for its provision of thrilling rides and novel experiences in a controlled and sanitised setting.[70]

In an entirely different spirit, Mass-Observation summed up a lot of the fairground amusements on offer at the Pleasure Beach and elsewhere, with their fascination for grottoes and exotic underground journeys, as 'short exciting trips down dark passages'.[71] This side of popular amusement, from which the Pleasure Beach tried so hard to distance itself, was increasingly, and controversially, in evidence on the so-called 'Golden Mile', the area facing the Promenade between Central Station and Central Pier which had been attracting stalls and exhibitions of the freakish and the titillating since the late nineteenth century. This area attracted maximum publicity and controversy in the mid-1930s, when the imaginative entrepreneurial mind of Luke Gannon brought new kinds of show while the Corporation began to display growing impatience with its inability to control this disreputable area at the core of the resort. In 1935 the most famous Gannon exhibit, the Rev. Harold Davidson, former Rector of Stiffkey, was prosecuted for attempted suicide after being exhibited allegedly starving himself to death. He had lost his Church of England living for alleged improper conduct with prostitutes he was supposed to be reforming, and spent several years seeking publicity for his cause in bizarre ways at coastal resorts. Davidson was ideal grist to Gannon's mill, alongside starving honeymoon couples and women posing as men; and the Corporation's attempt in 1935 to obtain parliamentary powers to suppress shows deemed 'undesirable' came to nothing. Mass-Observation was particularly fascinated by the popularity of these and similar shows, which challenged accepted categories of gender, romance and authority, and drew in a steady flow of prurient or merely curious onlookers. The Corporation was merely embarrassed and dismayed.[72]

The Corporation and the holiday industry

The Corporation was, indeed, the most active investor in new development in inter-war Blackpool's holiday industry; and its central aim was to extend the available leisure space in new ways, making room for a higher class of visitor and improving the resort's image by the fostering of planning and respectability. In so doing it fell foul of the Pleasure Beach, despite the latter's own version of a 'respectable' agenda, as well as Luke Gannon and his Golden Mile allies; and its vision for a reformed promenade involved sunken gardens and fountains rather than stalls and sensational exhibitions. This was a strong theme of the inter-war years.[73]

As Mass-Observation commented, the Corporation was Blackpool's biggest business organisation, with (by 1938) its own 'gas and electricity works, ... tramways, buses, public baths, and markets as well as airport, cemetery, slaughterhouses, housing schemes, and salt water works', as well as owning the beach and letting off trading concessions there. For most of the inter-war years it had the lowest level of rates (local property taxes) in Britain, although there was continuing debate as to whether this was achieved partly by high levels of assessment of rentals to inflate the values on which the rates were levied.[74] During the inter-war years the social composition of the Council changed, as the entertainment companies' representatives dwindled away to nothing (although the Tower Company, in particular, kept large numbers of shareholders among the councillors and the Bickerstaffe brothers, John and Tom, remained influential as aldermen until their deaths in 1930 and 1934). The direct representation of the building trades had also fallen away, with only five remaining out of a 56-strong council in 1938. A substantial hotel interest remained (nine members in 1938), and the drink trade remained influential, though nowhere near as powerful as in its heyday in the 1890s. Tellingly, the contingent of professional men had increased to eleven by the eve of the Second World War. The Corporation was enduringly short of women (only one female councillor, Mrs Mabel Quayle, was elected in the whole of the inter-war period), and, relatedly, of boarding-house keepers, despite the importance of the female-dominated accommodation industry to the local economy.

After the turmoil of the post-war years, too, only one Labour representative appeared during the rest of the period, and he was the Ernest Machin who had earlier been branded as a Bolshevik. He subsequently became an enduring and respected pillar of the municipality, partly because, as the *Gazette* pointed out in 1933, 'There is no danger of socialism in Blackpool'. Nor, by that time, was there much danger of Liberalism: in that same year, which saw the demise of the town's Liberal newspaper, the *Blackpool Times*, the November elections left a party composition of 32 Conservatives, 15 Liberals, 2 Independents and 2 'Apartment Keepers', this last group reflecting the persisting efforts of the organised accommodation interest to keep a foothold in the council chamber. Their influence had grown since the First World War, but this typical political profile reveals its limitations.[75]

Despite the declining influence of (by now) traditional holiday industry interests, the Corporation as a body recognised the overwhelming importance of tourism to Blackpool's economy and to their businesses, and invested heavily in improved amenities on the ratepayers' behalf. Blackpool spent more than eight times the English and Welsh average *per capita* for county boroughs on parks and open spaces between 1919 and 1939, far more than anywhere else, and the town was also among the three top spenders on highways, which included promenades and sea defences, alongside Hastings and Brighton. Conversely, Blackpool scored comparatively poorly for municipal housing, despite its active start in the early 1920s. This expressed a continuing pattern of 'municipal capitalism', investing eagerly in the resort to boost its competitiveness against rivals, but sidelining social welfare expenditure or leaving problems to be solved through economic growth achieved by other policies.[76]

The most conspicuous public works of the period were the promenade extensions to north and south which were undertaken in the early 1920s, the South Shore swimming baths which opened in 1923, and the great expanse of Stanley Park which was formally opened in 1926, providing green space, flowers and sporting facilities which lured some visitors away from the sea-front commercial areas but added to the attractions of the town as a whole, not least for residents. This investment expressed a deliberate policy of going up-market, and the employment of the fashionable Lancaster landscape architect T. H. Mawson showed a commitment to trees, curves and soft outlines which was in sharp contrast with the bold, stark, red-brick Victorianism which prevailed in the older parts of the town. Particular pride was taken in the South Shore baths, which were presented as following the style of imperial Rome but outdoing the Romans themselves in the grandeur of their conception and execution. The spate of investment in the 1920s, when the Corporation embraced town planning with hitherto unimaginable fervour, aroused fears of financial over-extension, and W. G. Bean of the Pleasure Beach was an opponent of initiatives which seemed to threaten his own empire, which was also menaced by

A picture postcard view of the South Shore baths, which had opened in 1923 and offered ample accommodation for spectators as well as bathers.

road proposals which threatened to carve it into quarters and pose problems of management and safety. Tower Company interests were still powerful at this stage, and there was a long history of enmity between the Bickerstaffes and Bean; but there was also a municipal ideal of healthy, uncommercial recreation which led councillors into putting on shows in the park which seemed to conflict with private enterprise and incurred the wrath of Bean. The new initiatives celebrated an ideal of healthy, outdoor holidays which embraced the rising cults of fitness and sunbathing, and this extension of Blackpool's holiday agenda was resumed when spending revived in the later 1930s with the opening of the Derby Baths and the open-air pool at North Shore.[77] On the eve of the Second World War a great central development scheme was planned, under the Blackpool Improvement Act of 1938, which would demolish 'the oldest and least salubrious area of the borough', including the existing Golden Mile, set back Central Station and provide a boulevard, an extensive open space and a bus station. A £760,000 sewerage scheme was also in progress, involving the laying of over 18 miles of sewers and the installation of three new pumping stations; but the central issue of marine pollution was still not being addressed, despite occasional adverse comments in the local press and elsewhere.[78]

   This was ironical in the light of Blackpool's own municipal publicity. The official guide for 1939 followed the Corporation's inter-war agenda faithfully by highlighting the beach as a safe and healthy place for adults to exercise and children to play (although in practice, as Mass-Observation remarked, actual bathing as opposed to strolling or sitting on the beach was in rapid decline, as the remaining bathing-van proprietors complained). Extended illustrated coverage, some in colour, was given to the new gardens,

The Cliffs and New Promenade, (N.S) Blackpool.

The ornamental cliffs of artificial rock which adorned the northern promenade extension of the early 1920s

promenades, cliff walks and parks, and to the South Shore open-air bath, in whose controlled surroundings bathing *was* very popular, with large numbers of spectators. The sea-water here was said to be 'scientifically filtered ... aerated by the latest process'. Sport had high priority, including the newly promoted First Division football team, and as much space was given to the rather tame glories of the Fylde countryside as to the three piers and the Pleasure Beach combined, or to the rest of Blackpool's entertainments. This rhetoric of health and open-air exercise represented a conscious effort to bring in a new, national visiting public in competition with the south coast resorts; and to some extent it clearly succeeded.[79]

The Corporation also devoted its energies to extending the season. When the Illuminations returned in 1925, still organised from the Electricity Department, they revived the pre-war trend of targeting the autumn months, after the failure of the Carnivals of 1923 and 1924 to build an early season which outlasted their special attractions. Tableaux were introduced in 1930, and nursery rhymes became a strong theme, with primitive animation techniques spreading during the 1930s.[80] Mass-Observation revelled in the statistics of the 1937 show (650 flagpoles ... 27 miles of festoons ... 300,000 bulbs ... 2,000,000 visitors over the six weeks in September and October) and had no doubt about the success of the venture. Nor had the local press, despite reservations about motorists who drove through the Lights and left no money in the town. The Illuminations had no parallel elsewhere in scale or pulling power, and gave Blackpool traders of all kinds a tremendous advantage over rival resorts.[81] Not content with this, the Corporation

CARNIVAL REVELLERS, BLACKPOOL.

tried to encourage early-season visitors through 'Guest Weeks' which of-fered special concessions in June, but entertainment companies and landladies proved reluctant to co-operate, and the spring and early summer remained relatively quiet. The conference trade and the Christmas season continued to develop, however, and the role of the local authority in extending the season was unique in both its scale and its success.[82]

Revellers in fancy dress dance on Central Beach at the Carnival of 1924, which attracted huge crowds but was the last event of its kind.

Landladies and visitors

The extended season was particularly important to the accommodation industry. The number of landladies recorded in official sources declined from an artificial peak in 1921, but the unofficial back-street seasonal accommodation which Mass-Observation designated 'Kippaxes' (for im-penetrable reasons) proved popular with motorists and seekers after informality, while at the top of the scale more and more businesses were claiming to be 'private hotels' and even acquiring licences to sell drink to their visitors. A total of 134 of these were listed in a local trade directory for 1934, and 313 four years later. The opening of impressive new 'private hotels' on the northern and southern promenade extensions helped to account for this growth, but there were also upgradings of existing premises in the town centre, although bathroom and lavatory accommodation re-mained in short supply.[83] Not only were increasingly comfortably-off visitors in regular work wanting full board, which increased both work-loads and profits and generated more seasonal work in domestic service; they

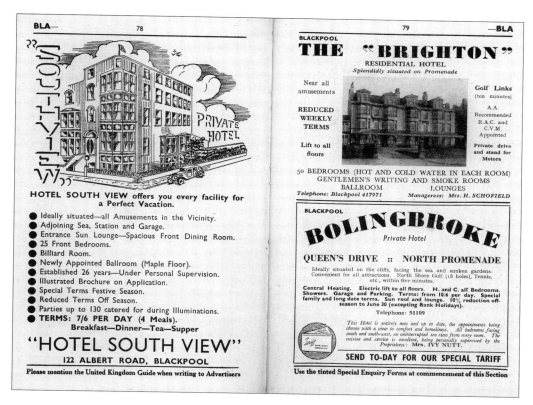

The aspiring end of the Blackpool accommodation market in 1939, as self-described in advertisements in the *United Kingdom Holiday Guide*, London, 1939, pp. 78–9.

were also aspiring to more comfortable furniture and even extra space. The landladies were also becoming better organised to defend their interests, a phenomenon which had begun in earnest during the wartime inflation. But there were limits to improvement. Mass-Observation described a down-market boarding-house interior: 'Bedrooms are eight feet by eight feet, the floor covered with oilcloth, ceiling with leafy wallpaper, the walls with pictures of Dolores Costello, crosses and scrolls ... Visitors come down to have breakfast in a room whose most compelling decoration is its card of rules ...'. But jokes and horseplay were possible in similar-looking settings, and landladies advertising in the 1939 holiday guide often promised 'no annoying restrictions', or a similar formula.[84] For those who sought the cheapest of holidays in an altogether freer atmosphere, there was the Squire's Gate holiday camp at the southern boundary of the borough, with its chalets, tents, treasure hunts and dancing. William Holt found a summer population of 8,000 there in 1934, and three young women from Pendlebury told him that, 'There is plenty of fun in the camp, and music – banjos and gramophones. We get up early and bathe in the sea. We cook our own food on an oil stove.' Here again, Blackpool was embracing the open-air, bronzed holiday ideal, and making it available to families with young children; but without apparently detracting from the popularity of the boarding-house for the older and more conventional visitors. In this respect as in others, there was something for almost everyone.[85]

Charabancs, cars and trams

Changing patterns of holiday accommodation partly responded to changing transport preferences, although in 1939 the overwhelming majority of visitors still came by train. The charabanc and later the motor-coach became particularly important for the Illuminations traffic, allowing for stops on the way and freer alcoholic indulgence; and one indication of the importance of the middle classes among Blackpool's visitors was the rapid inter-war rise in motor traffic. By the mid-1930s car parking in the town was becoming a major problem, and watching the queues of cars and coaches on the Preston to Blackpool road was a popular way of passing a Sunday afternoon. In 1939 the Town Clerk proudly announced that the Corporation had 'recently erected at a cost of £117,000 a large omnibus station and garage accommodation for one thousand cars' and 'maintains a central park to accommodate six hundred and fifty motor coaches'. But a traffic census on the main road from Preston on 20 August 1938, had counted 20,145 vehicles, and at times every street was tightly packed.[86] Much more needed to be done. Meanwhile, alongside the introduction of motor buses, the Corporation bucked the general trend in urban Britain and invested heavily in a new generation of trams. This owed something to the connections of Alderman Lumb, chairman of the Transport Committee, with the English Electric tram works at Preston; and in conjunction with a new tramways manager, Walter Luff, an extensive re-equipment programme began, with a complete new fleet in operation by 1935. This helped to sustain a tram network which was eventually, by virtue of survival, to become a tourist attraction in its own right. Meanwhile, Luff proudly described in 1939 how concessions for schoolchildren and the elderly, and ill-patronised high-frequency winter services, could be subsidised by the summer crowds, thereby adding to Blackpool's attractions as a place of residence.[87]

Poverty and insecurity

The growing importance of the residential sector of Blackpool's population was a strong inter-war theme, as we have seen, as it attracted retired people, commuters, commercial travellers and its own professional people. Not all such residents were affluent. Harold Palmer describes how his down-at-heel, down-on-its-luck family migrated by bus from the Potteries to Blackpool in 1930, buoyed up by his father's description of the 'Eldorado of the North', but struggling to survive through unlicensed toffee-selling on the beach, and humiliating recourse to the Chief Constable's clothing fund, as they lived on tinned pilchards and fruit in a new Taylor Woodrow 'wonder house' which they could not afford to furnish. It was only when Mr Palmer senior landed a commercial traveller's job, the children's earning power increased and the family was able to move close enough to the town centre to take in summer visitors, that fortunes improved. This was probably a more representative saga than a dispassionate look at Blackpool's 'official' social structure might suggest.[88] As Palmer also points out, the temptations and expensive distractions of the holiday season made bringing up children especially difficult, and the swirling insecurity of Blackpool life was compounded by the comings and goings of theatrical people, who had their own world of distinctive lodgings and irritable competitiveness, and by less glamorous seasonal workers of all kinds. Blackpool was much less secure and predictable than the most depressed of industrial towns, and it was seldom an easy place in which to live.[89]

The survival strategies of the Palmer family were reproduced, in different mixes, in many Blackpool households. Seasonal unemployment was endemic. During the inter-war years officially recorded unemployment in Blackpool at the end of January ran at between two and three thousand between 1923 and 1928, but the depression of 1929 soon bit deep, and by 1932 the figure was 8,253, about one in twelve of the total population. It then slipped back to just over 7,000 by 1934, but began to rise again, against the national and regional trend, to approach 10,000 in 1936 and top it at the beginning of 1939. For most of the 1930s even the late July figures hovered between three and four thousand.[90] This is a reminder that Blackpool was an industrial town – a 'pleasure factory', as Charles Graves called it – and the healthy dividends of the entertainment companies half-hid widespread misery.[91] Begging was repressed, and the streets were carefully policed from this point of view (although itinerant mouth-organ players and accordionists were able to keep moving and make a living); but Allen Hutt was right to comment in 1933 that, 'Unemployment and misery weigh no less heavily on the workers in the much-boosted holiday resort of Lancashire than on the workers in the factory town.'[92]

These problems were compounded by anomalies which restricted the availability of benefits to seasonal workers, and by the flood of seasonal migrants who came looking for work in Blackpool in the season. Welfare agencies worried about the moral fate of young women who came to work as domestic servants or waitresses, but problems of exploitation and sweated labour of a basic economic kind were endemic. Occasional demonstrations, and shocked reports on the numbers of people sleeping in the promenade shelters in the winter of 1933, made little impact on the problems, and it should be emphasised that the apparent prosperity of Blackpool's holiday industry rested ultimately on a grim foundation of insecurity and highly mobile, sweated labour.[93] Local charities struggled to help the 'respectable', but made scant inroads into a highly mobile problem. The rapid turnover of Blackpool's population, indeed, made it difficult for working-class organisations such as trade unions to sustain themselves, and only the Co-operative movement flourished, buoyed up by the support of visitors who had the 'Co-op habit' as shoppers in their home towns, with an impressive central store and a members' recreational culture. By 1935 Co-op membership added up to 75 per cent of Blackpool's households.[94] A lot of these would be middle-class, of course, and at this level it might be easier to sustain the amateur dramatic and other societies which flourished during the off season. But a concluding emphasis on the social problems behind Blackpool's summer crowds and prosperous façade would not be out of place.

On the eve of the Second World War, Blackpool was still growing and prospering impressively in terms of dividends, investment, population and housing. It was approaching the peak of the resort cycle, but stagnation was not yet looming. There was plenty of evidence of innovation, not least in the proliferation of smooth, modernist cinemas, pubs, entertainment centres and public buildings. Not far behind the façade, however, could be found the crumbling slums of the earliest uncontrolled development, while there was no shortage of poverty in back streets of more respectable appearance, compounded by the failure to carry through the early initiatives in municipal housing. Nor did the sea, the original source of Blackpool's fame and fortune, stand up to close or critical inspection. But Blackpool's future lay in its artificial attractions, as developed over the last half century; and this became even more the dominant note after the Second World War had brought a stimulating interruption to the rhythms of the crowded seasons. The impact of the Second World War will lead us into a critical analysis of the development of contemporary Blackpool.

CHAPTER SIX

War, prosperity and crisis: the remaking of Blackpool, 1939–1997

B LACKPOOL DID AT LEAST as well out of the Second World War as out of the first one, and its role as a military training centre introduced its delights to a further array of newcomers, some of whom returned as honeymooners in the post-war marriage boom. It also shared to the full in the last uncomplicated golden age of the English seaside resort in the post-war generation. At this time the seaside attracted huge crowds (alongside the great spectator sports) at a time when holidays with pay at last became general, while in the immediate post-war years rationing restricted access to most consumer goods and set a premium on entertainment, which was taxed but not rationed, and on service industries generally.[1] Competition from overseas resorts was reduced by exchange controls and transport problems. Even when the rise of the overseas package tour industry, first by coach, then by aeroplane, tended to cream off middle-class holidaymakers, they were replaced at the English seaside by working-class newcomers who could afford a seaside holiday for the first time. Some resorts were running into trouble by the 1960s, especially smaller and less distinctive ones which had shared in the general post-war lack of investment in ageing accommodation and amenities; and the rise of Devon and Cornwall brought a shift in domestic demand for seaside holidays away from the less-favoured northern coasts. But it was not until the 1970s that package tour competition offering guaranteed sunshine and improved amenities began to bite deeply into working-class markets, and British seaside resorts really began to feel the pinch across the board.[2] This was an increasingly fraught and competitive environment, with the rise of new car-based alternatives to the traditional seaside holiday. The motor-car offered additional flexibility and mobility and required accommodation providers to adjust to shorter stays. Holiday camps also provided competition for established resort economies, although many of them were attached or adjacent to existing resort towns. Blackpool itself had one on its doorstep at Squire's Gate. Under these conditions Blackpool was forced to adopt new strategies at municipal level and to encourage improvement and innovation among its mass of small caterers, trying to sustain its traditional attributes while taking steps to meet new expectations. This was a difficult juggling act, and successive reinventions and relaunchings of the resort and its flagship entertainments proved necessary to prevent Blackpool from sliding into the stagnation and decline which mark the usual final phase of the resort life-cycle. Such models allow for escape through renewal and reorientation, and Blackpool has tried to achieve this with a good deal of success. Meanwhile it has also clung on to the remnants of its traditional clientele, which has seen a steady erosion of its economic base and spending power through a mixture of economic decline, involving the loss of traditional jobs, and advancing age.[3]

The post-war years have also seen dramatic changes in Blackpool's own economy, masked by a static census population. The proportion of the elderly in the population has increased, commuting has continued to grow in importance, and jobs lost over the last thirty years in manufacturing industries have not been fully replaced by the growth of civil service and related posts. The holiday industry has continued to decline in relative importance to the local economy, despite the tenacious survival of the 'Blackpool landlady', and Blackpool has undergone a transformation of its entertainment industries. Many of the older enterprises have lost their distinctive local identity and fallen into the hands of national or multinational organisations, while finding it increasingly difficult to recruit high-profile entertainers in the television age. Blackpool also shares to some extent in the general seaside resort problem of sustaining a distinctive entertainment profile, as leisure centres proliferate in the towns from which visitors are drawn and domestic entertainment offers its own kind of access to the 'stars'. The rise of a gay and transvestite bar, cabaret and night-club scene in the 1990s has given Blackpool a novel kind of distinctiveness, which might be thought an unlikely bedfellow for its traditional clientele, but seems rather to have benefited from Blackpool's tradition of tolerating and indeed enjoying a diversity of holiday and leisure styles, in a relaxed and voyeuristic environment where some of the usual constraints on behaviour were suspended.[4]

This is just as well, for even the pulling power of the sea and the beach has been undermined in recent years by the growing visibility and popular awareness of sewage and other kinds of marine pollution, for which Blackpool has a particularly and conspicuously dismal record.[5] More recently the resort has also seen a wholesale transformation of its political identity, as more than a century of Conservative domination has given place to Labour control and an almost total eclipse of the old governing party.[6] On May Day 1997 Blackpool's anomalous, indeed extraordinary, condition of having two Conservative MPs and only a solitary remaining Tory town councillor was terminated by the election of the first two Labour MPs ever to represent the town.[7] These startling electoral events have been rooted in changes in the local economy and in the role of municipal government in the holiday industry; and further changes are foreshadowed by Blackpool's successful drive for unitary authority status, which will make it independent of the County Council and concentrate local power within the town itself. The half century or so since the Second World War has thus been fruitful in major changes and big issues; but before we tackle them we must begin by examining the more immediate impact of the war itself.

The Second World War

As in the First World War, Blackpool gained more than it lost by wartime conditions between 1939 and 1945, especially as many of its competitors on the east and south coasts were incapacitated for the duration by military occupation and the threats of invasion and aerial bombardment. The loss of part of the season after war was declared at the beginning of September brought initial dislocation, and there were more summonses than usual for unpaid rates early in 1940 as the absence of Illuminations income made itself felt. But many landladies – and others – were able to recoup their fortunes through accommodating Royal Air Force personnel in training. Over three-quarters of a million RAF recruits passed through the town during the war, with up to 45,000 in residence at a time at peak periods, spread through five thousand houses. This was familiar from the previous war, although the RAF itself was a novelty; but there were also child evacuees, whose billeting allowances were much lower and whose numbers soon declined sharply from the initial peak of over 30,000 in September 1939. Another innovation was the evacuation of large numbers of civil servants from London, amounting to more than 1,700 by January 1940, which was to have a lasting effect on the town's post-war economy.[8] All these extra inhabitants, spread throughout the year, gave a considerable boost to Blackpool's wartime economy, which is hinted at in the Registrar-General's estimate that the town's population increased from 128,200 in 1939 to 143,650 in 1945, despite the departure of local men for the war effort.[9] There were further concentrations of airmen at nearby bases, and the Americans at Warton not only spent their money generously in Blackpool, but also included Black personnel who brought ethnic and cultural diversity to the town. The Blackpool entertainment industry, with what amounted to a year-round season, enjoyed a prosperity which had not been seen since the latter days of the previous war.[10]

The war also brought a sequence of successful holiday seasons. Blackpool was geographically favoured by its distance from potential invasion coasts and enemy air bases, although this did not exempt it from bombing entirely, and given its concentration of potentially attractive targets it was lucky to escape so lightly. The reasons which made it a relatively safe place to house evacuees, civil servants and airmen in training were also attractions for holiday visitors. At the end of June 1940 the east and south coasts from the Wash to Bexhill were closed to holidaymakers, and by mid-August the

prohibited area ran from Berwick to Dorset, with only Brighton remaining
in business. Once the crisis of the spring and early summer of 1940 had
passed, holidaymaking again came to be recognised as legitimate and good
for morale. The Whitsuntide holidays were abandoned in 1940, but the
Wakes holidays of the textile towns resumed in July, and rolling-stock was
even made available to run 29 special trains over the August Bank Holiday
weekend. It was a short season but a busy one, and the Tower declared a
15 per cent dividend. The worst was over for Blackpool, and it had proved
endurable.[11] Subsequent seasons were decidedly prosperous, and a property
boom developed as boarding-houses came to be regarded as gold mines.
Some trebled in value during the war years, as prices rose to '£1000 a
bedroom'.[12] The advent of rationing gave additional impetus to the change
from the apartments system to full board which was already under way
between the wars, as landladies took charge of the ration cards of visitors
who could afford to pay for extra services and thereby contribute to extra
profits; but the extent of billeting in the main accommodation areas pushed
visitors out into residential districts, where householders developed 'con-
nexions' of their own which lasted beyond the war itself. These were further
indications of wartime prosperity, which were borne out by the shortage
of domestic servants for boarding-house work, and the high wages which
women could command here and in other sectors of Blackpool's wartime
economy.[13]

The most impressive change in Blackpool's wartime employment structure was the state-run aircraft factory at Squire's Gate, near the holiday
camp, which opened in 1940 to produce Wellington bombers and employed
more than 10,000 workers at its peak. The other great growth area was
'public administration and defence', which had 796 insured workers in the
Fylde registration sub-area in 1929, 3,356 in 1939 and 15,526 in 1944. Forty
per cent of the workers in this sector were women, and opportunities for
women in the civil service had knock-on effects elsewhere in the local
economy. Women rose from 37 per cent of the Fylde's insured workforce
in 1939 to 44 per cent in 1944. No doubt many women workers were not
insured. But employment in 'miscellaneous services', including boarding-
house servants, and the distributive trades fell sharply, as it did in the male
preserves of building, brickmaking and printing. Some of these changes
were to be solely for the war's duration, but others had lasting importance.[14]

Post-war prosperity

Despite the striking changes in its wartime economy and employment
patterns, Blackpool was able to make a rapid readjustment to the post-war
world. It was ready for the explosion of post-war holidaymaking in ways
which its competitors on the south and east coasts could not match,
although its neighbours in north-west England and North Wales had

similarly had a relatively easy time.[15] Elizabeth Brunner, writing in 1945 about the Sussex resorts, remarked on the problems associated with reopening small boarding-houses which had been forced out of business by wartime restrictions and hotels which had been damaged by military requisitioning, as well as the need to repair air-raid damage. She also reproduced a harrowing account of the state of Margate, from a *Times* report of 1943, which stressed accumulating damage, shabbiness and neglect in a town where only a handful of the more than 6,000 houses which had catered for visitors were still offering accommodation. Businesses needed financial and practical help before they could re-open, and the local Town Clerk thought this would be a widespread priority in seaside resorts. All this added to Blackpool's competitive advantage as it moved smoothly into the post-war world and sought to consolidate its national market.[16]

Blackpool dived into the first post-war holiday season with enthusiasm, and kept up the momentum thereafter. A record was claimed on the last July Saturday of 1945, when the London, Midland and Scottish Railway carried 102,889 passengers to Blackpool's stations in 24 hours.[17] Road traffic also increased enormously when motor-coach travel was derestricted, and for several weeks 1,200 coaches per week came in, with an average of 25 passengers each, most of whom were day-trippers.[18] A guidebook published in 1944 for American servicemen claimed that Blackpool now attracted between 8 and 10 million visitors a year, but that 'nobody can count them to a million'; and these developments can only have increased the numbers still further, although in 1969 8 million was still the Corporation's favoured figure.[19] In 1949 the return of the Illuminations marked a stage in the retreat from post-war austerity, reawakening from 'the years of darkness and depression'; and 'amazing', 'terrific', 'phenomenal' advance bookings were trumpeted in banner headlines. The Director of Publicity reported that enquiries were 50 per cent up on the best pre-war year and that 2 million autumn visitors were expected, with more coming by road than rail. The record road traffic was monitored by a police aeroplane, and hundreds of people were left to sleep on the beach and promenade after the last trains and coaches left at 2.30 a.m. on a September Sunday morning. Up to half a million people arrived for the busiest weekends, and in late October the local newspaper computed that the Illuminations had brought in 3 million excursionists and staying visitors, who had spent a neatly symmetrical £3 million in the town. Blackpool, to the envy of its rivals, was well and truly back in business, and beginning to reap the full benefit from the general entitlement to paid holidays. It was at this point, perhaps, that Blackpool really began to cater for a full cross-section of the working class.[20]

The return of the Illuminations set the seal on Blackpool's post-war success, extending the season for six weeks in the autumn and ushering in a prosperous decade for the entertainment companies and the accommodation industry. New records were proclaimed, just as they had been during the 1930s. The 1955 season saw deck-chair revenues 20 per cent higher than in the previous best year of 1950, and excursion trains for the Illuminations were booked from as far away as Dundee and Penzance, setting the seal on Blackpool's claim to dominate the United Kingdom

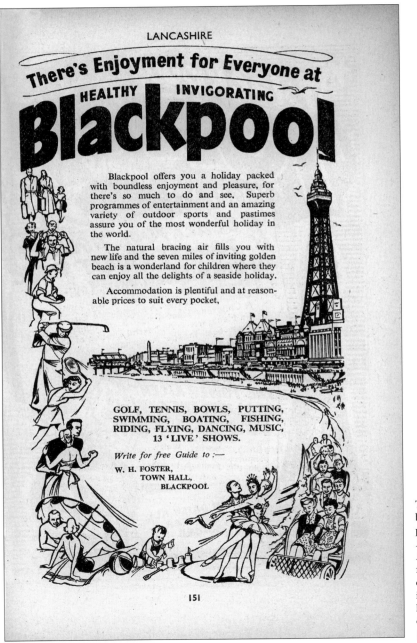

The mixture as before: Blackpool's publicity in the *British Railways Holiday Guide* for 1952 continued to emphasize the inter-war themes of health, sport and outdoor activity. (London, 1952, p. 151)

holiday market.[21] Good seasons continued into the 1960s, with British Railways and the Ribble/Standerwick coach group bringing over 4 million visitors between them in 1964, as the change in emphasis from the summer to the Illuminations season continued. This reduced the impact of emergent competition from continental holidays, as many people took their second holiday in Blackpool in the autumn, although such holidays were often shorter and some of the optimistic press comment may have been misleading, with visitors being redistributed through the season rather than growing in overall numbers. The conference trade continued to boost off-season takings, with regular appearances by the big political party conferences which attracted national publicity, while a full-scale Christmas season saw 'all the large and middle-sized hotels' full to capacity and special entertainment programmes being offered.[22]

Alfred Gregory's wonderful collection of spontaneous shots of holiday-makers enjoying themselves on and around the beach in the 1960s, in which local teens and twenties no doubt mingle with the holidaymakers, provides vivid visual documentation of these buoyant years. It illustrates the emergence of a distinctively dressed new youth culture, and of public manners which had the power to shock an earlier generation. Mini-skirts, girls ostentatiously smoking and passionate kissing on the beach among the crowds in broad daylight were novel extensions of the licence Blackpool granted to young wage-earners, but there is something innocent about the horseplay and endearing about curlers as beachwear which are on display here. Blackpool has long been a place for working-class teenagers to get drunk for the first time, in large groups self-policed by gossip; but as Graham Turner remarked in 1967, teenagers were less in evidence, and generated less perceived trouble (even during the Mods and Rockers era of the mid-1960s) than in most resorts. As the 1972 visitor survey suggested, the elderly, the middle-aged and the very young now predominated. But an enduring notion that somewhat older men expected to let themselves go in Blackpool is epitomised by a story from the 1960s, recounted by the cricket correspondent Matthew Engel. A county cricket team was playing at Northampton, and the next match was at Blackpool. Defeat was delayed by a heroic rearguard innings by a young player, which was received with something less than rapture. A senior professional said to him, 'You little effer. If it hadn't been for you and your effing batting, I'd have been effing pissed on the effing Golden Mile by now.' Something similar also applied to women. Blackpool's emblematic status as somewhere to get pissed was already of long standing, and has remained an important part of its appeal.[23]

Gregory's camera also caught an older generation, even in the central zone which was, and is, more the haunt of younger visitors. He captured families on the beach, still fully clothed in their deck-chairs, with ties, braces and jumpers much in evidence, and just a few decorous swimsuits. Crowds on the beach covered the full age-range, from babe in arms to

grandmother, and the elderly were as evident in the picture as the rest, sometimes wearing funny hats with no hint of self-consciousness. In one memorable vignette an elderly man paddles, trousers rolled up almost to the knees, wearing waistcoat, gold watchchain, jacket, tie, stiff collar and flat cap: he is a little too respectable to sport the classic knotted handkerchief, emblem of the 'grockle' or tripper. Even the staidest of demeanours can unbend a little. But these crowded beaches and inclusive family parties of

Teenagers romping on the beach in the early 1960s, as captured by Alfred Gregory. (*Blackpool: A Celebration of the '60s* (London, 1993), p. 72)

The respectable paddler, shoes under arm, enjoying the sea in the early 1960s (*Blackpool: A Celebration of the '60s* (London, 1993), p. 173)

the 1960s are close to the end of an era. Over the succeeding generation the ages have become more segregated and the beach less frequented. Gregory's seething shoreline crowds have become a thing of the past.[24]

Two more particularly telling Gregory photographs show a semi-circle of (mainly) sexagenarian women utterly absorbed in communal singing in a pub, and a similar party of cheerful ladies marching assertively arm in arm, six abreast, along a crowded central promenade, just as they might have done thirty years earlier when Mass-Observation commented wonderingly on this Blackpool phenomenon.[25] An enduring theme, as the drag artiste Lily Savage perceptively remarked thirty years later, is that Blackpool 'caters particularly well for the elderly. The old ladies of the southern cities cower behind net curtains waiting for another day-centre to close. In Blackpool, they waltz away the afternoon or have a sing-song in a cosy hotel bar.'[26] But Blackpool also finds room for the solitary observer, the social misfit who likes to listen to the conversations of others and finds amusement there, while trying out a variety of entertainments in a semi-

detached way. In this gregarious setting there is quiet satisfaction to be had at the fringes of the crowd, of a kind which has drawn people back over the whole long span of the post-war years, finding something new to interest them each time.[27]

Visitor trends in the 1970s and 1980s

This apparent prosperity masked a failure to recruit enough of the new generation of the 1960s, and a change in the social profile of the visitors, which if left unchecked might have generated a subsequent collapse of the holiday industry on the pattern which soon became widespread elsewhere.[28] At the beginning of the 1970s the local authority became aware of potential problems in the holiday market, and responded to them decisively.

In 1972, for the first time, Blackpool Corporation and the English Tourist Board commissioned a survey of the town's visitors, which was carried out by the British Market Research Bureau. It concluded, on the basis of heroic extrapolation from a national sample of 9,343 adults, that Blackpool attracted 3.24 million staying visitors and 12.8 million day-trippers during the season, although many of these were repeat visits drawn from a pool of nearly 6 million Blackpool customers. It also offered a social profile of the visitors, concluding that 4 per cent were from social groups AB (professional and managerial), 13 per cent from C1 (white-collar workers and foremen), just over half from C2 (skilled manual workers), and as many as one-third from groups D and E (unskilled manual workers and state pensioners). The survey's suggestion that Blackpool's visitors were overwhelmingly proletarian, and relatively elderly, rang alarm bells in the Town Hall, especially in the light of visibly increasing competition from overseas package holidays as well as caravans and holiday camps nearer home. The findings probably reflected a steady shift down-market over the previous twenty years or so; but the interesting thing is that over the following fifteen years the decline proved reversible. A second survey in 1987 found that the lucrative ABC1 groups, who were most likely to take second holidays, had increased from one in six to one in three of what was, astonishingly, an expanded staying visitor public (from 3.24 to 3.46 million). A further survey two years later claimed 4.2 million, with nearly 17 million visits if day-trippers were included; but many people came twice or even more often, and the familiar figure of 8 million reappeared for visitors, as opposed to visits. The average length of stay was three or four nights. This healthy situation had to do partly with new attractions and effective publicity, but above all it was prompted by the continuing advance of the Illuminations. A survey in 1987–8 showed room occupancy levels of 75 per cent in Blackpool hotels during September, and 71 per cent in October, compared with 62 per cent in July and 64 per cent in August. Guest-houses had more empty rooms but showed a similar pattern. The Illuminations,

Pub community singing embraced both sexes and all ages. (*Blackpool: A Celebration of the '60s* (London, 1993), p. 151)

Six assertive ladies march past Louis Tussaud's, on the Golden Mile. (*Blackpool: A Celebration of the '60s* (London, 1993), p. 39)

in particular, seem to have attracted growing numbers of more up-market visitors taking second holidays. The age-profile of visitors was still potentially disturbing, as nearly half were over 45 years old, and less than 20 per cent between 25 and 34. But to show growth in the holiday trade between 1972 and 1987 was a remarkable feat, as rival resorts went into terminal decline; and Blackpool's success was won at the expense of Southport, Morecambe and especially New Brighton, whose holiday industries suffered severely in these years. As the second survey pointed out, 'the British took more holidays in Blackpool in 1987 than they did in Greece, Italy, Yugoslavia and Turkey combined'. This was a remarkable performance. Meanwhile Blackpool was beginning to attract overseas visitors, especially from Ireland, but also growing numbers of Germans and even Russians and Saudi Arabians in the 1990s; and the ethnic mix of holidaymakers was enhanced by a growing Lancashire Asian presence from the old cotton towns.[29]

Gay Blackpool

One contributory factor in Blackpool's move up-market may have been a growing number of gay visitors, who were not only significantly younger than the visiting public at large (on the basis of a small sample which found that 73 per cent of respondents were under 35), but also much more likely to be middle-class (61 per cent of the sample were professional/ managerial compared with 9 per cent in the 1987 visitor survey). They were also drawn from a very wide catchment area within Britain, with one-third coming from Wales and the south and south-west of England, compared with 15 per cent of the general sample. They also spent significantly more than the average visitor. In short, they were very desirable customers, and in 1991 Blackpool's Director of Tourism Services assured the compiler of the survey that he welcomed their presence. Blackpool's popularity as a gay meeting-place is of long standing, and it may be that a well-established gay visitor presence has only recently become visible. Certainly, the development of the gay night-club scene which attracts them, concentrated into the district around North Station, has spawned the most numerous gay-oriented accommodation industry in any British resort, especially in the area around the Flamingo night-club. In 1991 there were perhaps 150 guest-houses catering mainly for gays, many of which advertised in the gay press; and expansion has continued since then.[30] In 1994 two grandmothers were using a pools win to set up themed gay boarding-houses in Milbourne Street, in an unpretentious late Victorian district near North Station, with aspirations to taking over the whole street.[31] Basil Newby, the entrepreneurial mastermind behind much of this activity, has drawn together a rainbow coalition of gay cultures and preferences, and at Funny Girls, his 'camp cabaret venue' featuring transvestite dancers, he seems to have succeeded in mixing straight and gay customers in an atmosphere of mutual tolerance and shared outrageous fun.[32] This inclusiveness seems to be a general theme of the Blackpool night-clubs. This is the kind of atmosphere that attracted *Times* columnist Matthew Parris, who assumed that nothing here was to be taken seriously and decided that Blackpool 'depends ... on an unspoken pact between the town and its visitors ... "We're only here for the laughs" '.[33] All this is founded on a long history of gender-bending, as chronicled with relish by Mass-Observation in the late 1930s, and a tolerance of sexual 'otherness' in Blackpool's traditional catchment area which was well captured by Bill Naughton's description of his neighbour the gay coal miner in the Bolton of the early 1920s, who was accepted as a workmate with unusual preferences and left to get on with his life.[34] Not that Blackpool is a trouble-free environment, and the lack of overt conflict where gay and straight customers mix may be helped by widespread heterosexual unawareness of a gay presence; but the Director of Tourism Services in 1991 was more worried about heterosexual 'lager louts' as generators of violence and disorder among themselves, in territory they had made their own, while the gays got on with having fun in their own way.[35]

A dauntingly assertive heterosexual culture which privileged aggressive masculinity was the side of Blackpool's visiting public that most struck the bilious London journalist Charles Jennings in 1993, when he was deterred from ordering himself 'a solitary pansy's glass of champagne' in Yates's Wine Lodge by the nature of his neighbours: 'The building was filled to the eaves with powerfully built young men in stonewashed denims and

Yates's Wine Lodge, the upper floor of which housed the original Public Library of 1880.

Millets trainers, squiring tough-looking blonde birds who clearly put their blusher on with the vigour of someone rubbing down a horse.'[36] This was stereotyping on the grand scale, although perhaps pointing usefully to the differences between leisure spaces in a Blackpool where holiday lifestyles and nights out were zoned by age and entertainment preference as well as being demarcated by time of the day and spending power. The complexities here, as Blackpool tried to cater for the maximum range of preferences in the 1980s and 1990s (with impressive but less-than-complete success) would be worth a book in themselves.

The end of population growth

From the 1960s, and perhaps from the end of the Second World War (despite bullish rhetoric from the local press at the season's height), Blackpool's visitor numbers ceased to grow in the old sustained and spectacular way, as well as becoming concentrated later in the year and less unevenly distributed through it. This indication of the arrival of saturation point (at least in terms of demand) was matched by the end of growth in the census population. In 1951 it reached 147,184, which reflected further increments of well over 20,000 per decade since the 1931 census; but ten years later it reached its peak at 153,185, and by 1971 a gentle decline had begun, as the population fell to 151,860 (though the number of houses increased markedly, from 49,960 to 55,385). In 1981 the total fell below 150,000 again, and the 1991 census counted 145,175 people, which was below the 1951 figure. The tide was ebbing. This was, increasingly, an elderly population, with nearly one in four Blackpool inhabitants having reached pensionable age by 1991, compared with one in six in 1951 and one in five in 1961. Throughout the post-war period well over half the population was over 40 years old; so the locals were as middle-aged and elderly in profile as the visitors. Blackpool also remained a women's town, with women outnumbering men by 13,000 in 1951 and nearly 16,000 in 1981, although the gap had narrowed sharply ten years later. The discrepancy was most strongly marked among the over–50s and especially the over–60s: the boarding-house keeping and retirement age-groups. Although the town continued to import more migrants than it exported, an important index of residual attractiveness, deaths were outnumbering births with increasing insistence. We shall see that by the early 1990s there was widespread evidence of an ailing economy, and of widespread poverty, within this distinctive population profile; but these problems had deeper roots.[37]

Making a living

After the war Blackpool's economy reverted to its long-established domination by the service industries. The aircraft factory at Squire's Gate switched to civilian use after the war, making prefabricated houses until closure in 1948. It then returned to its original use between 1951 and 1957, making military jet aircraft and reaching a post-war employment peak of 7,000. Final closure brought a sharp reduction in relatively well-paid manufacturing employment, which nothing else was able to replace. At the end of the war 5,980 people were employed in mechanical engineering and the manufacture of transport equipment; in 1950, when the plant was closed, the figure had fallen to 2,412; it rose again to 6,459 by 1955 when Hawker Hunters were being made, but fell again to 1,882 in 1960. Such was the impact of the ebb and flow of Blackpool's only large-scale manufacturing plant. Coach-building (which employed over 1,000) and confectionery provided the only substantial year-round factory employment. When the Squire's Gate factory was working in 1955, manufacturing and food-processing accounted for just over a quarter of Blackpool's employees. Five years later the proportion had fallen to less than 15 per cent.[38]

The Corporation's preference, formally expressed in late 1944, was to discourage what it called 'heavy' industry as incompatible with resort amenities. It also offered year-round employment which might undermine the cheap labour on which the holiday trades depended, of course, and this may have been in the minds of those who discouraged the engineering firm Platt Brothers, who expressed an interest in Blackpool in the following year.[39] Construction accounted for about one in twelve of the workforce during the 1950s, and transport fluctuated around 10 per cent, but there was little else outside services, which employed just over 50 per cent of the workforce in 1950 and nearly two-thirds in 1960. The Lancashire and Merseyside Industrial Development Association published a calculation in 1965 showing that 71 per cent of Blackpool's workforce had service jobs and only 19 per cent were in manufacturing, mainly in small local firms specialising in light engineering, sweets, biscuits and clothing. By the 1950s, when post-war readjustment had been completed, retailing accounted for between a quarter and a third of service sector employment, while public administration fell from one in four to one in nine during the decade, banking and finance hovered around 6 per cent, and miscellaneous services rose to 20 per cent. Retailing was increasingly important: already in 1951 Blackpool could be described as 'the dominant shopping and commercial centre of the prosperous Fylde', and it was to consolidate this status in the following decades. This apart, the biggest player was the hotel and catering sector, which employed more than a quarter of the service workers. This leaves out of account the large numbers of seasonal migrant workers, and above all it ignores the self-employed and employers in this sector. Blackpool was no longer a town of landladies, but they were still very important to the local economy.[40]

The decline of the Blackpool landlady has been a long and slow process. Numbers remain difficult to establish, with so many casual and occasional

operators on the fringe of the business. The war had encouraged the rise
of the so-called 'pirate' landlady on the frontiers of the main accommodation district, as so many houses in the purpose-built streets were full of
billeted service personnel; and many of these people remained in business
subsequently, with word-of-mouth advertising and minimal overheads.
This made official figures more than usually misleading. The census suggested post-war collapse, with 4,094 landladies recorded in 1951 and only
2,055 in 1971; but in the latter year the Fire Brigade, enforcing new
regulations, estimated a total of 5,000 which equalled the record census
figure of 1921, and in 1987 the Corporation itself counted 2,410 'serviced
accommodation establishments' and 1,100 self-catering premises, although
these accounted for less than one-fifth of the half-million people which
Blackpool was said by one authority to be able to accommodate at a time.
The statistics are a minefield; but the resilience of the industry is apparent.
Where many boarding-houses were part of complex family economies with
several sources of income, it was understandable that businesses should be
visible in some sources but not in others. Moreover, the nature of the
business changed over time. The immediate post-war years saw a rapid
shift to full board as the norm in Blackpool, as the old apartments system
went into terminal decline. Meanwhile the inter-war trend to upgrade to
private hotel status continued, and this entailed providing bars, television
lounges, late keys and a more flexible regime. As awareness of standards
on package holidays spread there was pressure to upgrade generally spartan
furnishings and amenities, but this ate into the number of letting rooms
and forced prices up. It was particularly difficult to increase the historically
tiny number of bathrooms, and when the Corporation introduced a voluntary minimum standards scheme in 1967 it required only one bathroom
per 25 guests and one water-closet per 15. The morning queues which had
fascinated Mass-Observation were still a reality. En-suite accommodation
was slowly making headway in the 1980s, but not in the back streets.
Meanwhile the imposition of stringent fire regulations for guest-houses in
1971 encouraged a developing trend to self-catering accommodation, as
proprietors took evasive action against a further boost to overheads. The
Hotel and Guest-House Association, in its various incarnations, continued
to struggle against what it saw as a rising tide of taxation and bureaucracy,
and it was powerful enough to defuse the threat of a new Pontins holiday
village on Corporation land, which was proposed in 1973. The growing
importance of short breaks and touring holidays disrupted the cosy regime
of regular weekly stays to which landladies had become accustomed. Their
numbers were sustained by newcomers investing redundancy payments or
pensions from early retirement, but this was an increasingly complex and
demanding business, and long-term survivors were still relatively few. The
regular incomes generated by switching into retirement and convalescent
homes, and even catering for DSS claimants, became increasingly attractive

to some. Nevertheless, the industry seemed set to remain an important part of the town centre economy into the new millenium.[41]

From rail to road

The accommodation industry's problems were worsened by Blackpool visitors' growing preference for road over rail transport, and the increasing popularity of the private car. This not only made for shorter stays and more day-trippers: it also generated access and parking problems for guesthouses whose proximity to the railway stations and the town centre began to be a mixed blessing when forecourt and street parking became insufficient. The decline of rail transport began in earnest in the 1950s and accelerated in the following decade, when the Beeching cuts in services hit excursion traffic especially hard, as it became impossible to justify keeping rolling-stock in store through the year to satisfy peak demand. Central Station closed in the autumn of 1964, liberating the site for long-awaited redevelopment, and the direct cut-off line for excursions from Kirkham to South Shore was also abandoned. Meanwhile traffic on Blackpool's roads increased by 70 per cent between 1960 and 1973, and planners considered central relief roads which would have gouged out part of the Victorian heart of the town. In the end large-scale road-building was limited to conversion of the rail route to the old Central Station to provide rapid access to the central entertainments district from the newly built M55, a solution which also offered ample parking spaces on the old excursion and engine shed sidings. The opening of this motorway in 1975 gave a noticeable boost to the holiday season, and followed the demolition of the original North Station for retail development, and its replacement by a smaller building on the site of the excursion sidings. The famous tramway system along the sea-front survived, sometimes controversially, to become an additional tourist attraction by virtue of its uniqueness, although the inland routes through the streets were closed in 1961. In general, however, Blackpool came to terms with the full-blown motor age of the later twentieth century more smoothly than might have been expected, despite recurrent traffic jams on the M55 approaches at peak periods. What the town never developed, however, was the huge international airport which was envisaged at the end of the war, and Blackpool's passenger links from the airport which developed at Squire's Gate were largely confined to the Isle of Man and Ireland, as earlier aspirations were unfulfilled. This had its own limiting effect on the visitor catchment area, and Blackpool, like other British seaside resorts, was unable to tap a significant share of the foreign tourist market, which the tourist boards directed towards scenic and cultural attractions inland.[42]

The entertainment industry

Blackpool's entertainments also changed in significant ways. The Pleasure Beach remained locally-owned and family-run, and after a post-war hiatus consistently led the way in innovations and growing popularity as the Corporation and the older pleasure palaces flagged. It was not until 1957 that the first new rides were installed, and in 1960 a chairlift system linked the two halves of the divided site. After this regular innovations were made, as the management strove to outflank potential competition. The monorail and Log Flume opened in 1967, the Space Tower in 1974, and the Avalanche in 1988, as the Pleasure Beach became one of Britain's most popular attractions, with 6½ million visitors per year at the end of the 1980s.[43] This built on Blackpool's distinctiveness, which was undermined in other respects. The Tower, which had paid an astonishing dividend of 35 per cent in 1948, rebuilt its famous ballroom in all its original turn-of-the-century splendour after a fire in 1956, reflecting an attachment to an existing entertainment culture which would not have been sustained a few years later, but eventually created a vehicle for late twentieth-century nostalgia to match the trams. In 1961, however, over-capacity in the established live entertainment diet was reflected in the closure of the Palace next door and its replacement by Lewis's department store, reflecting the new primacy of shopping as entertainment. The key central entertainment complexes, the Tower and Winter Gardens, along with Matcham's Grand Theatre, moved out of local control when EMI took them over in 1967, and a fierce local campaign had to be mounted to save the Grand from closure and demolition.[44] Meanwhile the three piers were taken over by Forte's entertainment subsidiary Entam between 1963 and 1967. In 1982 First Leisure took over the dominant role in Blackpool's entertainments, controlling the three piers as well as the Tower and Winter Gardens, and local entertainment programmes and initiatives came even more firmly under the scrutiny of London accountants.[45]

The growing importance of television from the 1950s both pushed a national rather than a regional entertainment culture and, eventually, made it impossible to afford the great star names who had still made regular appearances in the immediate post-war years. Frank Sinatra played Blackpool twice in the early 1950s, and Gladys Cooper appeared in 1953. The town's numerous outlets at the Tower, Winter Gardens, piers and various theatres made it 'the finest centre for live entertainment outside London', and Blackpool benefited from national publicity when films were premiered and there was radio and then television coverage of live shows.[46] But there remained a distinctive tradition of down-to-earth and often vulgar Lancashire humour, exemplified in the lewd and belching carnivalesque of Frank Randle, which gave the South Pier pavilion over to the celebration of bodily orifices and functions and released Lancashire audiences from the

puritanism of everyday life.[47] Comedians like Randle rarely 'travelled' successfully, however, and the regional flavour of Blackpool's low comedy
became less pronounced with the passage of time. By the early 1970s local
journalists were beginning to worry that the town could no longer command
the stratospheric fees necessary to attract star entertainers; and although
Mike Yarwood and Danny La Rue, who then fell into this category, were
engaged in 1972, the days of Sinatra were past. Blackpool increasingly
depended on second-rank acts, or those which had seen better days, while
at the same time improved home entertainment technologies increased
audience expectations. A version of the Frank Randle tradition survived
through such acts as Roy 'Chubby' Brown, and even within the 'family
entertainment' provided by the Grumbleweeds' South Pier show, which in
1997 interspersed nostalgic references to the television and radio of the
1960s and 1970s with jokes about sexual performance and bodily functions
which conjured up descriptions of Randle's act; but the tone of Emily
Barr's 1997 *Guardian* piece on Kid Creole at Blackpool speaks volumes:
'We are not ... backstage at a major gig, or one of Europe's leading concert
venues. We are at the Blackpool Opera House, where Kid Creole ... is
starring in the summer show ... More unlikely still, he is pleased to be
here ...' Barr quotes the man himself: 'He admits that "they didn't say
Blackpool" when they offered him the role. "I'll survive ... You follow
your heart in life, and you can end up in the strangest places." ' This was
a far cry from the Blackpool of the 1950s and its widely shared self-
perception as the centre of an entertainment universe. Meanwhile, another
live entertainment attraction which had generated tremendous national
publicity for Blackpool in the 1950s, the town's football team, went into
decline after the famous epic Cup Final of 1953. The end of the Stanley
Matthews era was followed by relegation, short-lived revivals and long-term
residence in the obscurity of the Football League's lower divisions; while
the Rugby League side, whose aspirations had seldom passed beyond survival, eventually disappeared into oblivion by way of Chorley. In sport as
in entertainment, the 1950s had given Blackpool a primacy it was never to
reclaim.[48]

Blackpool's live entertainment theatres have survived in remarkable
strength, however, which is more than can be said for its cinemas. The
revitalised Grand, in particular, seems to be flourishing. Unlike most resorts,
the vexed question of whether the Corporation should intervene to subsidise
or take over ailing entertainment venues has hardly been an issue.[49] There
was debate, especially in the mid-1970s, over whether the Corporation
should boost the already thriving conference trade by investing in a big
new conference centre, as occurred in some rival resorts; but the hoteliers'
lobby on this issue was repelled, and the existing facilities offered by private
enterprise at the Tower and Winter Gardens were deemed sufficient. But
on the broader entertainment front, even the three piers, representing an

essential feature of the traditional seaside which has become increasingly vulnerable and expensive to maintain elsewhere, continue with their shows, slot machines and even innovations like the Central Pier's Ferris Wheel. Where the Corporation did intervene directly in the holiday industry was in publicity, planning and the provision of new amenities; and most conspicuously of all, through the Illuminations. The great free show continued to grow in scope and technical complexity, and an infrastructure of new sub-stations was constructed to support it, while the Corporation's Illuminations Department continued to develop new methods and sell off surplus stock in its role as unique repository of expertise. There was recurrent controversy among councillors, hoteliers and the ratepayers at large over how the cost should be spread, and an Illuminations appeal fund supplemented the Corporation's contribution, while from 1975 visitors were invited to make donations. The declining relative importance of the holiday industry in an increasingly residential town with a widespread poverty problem made municipal spending harder to justify, and in 1991 a critic complained that the Illuminations benefited only 3 per cent of the electorate. But the show, and the publicity generated by the annual switch-on ceremony, still goes on.[50]

The changing role of local government

The Corporation's role in developing attractions and infrastructure was much less prominent than in the inter-war years, especially the hyperactive 1920s. It took charge of the Airport in 1961 and launched an abortive scheme for a nearby hoverport five years later. It did address the twin problems of how to attract families with children, and what to do with the old airport site in Stanley Park, by opening a successful Zoo there in 1972; and subsequently it replaced the South Shore open-air pool with the all-weather Sandcastle complex, in a deal with private enterprise which generated embarrassing losses and fierce criticism. It also shed the Derby Baths at North Shore, another jewel in the inter-war investment crown. These were controversial decisions. Meanwhile the £180,000 sea defence works scheme at South Shore in 1973 was the most expensive improvement of its kind in Blackpool since the Second World War, and paled into insignificance beside the inter-war promenade and sea wall extensions.[51] The most conspicuous redevelopment scheme was the long-delayed Central Station and Golden Mile rebuilding, which had been on the drawing board in 1938 but was aborted by the war and proved very difficult to revive when the Corporation addressed the problems in 1956.[52] It was not until 1964, as the closure of Central Station became imminent, that a serious scheme could be put forward to replace the railway complex, the ramshackle and disreputable Golden Mile frontage to the south, and the decaying slums behind it with a new, sanitised layout; and it was not until 1976–7, after many vicissitudes, that redevelopment reached the sea-front, after the completion of law courts, a police headquarters and a multi-storey car park at the back of the site, in the fashionably uncompromising brutalist style of the early 1970s. The loss of the old Golden Mile unleashed a flood of nostalgia for its scruffy informality and the variety offered by its medley of small businesses. There was much criticism of planners and corporate developers (despite the protestations of EMI and Coral, the main investors) for undue formality and uniformity, as space-age presentations shouldered the old freak shows aside; and it did seem to some that fun had been sacrificed to tidiness. The face of an emblematic part of central Blackpool had been transformed; but the visitors continued to flood in, and many seemed to enjoy the new attractions.[53] Meanwhile, the nearby Hounds Hill redevelopment gave more attention to Blackpool's red-brick Victorian architectural

The last days of the old-style Golden Mile. (Alfred Gregory, *Blackpool: A Celebration of the '60s* (London, 1993), p. 114)

traditions, foreshadowing a growing concern with 'heritage'; but generally, in Blackpool as elsewhere, trends to uniformity were in the ascendant, in architecture as in entertainment. The Corporation, once so powerful, was being outflanked by regional, national and international entities. Its publicity department, heir of the most innovative and financially best-endowed municipal set-up in Victorian and Edwardian England, moved eagerly into television advertising in the early 1970s, but lacked the spending power to compete with international tour operators such as Thomson, and came to depend heavily on television coverage of Blackpool events.[54]

Development and disgrace

The Corporation was a busy developer of council estates on the urban fringe during the 1950s and 1960s, but it lost some of its functions to other bodies in the local government legislation of 1974, including its responsibility for the state of the sea, on which the town increasingly turned its back as pollution became more apparent and more openly discussed. The declining powers of local government in the 1980s and 1990s were evident here as elsewhere in the country. To make matters worse, the single-party politics which prevailed in the council chamber until 1991 encouraged a climate of faction-fighting and corruption allegations, which were endemic at regular intervals through the post-war period. The continuing preponderance of builders and the development-related professions among councillors helped to encourage a climate of suspicion. In 1956, for example, the fall-out from the strange suicide of the Town Clerk, after fires at the Town Hall, included an extended campaign by the Liberals for an enquiry into unspecified allegations of bribery and corruption, which encountered passive resistance from the Home Office and the Ministry of Housing and Local Government but rumbled on for two years in various guises after a spate of publicity in January of that year. In February 1958 an all-party committee of the Corporation reported that more than a quarter of a million pounds' worth of business had been transacted between individual councillors and the Corporation.[55] In the same year came the resignation of the Chief Constable and Deputy Chief Constable after investigations into the local police force. There were further allegations of corruption within the Town Hall over building applications in 1973, for example, and in 1977 Lancashire's Chief Constable, who had previously held the Blackpool post, was dismissed for (among other things) intervening in the judicial process on behalf of friends. The Director of Public Prosecutions spent four years investigating alleged corrupt deals in planning and commercial franchising between 1976 and 1980, eventually closing the file after a councillor was cleared of planning irregularities.[56] This climate of scandal accumulated a sense of unease about the legitimacy of the exercise of municipal power, which eventually came to a head in the 1990s.

Meanwhile, residential Blackpool continued to expand, although the post-war private estates were criticised in 1964 for their lack of 'variety and architectural appeal', which was said to be pushing the best class of residents out to Poulton-le-Fylde, Lytham St Annes and Thornton-Cleveleys.[57] There was certainly nothing to match the inter-war housing around Stanley Park, with its distinctive layout and features orchestrated by T. H. Mawson and Sons, whose conservation was a high priority in the Corporation's planning consultation document of 1993.[58]

Poverty and unemployment

At the other end of the social scale, problems of poverty and seasonal unemployment remained endemic. Blackpool's unemployment rates rose sharply in 1952, after the closure of the Squire's Gate factory, reaching 8 per cent in three winter months and averaging 6.6 per cent over the year, significantly higher than in Liverpool, Manchester, Blackburn, Bury and Preston. They remained higher than those of most north-western towns and all rival seaside resorts between 1954 and 1964, with winter peaks of 7.5 per cent in January 1959 and 7.3 per cent four years later. The July figures stood at 2.5 per cent in each of these years, the lowest of the decade being the 0.4 per cent recorded in July 1955.[59] The figures worsened considerably during the 1960s, with winter levels fluctuating between 6 and 9 per cent; and this reflected much wider ripples of unease, insecurity and intermittent unemployment, while the figures themselves err on the optimistic side, especially with regard to women's work.[60] Unemployment was disproportionately weighted to the over–55s, and the poverty of old age and low wages remained much in evidence in the back streets, and especially in the casualised service sector.[61]

Crime and the 'black economy'

Survival strategies under difficult conditions included multiple occupations, not all of which might be declared to authority. Gerald Mars, an anthropologist whose Blackpool upbringing (from the age of 12) seems to have influenced his career as an analyst of illicit workplace practices, commented on first impressions of Blackpool's Palatine School in 1946:

> I ... came from a school [in Manchester] where boys chased each other round the playground, played games or fought ... Here, however, they gathered at the playground's edge in small, inward looking groups. They were playing brag or pontoon for cash. One or two of the older boys moved about with attache cases offering scarce exotics like nylon stockings and art silk ties. If they hadn't got what you wanted they would take orders for future delivery.

This precocious petty trading was, thought Mars, emblematic of the 'entrepreneurial fever' which ruled in the Blackpool of the 1940s through the 1960s, offering 'an exhilarating mix of rules being bent, rampant short termist exploitation, corruption and the promise of unlimited personal gain'. One of the concrete forms this took was the hustling which prevailed on the Golden Mile, as spielers attracted the crowds and decoys in the audience led the rush to see the shows or buy the products.[62] Another was the way in which the same building plans for stalls and temporary exhibition buildings were submitted year after year, being duly rejected after the season was over and the profits in the bag.[63] Blackpool's 'black economy' is in the nature of things difficult to research – as is the influence of Freemasonry in the town – but none the less important for that. The losers in the desperate struggle for summer loot still had to survive in the winter, however, in a town whose dog-eat-dog scramble for existence was in stark contrast to what were, until perhaps the 1970s, the more ordered, structured lifestyles of the inland industrial towns.

What did become increasingly visible in post-war Blackpool was crime. Its importance had hitherto been played down, but problems were being acknowledged in the local press at the war's end. In 1945 Blackpool was said to have a particularly serious problem of indictable crime among 'boys, youths and young men', which had come to the fore during the war years; and by this time the tramways and buses were suffering from vandalism, with damage to shelters, lighting and seats. Convictions for drunkenness, on the other hand, had fallen dramatically even as the population grew, from 332 in 1904 and 148 in 1934 to 34 in 1944, but the cultural meaning of this statistic was unclear.[64] By 1959 Blackpool was acquiring a literary reputation for gangsterism and protection rackets along the Golden Mile, through works like Rupert Croft-Cooke's *Smiling Damned Villain*, which featured Scarface Jack and his razor mob. More prosaically, the chair of the parliamentary Select Committee on Estimates said in 1957 that Blackpool was 'the least policed of any county borough, with the highest in known indictable offences per police officer', and two years later the Chief Constable used this evidence to argue for additional staff. Comments on 'hooligan elements' posing problems for publicans added fuel to debate, and the Deputy Mayor complained of 'outbreaks of violence and rowdyism' which threatened the conference trade.[65] Gerald Mars has argued that towns like Blackpool, with a high throughput of people and limited opportunities or incentives for basing commercial and other relationships on trust and reliability, are 'crimogenic' environments of a sort which will generate high 'dark figures' of unrecorded crime; and the wonder is that it took until the post-war years for Blackpool to develop such a reputation, with the notorious temptations it offered to young residents as well as visitors.[66] A further dimension to the new reputation was the revelation, also in 1959, that Blackpool had the highest proportion of illegitimate births of any local authority, at 8.5 per cent, ahead of Brighton and Bournemouth. The figures included outsiders who came to Blackpool to give birth in anonymous surroundings, and seasonal workers who became pregnant and stayed; but this salved local pride without denying the existence of the evidence.[67]

Post-war Blackpool thus not only inherited an array of social problems from earlier times – including, it was alleged, jerry-built housing from the inter-war years – but also gained a reputation for distilling and concentrating certain perceived social pathologies of the 1950s and onwards. The endemic and worsening problems of seasonal unemployment, the poverty of old age and low wages, child labour, competition and temptation, were both worsening and becoming more visible. Crime figures are always more problematic, but the fear of anti-social behaviour was being more widely and anxiously expressed, and this in itself eventually warped lifestyles and depressed expectations. These trends came to a head in the late 1980s and early 1990s, with consequences on a broad front which extended to the control of the local political system.

Economic crisis

The extent of Blackpool's social problems in the last decade of the twentieth century was mapped out with stark precision in a national atlas of social characteristics based on the 1991 census. A Material Deprivation Index, calculated from the proportion of the population living at more than one to a room and the percentage of households without cars, central heating and 'basic amenities', put Blackpool twenty-first out of 366 local authorities, behind 15 Inner London boroughs, Liverpool, Knowsley, Birmingham, Hull and (for unexplained reasons) the Scilly Isles. The Social Deprivation Index, which based its league table on unemployment, lone parenthood, youth unemployment, single pensioners, long-term limiting illness and dependency, gave Blackpool thirtieth place, as did the Department of the Environment's multiple deprivation index. It is therefore not surprising to find Blackpool 337th in the table of average income per household, and 333rd in the national wealth index table (sharing this rung with Bolsover and Burnley). This relative impoverishment was based on having a high proportion of pensioners and people in shared accommodation, an ageing housing stock and high levels both of unemployment and of households with young children in which both parents work outside the home. Interestingly, Blackpool was now in the bottom quartile nationally for employment in the building industry, but in the top quartile for service sector employment. It was also forty-seventh out of the 366 localities for the proportion of economically active people who were self-employed (one in six). Such people were independent, but the indications are that few of them were prospering: many were obviously in the boarding-house sector. Nor was impoverishment confined to material possessions and opportunities for sociability: it extended to education, where the 2.4 per cent of Blackpudlians with degrees put the town in 354th place nationally, and to the development of the 'informational economy', the sunrise computer-based sector in which Blackpool fell into the bottom quartile.[68]

In perspective, this picture of almost unrelieved misery was hard to square with Blackpool's role as leisure, residential and commuter town. Other resorts shared some of the key characteristics, especially in terms of concentrations of pensioners, the long-term sick and the elderly; but none could begin to match Blackpool's across-the-board display of impoverishment. Most of the problems were of long standing, but they had worsened or stagnated while improvements were made elsewhere. None of this was news to Town Hall staff. William Turner, the Chief Planning Officer, was arguing against proposals for retail expansion on land zoned for industry on the urban fringe when he described Blackpool as 'an unemployment blackspot with an acute shortage of industrial land', and said, 'The image of Blackpool as a successful resort diverts attention from a proper assessment of its economic problems and the underlying weakness of the local economy'; but he carried more conviction than the developers' spokesman who described Blackpool as 'relatively prosperous'. It was, in fact, easy to see why many Blackpool people might be discontented with their lot and fearful for the future.[69]

Over the next five years matters continued to worsen, as visitors preferred to use the motorway network for day-trips rather than stay overnight, and the small boarding-houses in the back streets fell on very hard times. One symptom of this was the deepening conflict over the conversion of such establishments into hostels for social security claimants, whose £12 per night allowance (in 1994) paid better than holidaymakers in the cut-throat setting of the back streets, while offering a regular year-round income. The claimants were held to bring drink, violence, burglary and begging to the affected areas, and legislation was called for to curb the trend. This was a widespread problem in seaside resorts, but Blackpool was perhaps the worst-affected by this manifestation of a more general housing crisis. Both the local MPs joined a campaign which was led by hoteliers who wanted to preserve their status in threatened areas, and in 1995 it emerged that Blackpool had more than 3,000 'houses in multiple occupation', one in nine of which were classed as boarding-houses, with concentrations in the late Victorian accommodation areas around the old stations and behind the sea-front.[70] This was a threat to self-esteem as well as living standards, and it was part of a more general unease. When Blackpool put in a successful bid for £19.3 million of urban regeneration funds in 1996, targeting expenditure at four Victorian wards surrounding the Tower, it was revealed that the town had lost 45 per cent of its manufacturing jobs over the past thirty years and now relied on the service sector for 90 per cent of remaining employment. It consistently had the highest unemployment in Lancashire, a county which provided plenty of competition, and was described as the third most deprived town in the North-West. Seasonal employment and low wages in the holiday industry were more of an issue than ever, and there was widespread support for a minimum wage.[71]

The collapse of the Conservative Party

It was against this background that Blackpool's seismic political shift to Labour took place. In 1991 Labour gained 12 seats in the municipal elections, becoming the governing party on the Corporation for the first time, with 27 seats out of 44.[72] This reflected (among other things) a loss of confidence in the Conservatives' handling of the holiday industry, but it marked a broader political sea-change in Blackpool. Four years later the Conservative defeat turned into a rout, as they were reduced to two elected repre-sentatives, and then to one after a subsequent by-election.[73] The Conservatives had ruled Blackpool from 1876 to 1991, with an interlude in the late 1950s when a Liberal victory in 1958 was followed by a 'hung' council, and another after the 1987 elections when no party held control until the Tories gained seats in by-elections. Now, within four years of losing office locally, the party was reduced almost to extinction in the council chamber.[74]

This was spectacular; but it had deeper roots than appears at first sight. We have seen that accusations of municipal corruption within the ruling group recurred throughout the post-war years, as indeed they had done previously. The Liberals' local secretary, J. W. Wyers, commented in 1959 that Conservative control 'had, in the main, been in the interest of vested interests. It was at times ruthless, arrogant and intolerant, and it had reached a point where it deserved to be broken.' But the Liberals had broken it not only by exploiting corruption allegations, but also by promising to reduce local taxation, pursuing this through stringent economies to the fire and education services. They were alleged to have failed to repair the fire-engine turntable ladder as part of this philosophy. This left the Liberals vulnerable to a Conservative backlash, and the outspoken Labour candidates who attacked the Tories' record were as yet on the fringes of borough politics. Jimmy McCrae, standing for Layton Ward, might accuse the Conservatives of doing nothing 'except to tell us what their grandfathers had done for the town', and the Liberals of being 'more reactionary than the Tories ... a crowd of smart Alecs masquerading under a respectable name'; but this rhetoric was more enjoyable than efficacious.[75] Labour had only gained four seats on the council, making five in all, in the parliamentary landslide year of 1945, despite a doubled municipal electorate. The party had made no headway since: there was enduring propaganda value in the *Gazette*'s claim in 1945 that 'a predominantly Labour Town Council would be a blow to the spirit of enterprise which has transformed cliffs and dunes into the most popular British resort'. It was not until 1965 that Labour acquired more seats than the Liberals and became the official opposition.[76] By the early 1970s, however, the Conservatives' huge municipal majorities were based on the divide and rule principle: they only had just over 50 per cent of the popular vote in the elections of 1973 and 1976, despite taking 40 out of 56 and 35 out of 44 seats (after local government reorganisation in 1974) respectively; and their share of the vote fell steadily while they retained control with apparent comfort in 1979 and 1983. Their loss of overall control in 1987, when their share of the vote fell below 40 per cent for the first time, did not come from a clear sky; and the Labour victory in 1991 came partly from a continuing squeeze of the Liberal vote, and partly from a further decline in Tory popularity to 32.3 per cent of the votes cast. But there were specific as well as long-term reasons for the transformation of the town's municipal politics at this point.[77]

The watershed election of 1991 came at a bad time nationally for the Conservatives, as they struggled to recover from the Poll Tax and the fall of Thatcher. On top of all this, the month before the election produced a rich harvest of local conflict whose origins could be found in local as well as national government policies. There were strikes over pay cuts resulting from the contracting-out of hospital cleaning and municipal refuse services, and over threatened 'redundancies' in further education. The *West Lancashire Evening Gazette* was critical of the 'brave new world of privatised public services' as disputes escalated. Well-publicised intimations of local *malaise* included a big feature on 'Blackpool's drug menace', with more than 800 'addicts' registered at a new clinic, and 45 convictions for heroin abuse in the previous year; a sustained campaign against high levels of car theft; the postponement of a plan by recently privatised North West Water to disinfect the sewage in the sea, while prosecutions threatened from Brussels over unacceptable beach and sea pollution; a retailing crisis as attempts were made to rescue Lewis's sea-front store from permanent closure, and traders complained of litter and 'roaming drunks'; and the revelation that adult male unemployment in four central wards was hovering around 30 per cent, with the prospect of continuing high levels over the summer. There was also the latest in a series of campaigns against council policies, this time a scheme for a golf course and hotel complex on neglected public land off East Park Drive, which drew the fire of those who wanted it to remain a public open space. Opponents of this scheme accused an inner clique of councillors, the 'Happy Club', of deploying 'bully-boy tactics', and made links with earlier policy disasters including the financial scandals surrounding the Sandcastle indoor baths and amusement complex and the demolition of the Derby Baths. There were echoes of previous patterns of local scandal here, but in this environment there were political consequences. A self-described 'life-long Tory' stood as an

Independent to express his disillusionment over precisely these issues, and a newly formed Pensioners' Party contested five wards, advocating economies in holiday trade expenditure and free bus passes for the elderly. A letter from T. S. Fearnley brought all these grievances together in attacking a 'decade of deterioration, dereliction, destruction'; and his concentration on misguided and frivolous expenditure, as well as the need to cut Illuminations costs, confirmed that the ripples of anger had spread beyond supporters of the usual Labour agenda. Fearnley quoted Blackpool's longest-serving councillor (a Liberal Democrat) as saying that the Tories 'could not run a winkle stall'. This was a far cry from the heyday of municipal enterprise in Victorian and inter-war Blackpool; and the perceived offenders were punished at the polls.[78] Four years later, the complete collapse of Blackpool's Conservatives followed a much more low-key election campaign, which focused on Labour's local achievements and the threat to Civil Service jobs at the recently rebuilt DSS offices at Warbreck Hill. Councillor Wynne of the Liberal Democrats said that 'local people will never forget the things the Conservatives did to this town'; and the election results of 1995 showed that such sentiments had wider currency.[79]

Labour took a little longer to end the traditional Conservative dominance of Blackpool's parliamentary seats. In the Labour 'landslide' of 1945, after all, the Tories won Blackpool North by 12,394 votes, and Blackpool South (which then included residential St Annes) by 16,043.[80] These were handsome majorities in their context. Subsequently the best Labour performance came in the Blackpool North by-election of March 1962, but it was the Liberals who nearly won the seat, on a low poll, with Labour not far behind in third place.[81] At this point the Liberals were still the leading opposition party on the Council. Thirty years later, General Election expectations were raised by the previous year's municipal results, but Gordon Marsden, editor of *History Today*, failed narrowly to win Blackpool South for Labour, while Harold Elletson held on comfortably for the Tories in Blackpool North. It took the unprecedented landslide of 1997, which pushed the Conservatives out of seaside strongholds all over Britain, to pull Blackpool's parliamentary representation into line with its local government, in the guise of 'New' Labour and under the leadership of Tony Blair, who had captivated the local press two years earlier. The true significance of the change of label is still a matter for debate.[82]

The political transformation was one of several concurrent changes in Blackpool's identity and fortunes in the early 1990s. It coincided with an increasing awareness of poverty and economic problems which generated a sense of sustained crisis. Meanwhile, the holiday industry was also changing in novel and (for some) potentially threatening ways, and the seriously polluted state of the sea, the town's original reason for existence, was a growing preoccupation. The image of carefree enjoyment and fun was increasingly at odds with a publicly acknowledged reality of poverty, dilapidation, crime and pollution. In the midst of all this, however, a new attempt to remake the town's tourist identity reached a well-publicised climax in 1994, when the Tower was gilded as part of its centenary celebrations. Meanwhile, as befitted what was by now a traditional rivalry, the Pleasure Beach introduced its spectacular new ride, the Big One, which provided the most striking competing accent on Blackpool's skyline since the demolition of the Gigantic Wheel in 1928. The Tower was celebrated in ways which emphasised heritage as well as keeping up with the times, while the Big One emphasised novelty and the sheer scale of thrills and investment.[83] Whether the new momentum can be sustained is still a matter for debate, as is the nature of Blackpool's future more generally. Prediction would be foolhardy, especially in the light of the vitality of the Pleasure Beach and other aspects of Blackpool's entertainments, and the town's recurrent ability to make Houdini-like escapes from what seem to be dead ends in the resort cycle; but in the concluding chapter an attempt can be made to set Blackpool's current fortunes in the context of its long-term development.

CHAPTER SEVEN

Blackpool in perspective

BLACKPOOL REMAINS UNIQUE. It has been a magnet for the English (and increasingly the British) working class, while symbolising the brash, open-handed, cheerful, vulgar and hedonistic incarnations of the North of England, for well over a century. It has defied predictions of stagnation and decline by persistently reinventing itself and reaching out to new constituencies, although this has been happening with increasing frequency and an air of the frenetic and even desperate in recent years. It has even begun to reach out to overseas markets, with some disasters but also some success, although the Irish have been the most receptive of the target groups. It is difficult to sustain a holiday economy based on heavy Victorian infrastructure and modernist top-dressing, and depending on the reproduction of consumer loyalty in succeeding generations, in the fleeting, evanescent, fashion-conscious, post-structural world of end-of-the-century tourism and consumerism. Recent developments in entertainment have been lavish and imaginative, but more vulnerable than ever before to the fickleness of the trend-seeker. If Blackpool were to lose its balance on the high-wire it is walking, with a skimpier safety-net of loyal regulars and municipal intervention than ever before, its fall into the abyss would be irreparable. It would have to fall back on its alternative identities as retirement centre (but with the pool of potential retirers steadily drying up as other locations were preferred), centre for administrative employment in Civil Service-related work, and dormitory town. Its existing problems of unemployment and decaying infrastructure would no doubt be exacerbated. As a resort, its strong identity and high profile have enabled it to weather the storms of the late twentieth century more confidently than its British rivals; but a sense of recurring or even enduring crisis has been apparent over the last few years, despite the inventive resilience of the Pleasure Beach and the extensive media coverage of Funny Girls and related phenomena. This urban history of Blackpool is being completed at a point of apparent transition and palpable unease, as the sea-change in the resort's political complexion suggests, even though it has coincided with a marked rightward shift in the Labour Party nationally, and similar developments have occurred in other seaside resorts.[1]

Symbols of transition are not hard to find. Perhaps most poignant, during a walk through the town in July 1997, was the 'For Sale' sign on the Lancashire and Cheshire Miners' proudly palatial convalescent home on the northern cliffs, built in 1925–7 and now as redundant in post-industrial Britain as the men who paid for it and used it.[2] The sound system on the North Pier was playing plangent laments from the 1960s by Brenda Lee and Billy Fury, and the sense of a predominant generation of fiftysomethings was reinforced by the legend 'Peggy Sue's' on the roof of the pavilion on Central Pier, indicating the nature of the end-of-the-pier show. Much of the sea-front entertainment had a similar flavour. Not that the young are absent, especially at the Pleasure Beach and at night, and Blackpool has thoroughly updated its celebrations of the vulgar, the lewd, the sexually ambiguous and the transgressive; but there was a recurrent sense of unambiguous closures and insecure beginnings. On the Bispham cliffs sea campion and thrift are reasserting nature above concrete, as the sterile tidyings, reinforcements and 'rockifications' of the 1920s and 1930s begin to feel their age. Is a 'melancholy long withdrawing roar' beginning, as Blackpool's tide goes out and its resort area contracts? The sea itself is still the unfortunate colour which the journalist William Holt remarked on in 1934, viewing 'the brown waters ... almost the same colour as the sands', and awareness of pollution is more widespread, although visitors still paddle and even swim in the unappetising liquid.[3] The modernist buildings of the 1930s, so beloved of the Borough Surveyor and of the Pleasure Beach architect Joseph Emberton, have suffered more casualties than the Victorian and Edwardian standard-bearers of the making of popular Blackpool, but neither the Golden Mile nor the Derby Baths have been

A vivid image of continuity and change in the accommodation industry: the turn-of-the-century Regent, facing the Pleasure Beach, is incongruously joined to the smooth 1960s façade of the Gables, on the site of the original Blackpool home of Pleasure Beach founder W. G. Bean.

adequately replaced: indeed, the central redevelopment at the back of Bonny Street is a piece of 1970s' brutalism which drew gasps of horror from a party of German academics when I showed them the delights of Blackpool in 1997. The saga of the demolition of the Derby Baths, together with the financial controversies surrounding the replacement (in effect) of the great South Shore bathing pool of 1923 by the Sandcastle, have been important contributors to Blackpool's political transformation, undermining the Conservatives' reputation for imaginative or at least competent management of the holiday industry.

A characteristic jumble of boarding-houses, workshops, gasworks, working-class housing and holiday industry offshoots a few yards inland from the central promenade.

While so much in which Blackpool once took pride has vanished, it is an irony to find the Sea Water Company's original water tower, emblem of an enterprise which was outdated at its inception, still in place behind the Imperial Hotel. Meanwhile, all that is left of Central Station, at which so many visitors arrived, is the enormous gentlemen's urinal which provided desperately needed relief after interminable journeys on non-corridor trains. Nearby, the big boarding-houses of the Albert Road area bear enduring witness to the former power of railways to shape the social topography of

resorts. Many of these establishments have moved up-market and become 'private hotels' with varying degrees of conviction, but remnants of the old Lancashire working class, now an endangered species, still head for the smaller ones of 1870s' vintage in Bairstow Street or Yorkshire Street, by the Central Pier. Sadly, in 1997 I was unable to find the disarmingly named Gas View, a little further south, which two years earlier had offered a grandstand view of the gasometers for £6.50 bed and breakfast. Some of the boarding-houses near the gasworks and tram depot, as elsewhere, are interspersed with back-street workshops whose working conditions would not be out of place in Tunis. Cheapness remains a dominant concern here and in the back streets around North Station, where the DSS hostels are making inroads, although elsewhere attempts to go up-market have had some success. Satellite television, sometimes metered, sometimes not, is the current fashionable draw. How much further this scissors movement can be taken remains to be seen. Here again are impending endings without visible new beginnings.

Visitors from outside the cultures it celebrates and caricatures are capable of embracing end-of-the-century Blackpool as loud, vivid, kitsch and camp, as did the *New York Times* correspondent William E. Schmidt for an American audience in 1994;[4] but they can also be simply appalled by it, to an extent that would be unthinkable in the 1930s or even the 1960s. The loathing expressed by *Guardian* political correspondent Peter Jenkins in 1970 was unusual in its outspokenness at the time, although he noted that his colleague James Cameron had once compared his hotel to Buchenwald and that Bernard Levin had publicly likened the town to 'an elephant's anus'.

> Those who hate the place gain a good deal of enjoyment from its horrors. After all these years it would be a grave disappointment to discover a tolerable hotel, consume a passable meal or encounter prompt service. Blackpool is the nearest a lot of us get to experiencing the hardships and depravations [sic] of working class life.[5]

His complaints, intriguingly, were focused on the Imperial, not on some hapless bed-and-breakfast establishment in Caunce Street or Lord Street, where he might have found even more to complain about. Twelve years later the globe-trotting travel writer Paul Theroux found Blackpool's buildings to be 'not only ugly but also foolish and flimsy', and decided that the town was 'perfectly reflected in the swollen guts and unhealthy fat of its beer-guzzling visitors', a perception which was a far cry from the idealisation of the restless, energetic crowd which had prevailed in the 1930s.[6] Three years ago the London correspondent of Austrian television, like Peter Jenkins a victim of the political party conferences, interviewed me to explain Blackpool to her viewers, because she was completely unable to comprehend how anyone could choose to go to such a dreadful place in search of holiday pleasure. Most recently of all, the best-selling American travel writer Bill Bryson described Blackpool as 'ugly, dirty and a long way from anywhere ... its sea is an open toilet, and its attractions nearly all cheap, provincial and dire'. He was deeply unimpressed by the Illuminations.[7] What all these people had in common was that they could not get away fast enough: Blackpool had no power to interest them even at an anthropological level.

The most spectacular response I have found was that of London journalist Charles Jennings, reporting on a southerner's expedition to unknown (and usually alien) territories in 1993. He was outraged:

> [Outside the Tower] I was overcome by exhaustion and fumes. Blackpool is the first place I've been to where the whole town has halitosis. I don't mean the people, specifically, I mean the environment, the air, the very buildings themselves. The whole settlement reeks of chip fat, beer and ice-cream, uniformly and without let-up. I felt as if I were wading through the contents of somebody's stomach.[8]

But this was only the most outspoken example in a developing genre. Blackpool's capacity for revolting as well as exciting and amusing is new and dangerous. It has prospered for so long on its capacity to provide something for almost everyone, but the flavours it is now providing may be strong enough to alienate potential customers. On the other hand, they may be necessary to attract others. Jennings's jaundiced view of parts of the town centre and the Pleasure Beach is a savage journalist's angle on Blackpool's shop window, which, although emblematic, is only a small and distinctive part of the town; but it may be disturbingly significant that he chose to write it. A more usual tone has been affectionate disbelief tinged with awe. Jennings was awed, but only by Blackpool's sheer enormity. Substituting his reading for the earlier ones would be very damaging to the town's future.

That future is bound up with continuing to deny the logic of the Butler model of the resort cycle, with which we began this book. Goodall's emphasis on the variety of possible exits from the 'stagnation' phase of the proposed cycle, including 'rejuvenation' (which may be imagined as refurbishing existing amenities and images, and/or creating new ones for rising or more attractive markets), adds flexibility to this very generalised model in useful ways.[9] But Blackpool's experience complicates matters. Its resident population reached its peak after the Second World War, and has been stagnating and then gently declining subsequently, although the snapshot figures hide a persistent flux of rapid migratory currents. Visitor numbers probably reached a peak in the 1960s, and the subsequent problem has been to sustain them. Blackpool has been rejuvenating and relaunching itself to respond to new tastes and new markets throughout its career: this has been one of the keynotes of its sustained growth and commercial success. But for most of its history these developments have been geared to promoting further growth, and have furthered advancement through the stages of the resort product cycle. Over the last few decades, however, they have been directed towards survival at the existing level rather than a further advancement which hardly seems possible, except perhaps through further extensions of the season. Blackpool has been working hard to stay at the stagnation stage, and it is difficult to imagine an exit which did not involve decline. By sustaining itself at the top of the cycle, having grown and consolidated on a remarkable scale, Blackpool is defying the logic of economic gravity; and there are indications that the suspension of disbelief is no longer tenable. Sustaining sufficient vitality and openness to innovation to avoid a cata-strophic fall, in a climate of intensifying change, constitutes a distinctive kind of success. It also makes for continuing insecurity.

There are, of course, other and less stressful routes through all or part of the resort cycle, to an easy-going stagnation which might also be defined as success, on a definition which goes beyond mere size and profit margins. They might entail limited and controlled growth which preserved landscape and other amenities, and attracted a visiting public whose spending power and numbers in relation to the host population were sufficient to sustain a comfortable standard of living for all concerned. Small resorts with up-market visiting publics and strong planning controls might fall into this category. Part of Blackpool's distinctiveness is that it followed a more dangerous and demanding route. From the 1870s onwards its leading citizens swam with a new tide, recognising the openness of the town to a hitherto unthinkable volume of working-class spending power, and en-couraging it rather than putting up resistance. Islands of respectability survived to north and south, but this was uncharted territory, and Blackpool was making itself vulnerable to economic decline and changes in popular taste and fashion, although events elsewhere were to show that elite loyalties could be just as fickle. Dynamism, awareness of new trends, and the capacity to anticipate and promote them, were all forced upon Blackpool by the need to keep following a path which admitted of no retracing. If Blackpool was to grow beyond the status of a provincial backwater, and indeed to sustain itself in the face of growing competition from places which were better endowed for the satisfying of middle-class preferences, this diversion from the high road of resort development was necessary; and it has been particularly interesting to chart the way in which it was taken and the nature of the journey. Blackpool differentiated itself from all its rivals in northern England by embracing the new working-class market so eagerly and wholeheartedly, and this, above all, enabled it to outpace them and dominate its chosen field, first regionally, then nationally. The nature of this experience in many ways transcends the unduly simple and economi-cally reductionist resort cycle model, which needs to be adjusted in complex ways to allow for different kinds of markets, contrasting social experiences and the variety of ways in which development, success and stagnation can be interpreted. Blackpool is, perhaps, the exceptional case that most obviously tests this particular rule to destruction.

Blackpool's place in the social history of popular culture is both assured and controversial. The nature of the dilemma it poses (to celebrate, criticise, condemn or possibly condescend) is encapsulated by Bernard Newman, writing at the end of the Second World War as one who was brought up on Blackpool (the goal of the annual long-distance excursion from his Leicestershire village), but who found it diminished after returning to it with a broader range of experience:

> Most of the people who sneer or gibe at Blackpool have never been there. It fulfils a function in our contemporary civilization. It collects the blatant, noisy holiday crowds in one huge dump, when they might otherwise be spread all over the land to clash with the quieter folk. Before we part with Blackpool we have to amend a good many ideas of methods of enjoyment: they have taken generations to mature, and will take many years to dispel.[10]

This defence of Blackpool damns with reluctant and rationed praise, regarding it as a necessary evil but recognising that it gives pleasure to millions, and at the same time doubting and almost denying the higher validity of that pleasure. The enhanced civilisation of the crowd, to which Newman (and some of the Mass-Observers of the late 1930s) looked, would make Blackpool obsolete in the form in which he saw it. A dialogue between Newman and Jennings, fifty years on, would be both pointed and poignant.

Such interest in the cultural significance of the Blackpool holiday is of long standing, and intertwines with questions about Blackpool's relationship, for good or ill, with something labelled 'mass tourism', about how far Blackpool can be regarded as a distillation of a broader Lancashire, Northern or national popular culture, and about how far it followed, and how far it helped to shape, the nature of perceptions of enjoyment, consumerism and the demand for entertainment. In the first place, 'mass tourism' is far too simplistic a description of what occurs, and has occurred, in Blackpool. The expression is bandied about indiscriminately in the literature on tourism studies, used for everything from early railway excursions to the Mediterranean and more exotic package holidays of the 1960s onwards. It would be tempting, but misleading, to lay claim to Blackpool's place as the pioneer centre for such an ill-defined set of practices. We have seen that its holidaymakers were, and are, culturally diverse, drawn from a cross-section of ages and social strata, enjoying different parts of the town in contrasting ways and adopting different roles and pursuing varied pleasures as the hours ticked by and the context changed. But to label the teeming diversity of Blackpool holiday crowds as 'mass tourism' is demeaning and reductive, regarding the holidaymakers as puppets manipulated collectively by exploitative leisure capitalists, and as lacking the capacity to make their own enjoyments and create their own identities from what is on offer.[11] There is, and has been, much more to Blackpool than that. Its visitors have often been conspicuous by their ability to use amusements and amenities in creative and unexpected ways, a theme which was never better illustrated than at the Carnivals of 1923 and 1924, but which was still highly visible in the 1990s.[12]

Blackpool as an embodiment of a rich and enjoyable popular culture, in distinctive seaside guise, carries much more conviction. It was, in many undeniable senses, Britain's and the world's first working-class seaside resort, viewed both in terms of visitors and (in many senses) residents, despite its recruitment of migrants from working-class backgrounds into back-street capitalism and an enduring politics of competitive individualism;[13] but some weight must be given to Patrick Joyce's suggestion that the vocabulary of class is insufficient to convey the complexity of the popular values which Blackpool has celebrated.[14] The Blackpool of the growth years between the 1870s and the 1930s, and in many ways beyond, celebrated the annual release of millions of manual workers of both sexes, and their families, from the constraints of the need to earn a living, observe time- and work-discipline, keep a home going and present an appropriate face to workmates and neighbours; but many of its visitors brought such constraints with them as part of an inescapable cultural baggage, while its amusements and shared cultural practices embraced workers in shops and offices as well as mills, mines and foundries, and found room for shop-keepers and the owners of other businesses as well. These are people who know their place and take pride in it, challenging assumptions of superiority in outsiders and making fun of pretensions, often by playing up and exploiting their own apparent simplicity. They are secure in their respect-ability, and lay claim to understanding their chosen spheres (brass band music, choral singing, pigeon-flying, crown green bowls). But they can also sustain a self-confidence which allows for feasting on innuendo and direct rudery in the special surroundings of the pier pavilion, or of the pleasure palace on the shoreline, celebrating the loosening of safety-valves which are kept tight for most of the year, while at the same time stopping short of explosion because of the restraining, visible presence of friends and neighbours.[15] Any such attempt at distilling a collective character from such an assembled throng runs its own dangers of exalting or excluding minorities within the broader culture, but the effort needs to be made. Blackpool's predominantly working-class identity, meanwhile, is unde-niable, but there is more to the story than that.

The same applies to Blackpool as the quintessence of Lancashire or Northern regional identities at play. Tony Bennett, in particular, has ar-gued that the Blackpool of the years between the late nineteenth and mid-twentieth centuries represented one aspect, and a highly potent one, of a northern counter-culture which laid claim to a rough vitality, a spirit of enterprise and a sense of purpose and material achievement which made the dominant southern (and especially metropolitan) ethos, based on aristocracy and high finance, look pallid and effete. Blackpool epitomised all that was lively and participatory in this full-blooded, disrespectful, carnivalesque industrial popular culture in its phase of playing hard, as it worked off the pent-up emotions of a year's disciplined toil. Only in recent years, with the decline of its industrial hinterland, has it moved over to embracing less distinctive, more international and specifically American pleasure styles, as its identity, and the fare it offers, have become more assimilated to a transnational popular culture associated with leisure corporations with a global reach.[16] There is something in this account, although metropolitan and indeed international influences have always had their place in Blackpool's popular entertainment culture. William Holland, after all, came from the metropolitan music-halls and thrived as the Winter Gardens' impresario in the late nineteenth century, and specifically American inroads can be traced to the turn of the century (on the Pleasure Beach, especially, as Bennett acknowledges), and were the source of increasingly tart comment in the 1930s. J. B. Priestley, for example, had this to say in 1934:

> Its amusements are becoming too mechanised and Americanised. Talkies have replaced the old roaring variety turns. Gangs of carefully drilled young men and women (with nasal accents), employed by the music publishers to plug their 'Hot Broadway Hits', have largely replaced the pierrots and nigger minstrels. The entertainers are more calculating, their shows more standardised, and the audiences more passive. It has developed a pitiful sophistication – machine-made and not really English – that is much worse than the old hearty vulgarity.

Priestley contrasted his sad vision of an anaemic, manipulated Blackpool visiting public with a nostalgic rendering of the pre-1914 holidaymakers, 'vital beings who burst out of their factories for the annual spree as if the boilers had exploded and blown them out'.[17] This was too obviously impressionistic and uneasily value-laden to convince, and it certainly contrasted with Mass-Observation's portrayal of a rumbustious and idiosyncratic Blackpool popular culture a few years later.[18] And when Gerald Mars emphasised growing American influences on the Golden Mile's amusements twenty years later, the hamburgers, Wyatt Earp hats and fake American accents were of little account compared with Blackpool's mainstream live entertainment scene, which featured regional performers whose acts often played up to the local loyalties of Wakes Week holidaymakers.[19] Bennett's version of Blackpool as (until perhaps the 1970s) the embodiment of a distinctive and assertive northern popular culture is too simple (and based on insufficient grasp of detail), but the countervailing evidence dilutes it rather than denying it altogether.

There would be room for a whole book on these issues, which are beyond the scope of an urban biography of the present kind. The same applies to the question of how far Blackpool made its own distinctive contribution to popular culture, and how far its success reflected its entrepreneurs' capacity to give the public what it already wanted. For some purposes Blackpool has certainly been a conduit of innovation which has later been taken up elsewhere, sometimes successfully, sometimes not. Its early entertainments were derivative: Raikes Hall, the piers, the Winter Gardens, the Aquarium. But towards the turn of the century the Tower, the Gigantic Wheel and the revamped Winter Gardens were authentic novelties, pleasure palaces new in nature as well as in scale. Meanwhile the Pleasure Beach brought in new American amusement technology, which raised the expectations of thrill-seeking customers and fed back into innovation elsewhere, although never on quite the same scale. The Tower had its imitators, none of which succeeded even in the medium term, even though New Brighton's was considerably higher. The great dance-halls of the inter-war years were imitated more successfully inland, but going to dance in Blackpool retained a special cachet. The town and its amusements brought people together from a variety of provincial cultures in a way that nowhere else could, disseminating fashions and novelties through display and demonstration, and increasingly providing shops in which the objects of desire could be bought and enjoyed, on holiday and then at home. Blackpool also provided space for parading, strolling, watching, which legitimised the woman as casual stroller, adventurous *flaneuse*, alongside the men and flirting with them, in what was a remarkably safe urban setting.[20] Its entertainment moguls and purveyors of consumer goods, at all levels, had to make provision within a strongly established, and in many ways very conservative, set of preferences, for people who were expected to return year after year; but they also had to innovate, even in unobtrusive ways, and the whole experience could hardly avoid widening horizons and bringing people into contact with new possibilities. Only in recent years have new developments made these things less important, especially to a rising generation; and this is central to Blackpool's current problems.

Enough has been said for Blackpool's wider importance to be apparent. It is interesting to speculate on what would have happened to Britain's seaside holiday industry without it. Could some other great honeypot have appeared, to engross the attention of the emergent working-class market from the late nineteenth century onwards? Or would the rise of the popular holiday habit have been delayed, diluted, diffused, as people preferred to spend their money in other ways? How would the lack of a developed popular market for seaside holidays have affected the international developments of the last thirty years? Blackpool was, after all, the only resort to open its arms to working-class demand and to cater for it in every respect, in the late nineteenth and early twentieth century. Take it away, and the

Last years of the old order at Blackpool: the Tower presides over a jam-packed beach in high summer in the early 1960s. (Alfred Gregory, *Blackpool: A Celebration of the '60s* (London, 1993), p. 167)

social history of British leisure and popular culture, and perhaps even that of popular politics, would look very different. Seaside resorts generally get short shrift, at best token treatment, in the standard economic and social histories of modern Britain. They deserve better. And Blackpool, like it or loathe it, deserves to be at the centre of the stage, getting the attention it craves, rather than being required to sulk uncharacteristically in the wings. This book has dealt with an important phenomenon. I hope it will be recognised as such.

Notes

Notes to Chapter One

1. J. K. Walton, 'Mass-Observation's Blackpool and some alternatives', in G. Cross (ed.), *Worktowners at Blackpool* (London, 1990), pp. 328–38.
2. N. Pevsner, *The Buildings of England: North Lancashire* (Harmondsworth, 1969), pp. 68–9.
3. Tony Bennett, 'Hegemony, ideology, pleasure: Blackpool', in T. Bennett, C. Mercer and J. Woollacott (eds), *Popular Culture and Social Relations* (Milton Keynes, 1986), pp. 135–54.
4. Three of my other works, in particular, provide additional detail and supporting footnote evidence to primary sources: J. K. Walton, 'The social development of Blackpool, 1788–1914', Ph.D. thesis, University of Lancaster, 1974; J. K. Walton, *The Blackpool Landlady: A Social History* (Manchester, 1978); J. K. Walton, 'The world's first working-class seaside resort? Blackpool revisited, 1840–1974', *Transactions of the Lancashire and Cheshire Antiquarian Society* 88 (1992), pp. 1–30.
5. J. K. Walton, *The English Seaside Resort: A Social History 1750–1914* (Leicester, 1983), pp. 71–2.
6. J. K. Walton, 'The seaside resorts of England and Wales, 1900–1950: growth, diffusion and the emergence of new forms of coastal tourism', in G. Shaw and A. Williams (eds), *The Rise and fall of British Coastal Resorts* (London, 1997), p. 27. This ranking is based on Southport's population being expanded by the inclusion of Birkdale, an adjoining resort which had not yet been amalgamated with its larger neighbour.
7. Even Torquay was developing a summer season by the Edwardian years and attracting some Lancashire working-class custom: N. Morgan, 'Perceptions, patterns and policies of tourism', Ph.D. thesis, University of Exeter, 1992, pp. 79–80.
8. J. K. Walton, 'Leisure towns in wartime: the impact of the First World War in Blackpool and San Sebastian', *Journal of Contemporary History* 31 (1996), pp. 603–18; J. K. Walton, 'Leisure towns in the aftermath of war: coping with social change and political upheaval in Blackpool and San Sebastian, 1918–23', in F. Walter and R. Hudemann (eds), *Villes et guerres mondiales au XXe siecle* (Paris, 1997), pp. 97–114.
9. J. K. Walton and C. O'Neill, 'Numbering the holidaymakers: the problems and possibilities of the June census of 1921 for historians of resorts', *Local Historian* 23 (1993), pp. 205–16.
10. Walton, thesis, chapter 7; S. V. Ward, 'Promoting holiday resorts: a review of early history to 1921', *Planning History* 10: 2 (1988), pp. 7–11; *Blackpool Times*, 24 August 1926.
11. Especially in the cases of Coney Island and Atlantic City: R. Lewis, 'Seaside holiday resorts in the United States and Britain', *Urban History Yearbook* 1980, pp. 44–52, and references cited there.

12. Charles Graves, *And the Greeks* (London, 1930), pp. 187–91; William Holt, articles on Blackpool in the *Daily Dispatch*, 3–7 August 1934; Cross, *Worktowners*.

13. Walton, 'Seaside resorts', pp. 29–30.

14. Blackpool Central Library (BCL), LM 89, *Blackpool Visitors and Tourism Survey 1972*, p. 3; *Blackpool Visitor Survey 1987*, p. 8.

15. J. Demetriadi, 'English and Welsh seaside resorts 1950–74', Ph.D. thesis, University of Lancaster, 1994; J. Demetriadi, 'The golden years: English seaside resorts 1950–74', in Shaw and Williams, *British Coastal Resorts*, pp. 49–75.

16. N. Essafi, *Some Aspects of Poverty in Blackpool 1945–60*, M.A. dissertation, University of Lancaster, 1990.

17. J. Porter, *The History of the Fylde of Lancashire* (Fleetwood and Blackpool, 1876), p. 311; Barrett's *Directory of Blackpool and the Fylde* (Preston, 1929), p. 11.

18. Walton, thesis, chapter 4.

19. R. A. Smith, 'Beach resort development: implications for planning', *Annals of Tourism Research* 19 (1992), pp. 304–22; S. J. Kirkby, 'Recreation and the bathing quality of Spanish coastal waters', in M. Barke, J. Towner and M. T. Newton (eds), *Tourism in Spain: Critical Issues* (Wallingford, 1996), pp. 189–211.

20. For general commentary on this, G. A. Parsons, 'Property, profit and pollution', Ph.D. thesis, University of Lancaster, 1996.

21. See especially D. Cannadine, *Lords and landlords* (Leicester, 1980), Part Three, and Walton, *Seaside resort*, Chapter 5.

22. H. J. Perkin, 'The "social tone" of Victorian seaside resorts in the north-west', *Northern History* 11 (1976), pp. 180–94.

23. Walton, *Seaside Resort*, p. 99; Walton, *Landlady*, chapter 1; J. K. Walton, 'The Blackpool landlady revisited', *Manchester Region History Review* 8 (1994), pp. 23–31.

24. Taken from the 1991 Census Report for Blackpool.

25. Sheila Johnston, 'Greetings from Blackpool', *The Independent* II, 19 August 1994, p. 25. Thanks to Neville Kirk for buying the paper.

26. B. Goodall, 'Coastal resorts: development and redevelopment', *Built Environment* 18 (1992), pp. 5–11.

27. Ibid., p. 8.

Notes to Chapter Two

1. W. Hutton, *A Description of Blackpool in 1788* (London; 1944 reprint of 1789 edn). For railways and resorts, J. K. Walton, 'Railways and resort development in Victorian England: the case of Silloth', *Northern History* 15 (1979), pp. 191–209; J. Simmons, *The Railway in Town and Country, 1830–1914* (Newton Abbot, 1986), chapter 8.

2. Walton, *Seaside Resort*, p. 53.

3. Porter, *Fylde*, pp. 316–17.

4. Harris Library, Preston, Baines Mss., vol. 6, p. 41. See M. J. Winstanley, 'Researching a county history: Edwin Butterworth, Edward Baines and the *History of Lancashire* (1836)', *Northern History* 32 (1996), pp. 152–72.

5. Walton, *Seaside Resort*, pp. 11–15.

6. J. Wilkinson, *The Langton Letters* (Preston, 1994), pp. 131, 133, 166.

7. Hutton, *Blackpool*, p. 19.

8. C. Hutton Beale (ed.), *Reminiscences of a Gentlewoman of the Last Century* (Birmingham, 1891), p. 56.

9. BCL, LM 851 (O), Account-book of Bonny's-in-the-fields lodging-house.
10. Porter, *Fylde*, p. 293.
11. Walton, thesis, p. 19; Baines Mss., vol. 6, p. 41.
12. Walton, thesis, p. 229 and footnotes cited there; Baines Mss., vol. 6, pp. 45–8.
13. Beale, *Reminiscences*, pp. 56–7.
14. Baines Mss., vol. 6, p. 39.
15. P. Whittle, *Marina* (Preston, 1831), pp. 9–10.
16. A. B. Granville, *The Spas of England, and Principal Sea-Bathing Places* (Bath, 1971, reprint of 1841 edn), vol. I, pp. 344–51.
17. Ibid., p. 351.
18. Beale, *Reminiscences*, p. 55.
19. Hutton, *Blackpool*, p. 13.
20. A. Corbin, *The Lure of the Sea* (Cambridge, 1994).
21. Baines Mss., vol. 6, p. 41.
22. Granville, *Spas*, I, p. 350.
23. Corbin's own presentation of Blackpool in 1841, which purports to be based on Granville, is so bizarre as to be worth reproducing in full (Corbin, *Lure*, p. 269): 'the recent and much appreciated resort at Blackpool, which in 1841 had some 1,500 houses of lovely appearance available, built below the cliff'. This would have added up to more than one house per inhabitant, and however lovely their appearance might have been, they would all have been washed away by the first high tide.
24. Cheshire Record Office, DDF/34/51, Samuel Finney to Catherine Mathias, 13 October 1789. Thanks to Jacquie Crosby for sending me this reference.
25. Letters of John Roberton to M., in Manchester, 11 and 13 August 1842. Joan Mottram of the Wellcome Unit for the History of Medicine, University of Manchester, kindly supplied photocopies from research material in her possession. Compare Hutton, *Blackpool*, p. 13.
26. Hutton, *Blackpool*, pp. 10–11; Baines Mss., vol. 6, p. 9.
27. Samuel Finney, letter cited above, note 24.
28. Hutton, *Blackpool*, pp. 18–22.
29. Baines Mss., vol. 6, p. 41.
30. *Preston Pilot*, 15 July 1854.
31. Baines Mss., vol. 6, p. 41.
32. P. Borsay, *The English Urban Renaissance* (Oxford, 1989); P. J. Atkins, 'The spatial configuration of class solidarity in London's west end 1792–1939', *Urban History Yearbook* 17 (1990), pp. 36–65.
33. Hutton, *Blackpool*, pp. 23–4.
34. Baines Mss., vol. 6, pp. 11–13; Lancashire Record Office (LRO), PR 2906/6/2 (1828–9).
35. Baines Mss., Vol. 6, p. 11; LRO, DRB/1/122; W. J. Smith, 'Blackpool: a sketch of its growth, 1740–1851', *Lancashire and Cheshire Antiquarian Society* 69 (1959), pp. 74–5.
36. For details, see Walton, thesis, pp. 22–9, and Smith, 'Blackpool', pp. 70–103. For the Clifton estate and Lytham, see G. Rogers, 'The nineteenth-century landowner as urban developer: the Clifton estate and the development of Lytham St Annes', *Transactions of the Historic Society of Lancashire and Cheshire* 145 (1996), pp. 117–50.
37. Baines Mss., vol. 6, pp. 45–8.
38. Whittle, *Marina*, is particularly critical of the lack of a uniform plan, although formally planned seaside resorts were most unusual at this stage.
39. Baines Mss., vol. 6, pp. 27–9.

40. Hutton, *Blackpool*, pp. 10, 19, 24–5.

41. Walton, thesis, p. 232, table 5.1; J. Whyman, 'Visitors to Margate in the 1841 census returns', *Local Population Studies* 8 (Spring 1972), pp. 19–39.

42. Walton, 'World's first', provides a wider context for the Bathing Sunday tradition. For popular sea-bathing at Liverpool in the later eighteenth century, and apposite comments on social emulation, H. Cunningham, 'Leisure and culture', in F. M. L. Thompson (ed.), *The Cambridge Social History of Britain* (Cambridge, 1990), vol. 2, p. 313.

Notes to Chapter Three

1. Walton, 'Railways', pp. 191–208; J. K. Walton, 'Railways and resort development in north-west England, 1830–1914', in E. Sigsworth (ed.), *Ports and Resorts in the Regions* (Hull, 1980), pp. 120–37; J. Simmons, *The Railway in Town and Country 1830–1914* (Newton Abbot, 1986), chapter 8.

2. J. H. Sutton, 'Early Fleetwood, 1835–47', M. Litt. thesis, University of Lancaster, 1968, pp. 42–3, 64; and see also Simmons, *Railway*, pp. 201–3.

3. Sutton, 'Early Fleetwood', p. 222.

4. *Preston Pilot*, 15 August 1840.

5. Walton, thesis, pp. 240–6 and footnotes cited there.

6. Ibid., pp. 375–83; *The Lankishire Loominary un Wickly Lookin Glass*, 21 May 1861 (thanks to Robert Poole for this reference).

7. Walton, thesis, pp. 375–83.

8. D. Cannadine (ed.), *Patricians, Power and Politics in Nineteenth-Century English Towns* (Leicester, 1982), chapter by Liddle on Southport; G. Rogers, 'Social and economic change on Lancashire landed estates during the nineteenth century, with special reference to the Clifton estate, 1832–1916', Ph.D. thesis, University of Lancaster, 1981.

9. Walton, thesis, pp. 23–9; and for contemporary rumours about the scale of Clifton's capital gains, J(ohn) B(ill), *The English Party's Excursion to Paris, in Easter Week 1849* (London and Leek, 1850), copy in Blackpool Central Library, p. 514. The title of this book is spectacularly misleading.

10. Walton, thesis, pp. 181–2. The quotation is from LRO, DDCl/2233/2.

11. Walton, thesis, pp. 182–4.

12. Ibid., p. 185.

13. Ibid.

14. Bill, *English Party's Excursion*, p. 487.

15. Walton, thesis, p. 387.

16. Ibid., p. 388.

17. Ibid., p. 187.

18. Ibid., p. 188; J. F. Wilson, *Lighting the Town: A Study of Management in the North West Gas Industry 1805–1880* (London, 1991), pp. 44–5.

19. Walton, thesis, p. 189; C. Arthur, *A History of the Fylde Waterworks Company, 1861–1911* (London, 1911).

20. Walton, thesis, p. 190.

21. Ibid., p. 19; P. J. Waller, *Town, City and Nation: England 1850–1914* (Oxford, 1983), pp. 4–7.

22. Walton, thesis, p. 107, using the census enumerators' books.

23. Ibid., p. 265, sampling from lists of visitors published in the *Fleetwood Chronicle*. See also J. K. Walton and P. R. McGloin, 'Holiday resorts and their visitors', *Local Historian* 13 (1979), pp. 323–31.

24. Walton, thesis, p. 121.
25. Ibid., pp. 306–7; N. Sheldon, 'Church and community in Blackpool, 1850–1880', BA dissertation, University of Manchester, 1977, pp. 9–15. Thanks to Ms Sheldon for sending me a copy of this excellent piece of work.
26. Walton, thesis, p. 32.
27. Ibid.
28. Ibid., pp. 36–40.
29. Ibid., pp. 306–7.
30. Ibid., p. 263. Passenger arrivals per year at Blackpool doubled during the 'cotton famine' years, 1861–5: p. 310.
31. Ibid., pp. 308–9.
32. Ibid., p. 309; Sheldon, dissertation, pp. 12ff.; Pevsner, *North Lancashire*, p. 69.
33. Walton, thesis, pp. 192–4.
34. Ibid., p. 195; B. R. Palmer and G. S. Turner, *The Blackpool Story* (Cleveleys, 1976), p. 26.
35. Walton, thesis, pp. 245–6; Palmer and Turner, *Blackpool Story*, p. 31.
36. Sheldon, dissertation, chapter 5.

Notes to Chapter Four

1. 21,970, to be exact. Population figures are taken from the decennial censuses.
2. P. J. Waller, *Town, City and Nation* (Oxford, 1983), p. 7, table 2.
3. Walton, *Seaside Resort*, pp. 65–8.
4. Calculated from Walton, thesis, p. 263, table 5.2.
5. Walton, *Landlady*.
6. Lynn F. K. Pearson, *The People's Palaces: The Story of the Seaside Pleasure Buildings of 1870–1914* (Buckingham, 1991); Walton, thesis, chapter 6.
7. Walton, thesis, chapter 1.
8. J. K. Walton, 'The demand for working-class seaside holidays in Victorian England', *Economic History Review*, 2nd series, 34 (1981), pp. 249–65.
9. Walton, thesis, p. 265, table 5.3.
10. Ibid., p. 266; and see, for example, T. C. Barker and J. R. Harris, *A Merseyside town in the Industrial Revolution: St Helens* (Liverpool, 1954), and E. Roberts, *A woman's place* (Oxford, 1985).
11. A. Davies, *Leisure, Gender and Poverty* (Milton Keynes, 1992), p. 41; G. R. Sims, 'A wonderland by the waves', *Pearson's Magazine* 1902, p. 204 (copy in LRO).
12. Walton, thesis, p. 273.
13. Ibid., p. 274.
14. Bill Naughton, *Neither Use nor Ornament* (Newcastle upon Tyne, 1995).
15. P. Wild, 'Recreation in Rochdale, 1900–1940', in John Clarke and Chas Critcher, *Working Class Culture* (London, 1979), pp. 145–8.
16. Robert Roberts, *The Classic Slum: Salford Life at the Turn of the Century* (Manchester, 1971); Davies, *Leisure, Gender and Poverty*, pp. 40–2.
17. Harvey Taylor, *A Claim on the Countryside: A History of the British Outdoor Movement* (Edinburgh, 1997), chapter 6 and especially pp. 193–5; Allen Clarke, *The Effects of the Factory System* (2nd edn, Littleborough, Lancs., 1985), pp. 134–6.
18. P. Joyce, *Visions of the People* (Cambridge, 1991), pp. 165–71.
19. E. H. Hunt, *Regional Wage Variations in Great Britain 1850–1914* (Oxford, 1973); A. McIvor, *Organised Capital* (Cambridge, 1995).
20. J. K. Walton, *Lancashire: A Social History 1558–1939* (Manchester, 1987), chapter

13; B. Lancaster and P. McGuire (eds), *Towards the Co-operative Common-wealth* (Loughborough, 1996), pp. 17–28.

21. P. Johnson, 'Conspicuous consumption and working-class culture in late Victorian and Edwardian Britain', *Transactions of the Royal Historical Society*, 5th series, 38 (1988), pp. 27–42.

22. Clarke, *Effects*, pp. 134–6.

23. M. Douglas and B. Isherwood, *The World of Goods* (London, 1979), chapters 3–4. I have modified my own earlier position on this: Walton, thesis, pp. 1–2.

24. Walton, thesis, pp. 246–50.

25. Ibid., pp. 250–8; and for a more favourable verdict, Simmons, *Railway*, chapter 8.

26. J. Urry, 'The "consumption" of tourism', *Sociology* 24 (1990), p. 31; Walton, 'Blackpool landlady revisited', p. 30.

27. Denis J. B. Shaw, *Selling an Urban Image: Blackpool at the Turn of the Century* (Birmingham, 1990), p. 12.

28. T. D. Carr, *Blackpool as a Health Resort* (Blackpool, 1901).

29. Shaw, *Urban Image*, p. 12.

30. The Sea-Water Company's water tower can still be seen at the back of Claremont Park.

31. R. Poole, *The Lancashire Wakes Holidays* (Preston, 1994).

32. E. J. Hobsbawm and T. Ranger (eds), *The Invention of Tradition* (Cambridge, 1983).

33. Cannadine, *Lords and Landlords*, for a classic study of Eastbourne; D. Cannadine (ed.), *Patricians*, including Bournemouth and Southport.

34. Walton, thesis, p. 33.

35. Ibid., pp. 389–90.

36. J. Liddle, 'Estate management and land reform politics: the Hesketh and Scarisbrick families and the making of Southport, 1842–1914', in Cannadine, *Patricians*, pp. 133–74; M. Gowling, 'Social changes in Southport 1841–1891', M. Phil. thesis, University of Lancaster, in progress.

37. Rogers, 'The nineteenth-century landowner as urban developer'; P.S.Peers, 'The development of St Annes-on-the-sea as a residential town and watering-place', MA dissertation, University of Lancaster, 1979.

38. R. Bingham, *Lost Resort ? The Flow and Ebb of Morecambe* (Milnthorpe, 1990).

39. J. D. Marshall, *Old Lakeland* (Newton Abbot, 1971), chapter 12; O. M. Westall (ed.), *Windermere in the Nineteenth Century* (2nd edn, Lancaster, 1991).

40. Walton, thesis, pp. 79–86. Detailed documentation based on press reports, deeds, rate-books and council minutes can be found in the footnotes to the thesis.

41. Ibid., pp. 50–4.

42. Ibid., pp. 54–6.

43. LRO, CBBl/2/56, 59, 63; Walton, thesis, p. 71, table 1.7.

44. Walton, thesis, pp. 27–9.

45. Ibid., pp. 41–4.

46. Ibid., pp. 46–7.

47. Ibid., pp. 44–5.

48. J. Urry, *Consuming Places* (London, 1995).

49. Walton, *Landlady*, pp. 74–5.

50. Ibid., pp. 72–3.

51. Ibid., chapter 6, and Walton, 'Blackpool landlady revisited', p. 30.

52. Walton, thesis, pp. 389–438, for this and most of what follows.

53. Ibid., pp. 422–4.

54. Ibid., pp. 413–22; Parliamentary Papers, Joint Select Committee on Sunday Trading, 1906, Q. 1901–1955.

55. Ibid., pp. 410, 412–13; R. Shields, *Places on the Margin* (London, 1991), chapter 2.

56. Walton, thesis, pp. 411–12.

57. *Blackpool Gazette*, 9 September 1887.

58. Walton, thesis, pp. 395–6.

59. Public Record Office, HO.45/22722.

60. Walton, thesis, pp. 402–4.

61. Ibid., pp. 396–9.

62. *Fleetwood Chronicle*, 6 June 1856.

63. Walton, thesis, pp. 402–3; Walton, *Landlady*, p. 144.

64. Shields, *Places on the Margin*, chapter 2.

65. J.-D. Urbain, *Sur la plage* (Paris, 1994), pp. 124–8.

66. Walton, *Landlady*, p. 140.

67. Walton, thesis, p. 333.

68. Ibid., pp. 387–8. Urbain, *Sur la plage*, is obsessed with the regulation of bodily exposure and pays no heed to the problems arising from beach entertainment, which were perhaps less pressing in the French and Belgian resorts with which he is concerned.

69. Walton, thesis, pp. 404–5.

70. Ibid., p. 406.

71. Ibid., pp. 406–8.

72. LRO, PLB 3/2.

73. Walton, *Seaside Resort*, pp. 192–3.

74. Shields, *Places on the Margin*, and references cited there.

75. See, for example, Tom Treddlehoyle, 'A Leeds loiner's leap inta luv at Blackpool', *T'Pogmoor Olmenack an Bairnsla Foaks Yearly Jottings* (Barnsley, 1904), p. 28. This typifies a whole *genre* of dialect writing about innocuous sexual encounters at the seaside, although some publications of this sort also sentimentalised holiday romances which might be read as more exciting sexual encounters: 'On Blackpool shore', *John Hartley's Clock Almanack* (Wakefield, 1905), pp. 42–3. These dialect almanacs were also full of advertisements for obvious abortifacients.

76. Walton, 'World's first', pp. 13–14.

77. Walton, thesis, chapter 4.

78. Palmer and Turner, *Blackpool Story*, p. 34.

79. Walton, thesis, pp. 201–5.

80. Ibid., chapter 4.

81. P. Askew, 'The origins and effects of the scholarship system as applied to Blackpool secondary school, 1907–1937', MA dissertation, University of Lancaster, 1977, chapter 2.

82. J. K. Walton, 'Municipal government and the holiday industry in Blackpool, 1876–1914', in J. K. Walton and J. Walvin (eds), *Leisure in Britain 1780–1939* (Manchester, 1983), pp. 158–85; P. Cooke (ed.), *Localities* (London, 1989), p. 175.

83. For this and what follows, Walton, thesis, chapter 7.

84. For the Illuminations see also Palmer and Turner, *Blackpool Story*, pp. 84–5.

85. Walton, thesis, pp. 209–10.

86. W. H. Wheeler, *The Sea-Coast* (London, 1902), pp. 307–10.

87. *Blackpool Gazette*, 24 March 1899.

88. Walton, 'Municipal government', pp. 166–70, and for a comparative perspective, *Seaside Resort*, chapter 6.

89. Shaw, *Urban Image*, pp. 15–18. Shaw points out that all the turn-of-the-century guidebooks continue to emphasise nature and health, especially the sea and its breezes, and buildings and architecture, before moving on to popular pleasures and the entertainment companies.

90. For full documentation, Walton, thesis, chapter 9.

91. Walton, *Seaside Resort*, chapter 7.

92. Pearson, *People's Palaces*.

93. Walton, thesis, pp. 312–13.

94. Ibid., pp. 314–15.

95. Ibid., pp. 315–18; and see also Joyce, *Visions*, pp. 165–71.

96. Walton, thesis, p. 319; J. K. Walton, 'The re-making of a popular resort: Blackpool Tower and the boom of the 1890s', *Local Historian* 24 (1994), pp. 201–2.

97. Walton, thesis, pp. 319–20; Walton, 'Blackpool Tower', p. 201.

98. Walton, thesis, pp. 320–1; Walton, 'Blackpool Tower', p. 202.

99. A. Laycock, *Warren of Manchester* (London, n.d., *c.* 1906), p. 101.

100. Walton, thesis, pp. 322–3.

101. I. Harford, *Manchester and its Ship Canal Movement* (Keele, 1994).

102. Walton, thesis, pp. 323–6; Walton, *Seaside Resort*, pp. 170–80.

103. Walton, thesis, pp. 326–9; P. Bennett, *A Century of Fun* (Blackpool, 1996), Chapter 2; K. Peiss, *Cheap Amusements* (Philadelphia, 1986), chapter 5; and for the gypsies S. Floate, 'The history of the gypsy encampment on Blackpool's South Shore 1840–1910', University of London Diploma in Genealogy and the History of the Family, 1993, chapters 2–3 (copy at LRO).

104. Walton, thesis, pp. 329–32; B. Band, *Blackpool Grand Theatre 1894–1930* (Lytham, 1993), p. 17; K. Berry, 'The changing nature of the theatre in provincial Lancashire, *c.* 1843–1900', MA dissertation, University of Lancaster, 1991, pp. 43–4, 99–105, 121–2.

105. Shaw, *Urban Image*, p. 17.

106. Joyce, *Visions*, chapters 11–13.

107. Walton, thesis, chapter 2, provides an overview.

108. Ibid., p. 108, Table 2.3., and Walton, 'Blackpool landlady revisited', p. 27, table 4. The location quotient for a particular occupation in a town or area is found by dividing the percentage of the local labour force in the occupation concerned by the corresponding national figure.

109. Ibid., pp. 115–17.

110. Ibid., p. 113, table 2.5.

111. Ibid., pp. 107, table 2.2, and p. 111.

112. Ibid., pp. 166–71.

113. Statistics taken from J. E. Adams, 'A study of infant mortality in Burnley, Nelson and St Helens, 1899–1914', MA dissertation, University of Lancaster, 1996, and from unpublished analyses of the 1911 census by Mike Winstanley. My thanks to both of them.

114. Walton, *Landlady*, chapter 1; Walton, 'Blackpool landlady revisited', pp. 23, 30.

115. Walton, *Landlady*, p. 216.

116. Laycock, *Warren of Manchester*, pp. 34, 43.

117. Walton, thesis, p. 113, table 2.6; Walton, *Seaside resort*, p. 99, table 20.

118. Walton, thesis, p. 114, table 2.7.

119. Ibid., p. 206, table 4.4.

120. Ibid., pp. 205–7; Adams, 'Infant mortality'.

121. British Parliamentary Papers, Committee on Partial Exemption from School Attendance, 1909, evidence of H. M. Richards, Q. 5493–5503, 5525, 5544–6. Thanks to Jim Pressley for this material.

122. Ibid., Q. 5516.
123. Walton, thesis, p. 121, tables 2.8 and 2.9; Walton, *Seaside resort*, p. 101, table 21.
124. R. Fuller, *Souvenirs* (London, 1980), pp. 91–2.
125. Floate, 'Gypsy encampment', pp. 13–16, 27, 39.
126. D. Claber, 'The Blackpool Industrial Co-operative Society, 1885–1910', MA dissertation, University of Lancaster, 1991.
127. Walton, *Landlady*, chapter 8.
128. Pevsner, *North Lancashire*, pp. 69–70, 230–2.
129. M. Huggins, 'Sport and the English seaside resort *c.* 1800–1914', *International Journal of Maritime History* 9 (1997).
130. A. Hailwood, 'The Blackpool Ladies' Sick Poor Association', MA dissertation, University of Lancaster, 1990, chapter 3.
131. Waters, *British socialists*; Taylor, *Claim on the Countryside*.
132. Walton, 'Blackpool Tower', p. 198.

Notes to Chapter Five

1. Walton, 'Leisure towns in wartime', pp. 603–18.
2. Walton, 'Leisure towns in the aftermath of war'.
3. J. K. Walton, 'Popular entertainment and public order: the Blackpool Carnivals of 1923–24', *Northern History* 34 (1998), pp. 170–88.
4. Walton, 'World's first', pp. 22–7.
5. Walton, 'Blackpool landlady revisited', pp. 23–31.
6. Walton, 'The seaside resorts of England and Wales, 1900–1950', pp. 26–7, 37.
7. Walton, 'Leisure towns in wartime', pp. 606–8.
8. Dave Russell, *Football and the English: A Social History of Association Football in England, 1863–1995* (Preston, 1997).
9. LRO, PLB 3/2, 26 March 1915.
10. Walton, 'Leisure towns in wartime', pp. 608–9.
11. E. W. Gilbert, *Brighton: Old Ocean's Bauble* (2nd edn, Hassocks, 1975), p. 219.
12. S. Norris, *Manx memories and movements* (3rd edn, Douglas, 1941), chapters 17–19.
13. Walton, 'Leisure towns in wartime ', pp. 610–13; *Blackpool Herald*, 8 November 1918; *Blackpool Times*, 9 November 1918, 31 December 1918.
14. See especially G. Moorhouse, *Hell's Foundations* (London, 1994).
15. Walton, 'Leisure towns in wartime', pp. 613–14; J. K. Walton and J. Smith, 'The rhetoric of community and the business of pleasure: the San Sebastian waiters' strike of 1920', *International Review of Social History* 39 (1994), pp. 28–30.
16. M. Dupree, 'Foreign competition and the inter-war period', in Mary B. Rose (ed.), *The Lancashire Cotton Industry: A History since 1700* (Preston, 1996), pp. 265–72.
17. *Blackpool Times*, 7–28 June 1919, 27 September 1919.
18. *Blackpool Times*, 15 October, 22 November 1919; 14 August 1920; 26 July, 9, 16 and 19 August 1921.
19. *Blackpool Times*, 1, 8, 22 and 29 July, 2 August 1921.
20. *Blackpool Times*, 5 August 1921.
21. *Blackpool Times*, 5 July, 30 August 1921.
22. Walton, 'Popular entertainment and public order'.
23. *Blackpool Times*, 31 May, 28 June, 3 September 1919.
24. *Blackpool Times*, 13–20 July 1918; 24 May, 9–16 August 1919; 7–11 August 1920; 19 August 1921.

25. *Blackpool Times*, 14 November, 31 December 1918.

26. Walton, *Lancashire*, chapter 13.

27. Walton, 'World's first', pp. 24, 28.

28. Blackpool Trades Council, *Diamond Jubilee History* (Blackpool, 1951), BCL, LM 08 (P), pp. 34–5; *Blackpool Gazette*, 8–15 May 1926.

29. See also Walton and Smith, 'Waiters' strike'.

30. T. H. Mawson, *The Life and Work of an English Landscape Architect* (London, 1927), p. 344.

31. M. Swenarton, *Homes Fit for Heroes: the Politics and Architecture of Early State Housing in Britain* (London, 1981).

32. *Blackpool Times*, 27 August, 13 September, 4 October 1919; 21 February 1922; LRO, CBBl 54, valuation books for 1923; Barrett's *Directory for Blackpool and the Fylde* (Preston, 1929); D. Beattie, 'The origins, implementation and legacy of the Addison Housing Act 1919, with special reference to Lancashire', Ph.D. thesis, University of Lancaster, 1986; 'Changing Blackpool: a record of recent progress', *Blackpool Gazette* supplement, 6 May 1939, BCL, LE 02 (P), p. 4.

33. J. K. Walton and C. O'Neill, 'Numbering the holidaymakers: the problems and possibilities of the June census of 1921 for historians of resorts', *Local Historian* 23 (1993), pp. 205–16.

34. Lancashire and Merseyside Industrial Development Association, *The Lancashire Coast Area* (Manchester, 1951), Appendix A, pp. 36–7.

35. *Blackpool Gazette*, 5–22 May 1928.

36. Lancashire and Merseyside Industrial Development Association, *Lancashire Coast*, pp. 25–6; E. Brunner, *Holiday Making and the Holiday Trades* (London, 1945), p. 42.

37. Ibid., p. 26. For location quotients see above, Chapter 4, note 108.

38. Walton, 'Blackpool landlady revisited', p. 27, table 4; Lancashire and Merseyside Industrial Development Association, *Lancashire Coast*, pp. 27–8.

39. *The Automobile Association Hotel Handbook 1939–40* (London, 1939).

40. Brunner, *Holiday Trades*, p. 26; Lancashire and Merseyside Industrial Development Association, *Lancashire Coast*, p. 28.

41. Brunner, *Holiday Trades*, p. 26.

42. Ibid., p. 45; J. Walvin, *Beside the Seaside* (London, 1978), p. 118.

43. New Century Publications, *Residential Blackpool* (Blackpool, 1939), unpaginated: CL, LEO2 (P).

44. 'Changing Blackpool: a record of recent progress', p. 2.

45. New Century Publications, *Residential Blackpool*.

46. *Blackpool Times*, 30 April 1926.

47. W. Dougill, 'The British coast and its holiday resorts', *Town Planning Review*, December 1935, p. 265, footnote; Brunner, *Holiday Trades*, p. 8; Cross, *Worktowners*, p. 19, for Mass-Observation's endorsement of the Blackpool figure.

48. William Holt, 'Mill-land folk on the Continent', *Daily Dispatch*, 17 and 22 August 1934.

49. S. G. Jones, 'The Lancashire cotton industry and the development of paid holidays in the 1930s', *Historic Society of Lancashire and Cheshire* 135 (1986), pp. 99–115; William Holt, 'The North on holiday', *Daily Dispatch*, 7 August 1934; M. Bragg, *Speak for England* (pbk edn, London, 1978), p. 372; *Blackpool Gazette*, 26 June, 31 July 1937.

50. *John Hartley's Original Clock Almanack* (Idle, 1929), p. 44; Cross, *Worktowners*, p. 42.

51. Ibid., pp. 67–8; Walton, *Landlady*, pp. 173–82.

52. Cross, *Worktowners*, p. 57.

53. Jones, 'Paid holidays', p. 111.

54. William Woodruff, *Billy Boy: The Story of a Lancashire Weaver's Son* (Halifax, 1992), pp. 41–4, 123–6.

55. S. Messenger, 'Youth culture in Blackpool between the wars', unpublished M. A. dissertation, University of Lancaster, 1993, chapter 4; E. Oliver, 'Women and leisure: working-class women in Bolton between the wars', unpublished MA dissertation, University of Lancaster, 1992, pp. 74–5.

56. Messenger, 'Youth Culture', chapter 5; Cross, *Worktowners*, pp. 172–7.

57. D. L. Murray, *Leading Lady* (London, 1947), p. 242. The book is set in the late 1930s.

58. William Holt, 'Round the clock with Blackpool's joy-seekers', *Daily Dispatch*, 7 August 1934.

59. William Holt, 'I watch the North on holiday: magic lure of Blackpool', *Daily Dispatch*, 3 August 1934.

60. *Blackpool Gazette*, 7 August 1937; Graves, *Greeks*, pp. 187–91.

61. Cross, *Worktowners*, pp. 151–71.

62. Ibid., pp. 180–91.

63. S. Humphries, *A Secret World of Sex* (London, 1988), pp. 165–92.

64. Cross, *Worktowners*, pp. 184–5.

65. Ibid., p. 128.

66. Ibid., p. 158.

67. Ibid., pp. 132–5. For the South Pier's Fred Walmsley, see Roy Fuller, *Souvenirs* (London, 1980), pp. 164–5.

68. Graves, *Greeks*, p. 188.

69. *Blackpool Gazette*, 14 May 1928; Palmer and Turner, *Blackpool Story*, pp. 119–20.

70. Bennett, *Century of Fun*.

71. Cross, *Worktowners*, p. 105.

72. *Blackpool Gazette*, 31 May 1935, 5 August 1935 (and later press references); Cross, *Worktowners*, pp. 192–201.

73. Bennett, *Century of Fun*, picks up on this well.

74. Cross, *Worktowners*, pp. 206–7; 'Wonderful Blackpool', *Blackpool Gazette* New Year supplement, 7 January 1933, BCL, LEO2 (P), p. 21.

75. Cross, *Worktowners*, pp. 206–7; Barrett's *Directory for Blackpool and the Fylde*, 1938; Walton, 'World's first', pp. 28–9.

76. S. V. Ward, *The Geography of Inter-War Britain: The State and Uneven Development* (London, 1988), pp. 158–67.

77. 'Changing Blackpool: a record of recent progress', p. 2; Palmer and Turner, *Blackpool Story*, pp. 117–19; Bennett, *Century of Fun*; K. Parry, *The Resorts of the Lancashire Coast* (Newton Abbot, 1983), chapter 15; Blackpool Corporation, *New Park and Recreation Ground for Blackpool* (Blackpool, 1922); Walton, 'Popular entertainment and public order', and newspaper references cited there.

78. Trevor T. Jones, *Redevelopment in Blackpool* (June 1939: BCL, LE 02(P)), p. 6; 'Changing Blackpool: a record of recent progress', p. 4.

79. Blackpool Corporation Publicity Committee, *Blackpool: Open the Door to Holiday Happiness* (Blackpool, 1939); Cross, *Worktowners*, pp. 89–94.

80. Palmer and Turner, *Blackpool Story*, pp. 86–9.

81. Cross, *Worktowners*, pp. 216–21.

82. Walton, *Landlady*, pp. 176–7.

83. Ibid., pp. 171–87; Walton, 'Blackpool landlady revisited'; Parry, *Resorts*, chapters 19–20.

84. Cross, *Worktowners*, p. 65.
85. Ibid., pp. 136–8; William Holt, 'The blonde & the brunette', *Daily Dispatch*, 10 August 1934.
86. Jones, *Redevelopment*, p. 4.
87. Parry, *Resorts*, pp. 92–7; 'Changing Blackpool: a record of recent progress', p. 20.
88. Harold Palmer, *Not a Sparrow Falls* (Preston, 1988), pp. 115–59.
89. Murray, *Leading Lady*, deals convincingly with theatricals.
90. Messenger, 'Youth culture in Blackpool', p. 104, Appendix 1.
91. Graves, *Greeks*, p. 189.
92. Allen Hutt, *The Condition of the Working Class in Britain* (London, 1933), p. 70.
93. Walton, 'World's first', p. 26.
94. Blackpool Industrial Co-operative Society, *Fifty Years of Progress* (Blackpool, 1935), in BCL, LM 97 (P).

Notes to Chapter Six

1. N. Fishwick, *English Football and Society 1910–1950* (Manchester, 1989).
2. Demetriadi, 'English and Welsh seaside resorts'; Demetriadi, 'The golden years', pp. 49–75.
3. B. Goodall, 'Coastal resorts: development and redevelopment', *Built Environment* 18 (1992), pp. 5–11; C. Cooper, 'Parameters and indicators of the decline of the British seaside resort', in Shaw and Williams, *British Coastal Resorts*, pp. 79–101.
4. R. Ambrose, 'Gay tourism in Blackpool: a geographical study', BA dissertation, University of Birmingham, 1992.
5. *The Guardian* G2, 13 May 1994, pp. 8–9; J. Hassan, *Environmental and Economic History: Lessons from the Beaches?* (Manchester Metropolitan University: Department of Economics and Economic History, 1995), for background and context.
6. C. Rallings and M. Thrasher (eds), *Local Elections in Britain: A Statistical Digest* (Plymouth, 1994), p. 271.
7. *The Guardian*, 3 May 1997.
8. Palmer and Turner, *Blackpool Story*, pp. 124–5.
9. Lancashire and Merseyside Industrial Development Association, *Lancashire Coast*, p. 37.
10. Palmer and Turner, *Blackpool Story*, p. 125.
11. Walton, *Landlady*, p. 188.
12. *Blackpool Gazette*, 29 September 1940, 14 September 1946, 13 January 1951.
13. Walton, *Landlady*, pp. 189–90; Palmer and Turner, *Blackpool Story*, pp. 126–9.
14. Lancashire and Merseyside Industrial Development Association, *Lancashire Coast*, pp. 17–19.
15. Brunner, *Holiday*, pp. 57–9.
16. Ibid., pp. 52–3; *Blackpool Gazette*, 20 January, 3 February 1945.
17. Palmer and Turner, *Blackpool Story*, p. 130.
18. *Blackpool Gazette*, 8 September 1945.
19. *Blackpool Gazette*, 19 May 1945; LRO, CBBl 32/4, Traffic and Transport Plan, 1969, p. 1.
20. *Blackpool Gazette* and *West Lancashire Evening Gazette*, 10 September–22 October 1949.
21. *The Times*, 10 September 1955.

22. *Blackpool Gazette*, 6 November, 24 December 1964.
23. Alfred Gregory, *Blackpool: A Celebration of the '60s* (London, 1993); Demetriadi, 'English and Welsh seaside resorts', p. 343; Matthew Engel, 'Stumped for the truth', *Guardian*, undated newspaper cutting in author's collection.
24. Gregory, *Blackpool*, especially pp. 167, 172–3.
25. Ibid., pp. 39, 151; Cross, *Worktowners*.
26. Lily Savage, 'Holiday greetings from Blackpool Pier', *The Observer Review*, 25 August 1996, p. 1.
27. J. Campbell, *Tower above All: Personal Memories of Blackpool from Holiday Diaries* (Upton-upon-Severn, 1991).
28. Demetriadi, 'English and Welsh seaside resorts', chapters 2 and 8; H. C. Stallybrass, 'The holiday accommodation industry: with special reference to Scarborough, England', Ph.D. thesis, University of London, 1978, p. 175.
29. BCL, LM 89, *Blackpool Visitors and Tourism Survey 1972*, and *Blackpool Visitor Survey 1987*; Blackpool Borough Council, *Blackpool Borough Local Plan* (Consultation edition, 1993), p. 37; Demetriadi, 'English and Welsh seaside resorts', pp. 321–2; Stallybrass, thesis, p. 348; Walton, 'Blackpool landlady revisited', pp. 25–6; *West Lancashire Evening Gazette*, 16 April 1991.
30. Ambrose, 'Gay tourism', pp. 36–42 and maps 1a, 1b.
31. Martin Wroe, 'Golden girls corner gay market', *Observer*, 27 November 1994.
32. Julian Keeling, 'Holiday camp atmosphere', *Sunday Times*, 11 December 1994.
33. Quoted by William E. Schmidt, 'Tacky, wonderful Blackpool', *New York Times*, 7 August 1994, sect. xx, pp. 8–9.
34. Bill Naughton, *Saintly Billy* (Oxford, 1989).
35. Ambrose, 'Gay tourism', p. 63.
36. Charles Jennings, *Up North: Travels beyond the Watford Gap* (London, 1995), p. 88.
37. National census returns.
38. Palmer and Turner, *Blackpool Story*, p. 135; N. Essafi, 'Some aspects of poverty in Blackpool, 1945–60', MA dissertation, University of Lancaster, 1990, table III. 2.
39. *Blackpool Gazette*, 6 January, 10 February 1945.
40. Essafi, 'Poverty', tables III. 2, III. 3; Lancashire and Merseyside Industrial Development Association, *The Problems of Seasonal Unemployment and Labour Supply in the Coastal Towns of Lancashire* (1965: mimeo at BCL, LQ 95 (P)), pp. 2, 7, 12–14; T. W. Freeman, H. Rogers and R. Kinvig, *Lancashire, Cheshire and the Isle of Man* (London, 1966), p. 243.
41. Walton, *Landlady*, pp. 191–206; Walton, 'Blackpool landlady revisited'; Stallybrass, thesis.
42. Demetriadi, 'English and Welsh seaside resorts', chapter 3; Palmer and Turner, *Blackpool Story*, pp. 82, 131–3; *West Lancashire Evening Gazette*, 25 June 1973.
43. Bennett, *Century of Fun*, chapters 7–8.
44. Palmer and Turner, *Blackpool Story*, pp. 134–5.
45. Demetriadi, 'English and Welsh seaside resorts', pp. 263–4.
46. Ibid., pp. 334–6.
47. Jeff Nuttall, *King Twist* (London, 1978); Jeffrey Richards, *Stars in their Eyes* (Preston, 1994).
48. Demetriadi, 'English and Welsh seaside resorts', pp. 340–1; Emily Barr, 'Coconut shy', *The Guardian* G2, 27 June 1997, p. 29.
49. N. Morgan, 'Perceptions, policies and patterns of tourism', unpublished Ph.D. thesis, University of Exeter, 1992, for Torquay and Ilfracombe.
50. Palmer and Turner, *Blackpool Story*, pp. 90–5; Demetriadi, 'English and Welsh seaside resorts', pp. 326–8, 331–3; *West Lancashire Evening Gazette*, 27 April 1991.

51. LRO, CBBl 118/2, which gives an overview of the Corporation's role in Blackpool's economy in 1969; *West Lancashire Evening Gazette*, 8 June 1973; Demetriadi, 'English and Welsh seaside resorts', pp. 347–8.

52. *West Lancashire Evening Gazette*, 13 January 1956.

53. Palmer and Turner, *Blackpool Story*, pp. 137–8; *West Lancashire Evening Gazette*, 2 December 1972, 20–22 July 1977.

54. Demetriadi, 'English and Welsh seaside resorts', pp. 337–40.

55. *West Lancashire Evening Gazette*, 17–20 December 1955; 6–12 January 1956; 27 February 1958.

56. *The Times*, 15 July 1958; 23 June 1973; 28 January, 3 March, 22 December 1977; 4 March, 21 May 1980.

57. *Blackpool Gazette*, 18 December 1964.

58. *Blackpool Borough Local Plan*, pp. 59–60.

59. Essafi, 'Poverty', p. 55 and table III. 7; Lancashire and Merseyside Industrial Development Association, 'Seasonal unemployment', p. 8, table II.

60. Essafi, 'Poverty', chapter 3; LRO, CBBl 118/3, p. 30.

61. Essafi, 'Poverty', chapter 4. Essafi's dissertation provides a full and sophisticated discussion of these issues.

62. G. Mars, draft 'Introduction' to 'We've Got to Live in the Winter: A Personal and Social History of Blackpool', unpublished autobiography. I am very grateful to Gerry Mars for letting me make use of this.

63. LRO, CBBl 89/1.

64. *Blackpool Gazette*, 13 and 20 January, 10 February 1945.

65. *West Lancashire Evening Gazette*, 14, 23 and 29 January, 19 March, 7 May 1959.

66. G. Mars, unpublished paper to the Centre for Social History, University of Lancaster, November 1994.

67. *West Lancashire Evening Gazette*, 19 March 1959. This was already a problem in Blackpool during the 1930s.

68. R. Forrest and D. Gordon, *People and Places: A 1991 Census Atlas of England* (Bristol, 1993), especially pp. 58–61; D. Gordon and R. Forrest, *People and Places 2: Social and Economic Divisions in England* (Bristol, 1995), especially pp. 22–9, 48–51, 60–1, 68–9, 76, 80–1, 84–5.

69. *West Lancashire Evening Gazette*, 10 and 19 April 1991.

70. *Guardian*, 14 March 1994; *West Lancashire Evening Gazette*, 22 July 1995.

71. *Guardian*, 6 January, 28 September 1996.

72. P. Norris, I. Crewe, D. Denver and D. Broughton (eds), *British Elections and Parties Yearbook 1992* (Hemel Hempstead, 1992), p. 212.

73. *Lancashire Evening Post*, 5 May 1995.

74. *West Lancashire Evening Gazette*, 25 March, 8 May 1959; Rallings and Thrasher, *Local elections*, p. 271.

75. *West Lancashire Evening Gazette*, 26 March, 5 and 6 May 1959.

76. *Blackpool Gazette*, 20 October, 3 November 1945; Blackpool Trades Council, *75th anniversary history*, p. 48.

77. Rallings and Thrasher, *Local Elections*, p. 271.

78. *West Lancashire Evening Gazette*, 10 April to 3 May 1991; *The Times*, 15 July 1993.

79. *West Lancashire Evening Gazette*, 12, 19 and 20 April 1995.

80. *Blackpool Gazette*, 28 July 1945.

81. *The Times*, 14 March 1962.

82. J. K. Walton, 'Seaside resorts and maritime history', *International Journal of Maritime History* 9 (1997), p. 131.

83. J. K. Walton, 'The remaking of a popular resort: Blackpool Tower and the

boom of the 1890s', *Local Historian* 24 (1994), pp. 194–7; Bennett, *Century of Fun*, chapter 9.

Notes to Chapter Seven

1. Andy Beckett, 'Think-tank running on empty', *The Guardian* G2, 31 July 1997.
2. Pevsner, *North Lancashire*, p. 72.
3. William Holt, 'I watch the North on holiday', *Daily Dispatch*, 3 August 1934.
4. Schmidt, 'Tacky, wonderful Blackpool', pp. 8–9.
5. *The Guardian*, 7 October 1970.
6. Paul Theroux, *The Kingdom by the Sea* (pbk edn, London, 1984), pp. 212–15.
7. Bill Bryson, *Notes From a Small Island* (London, 1995), pp. 268–70.
8. Jennings, *Up North*, p. 82.
9. B. Goodall, 'Coastal resorts: development and redevelopment', *Built Environment* 18 (1992), pp. 5–11; and for a related approach, C. Ryan, *Recreational Tourism: A Social Science Perspective* (London, 1991), pp. 51–4.
10. B. Newman, *British Journey* (London, 1945), p. 133.
11. For an example (among many) of the looseness and contradictory usage which this terminology entails, A. Williams, 'Mass tourism and international tour companies', in M. Barke, J. Towner and M. T. Newton (eds), *Tourism in Spain: Critical Issues* (Wallingford, 1996), pp. 120–1. For a particularly strong (indeed extreme) argument for the sovereignty of consumer choice in popular culture, J. Golby and W. Purdue, *The Civilization of the Crowd* (London, 1984).
12. Walton, 'Popular entertainment and public order'.
13. Walton, 'World's first', pp. 1–30.
14. Joyce, *Visions*, chapter 6.
15. Cf. Shields, *Places on the Margin*, pp. 84–97.
16. Bennett, 'Hegemony, ideology, pleasure', chapter 7.
17. J. B. Priestley, *English Journey* (London, 1934), p. 267.
18. Cross, *Worktowners*.
19. G. Mars, 'Blackpool's "Golden Mile"', unpublished essay, 1959, pp. 14–15. Thanks to Gerry Mars for sending me this.
20. Cf. J. Walkowitz, *City of Dreadful Delight* (London, 1992).

Index